Tourism for Development

For my parents, Harry and Josie

Themes in tourism

Series Editor: Professor Stephen J. Page, *Scottish Enterprise Forth Valley Chair in Tourism, Department of Marketing, University of Stirling, Stirling, Scotland FK9 4LA.*

The Themes in Tourism Series is an upper level series of texts written by established academics in the field of tourism studies and provides a comprehensive introduction to each area of study. The series develops both theoretical and conceptual issues and a range of case studies to illustrate key principles and arguments related to the development, organisation and management of tourism in different contexts. All the authors introduce a range of global examples to develop an international dimension to their book and an extensive bibliography is complemented by further reading and questions for discussion at the end of each chapter.

Books published in the Themes in Tourism Series

S.J. Page *Transport and Tourism*
C.M. Hall *Tourism Planning*
S.J. Page and R.K. Dowling *Ecotourism*

Forthcoming titles

Tourism and Recreation
Heritage Tourism
Urban Tourism

Tourism for Development

Empowering Communities

Regina Scheyvens

An imprint of **Pearson Education**

Harlow, England · London · New York · Reading, Massachusetts · San Francisco · Toronto · Don Mills, Ontario · Sydney
Tokyo · Singapore · Hong Kong · Seoul · Taipei · Cape Town · Madrid · Mexico City · Amsterdam · Munich · Paris · Milan

Pearson Education Limited
Edinburgh Gate
Harlow
Essex CM20 2JE
England

and Associated Companies throughout the world

Visit us on the World Wide Web at:
www.pearsoneduc.com

First published 2002

© Pearson Education Limited 2002

ISBN 0 130 26438 5

British Library Cataloguing-in-Publication Data
A catalogue record for this book can be obtained from the British Library

Transferred to Digital Print on Demand 2011

Typeset by 35 in 10/12pt Sabon
Produced by Pearson Education Asia Pte Ltd.
Printed and bound by CPI Group (UK) Ltd, Croydon, CR0 4YY

Contents

List of figures

List of tables

List of boxes

Preface

The idea of writing a book on tourism and development appealed to me, particularly in terms of emphasising ways in which tourism could provide a sustainable livelihood option to local communities. Most other texts covering this subject area have been very critical of the impacts of tourism and have had a negative focus, as noted by Ashley: 'The common gloomy picture from tourism case studies around the world is of local people disempowered by alien tourism developments and disenfranchised from their resources' (2000: 22). While individual chapters in books and some journal articles provide a more positive focus, there did not appear to be a text which aimed explicitly to examine how tourism could work *for* development. Thus this is what I set out to do. While there is clearly an important place for thorough analysis and critique of problems associated with tourism development, there is also a time and a place to start looking for constructive approaches to tourism which can benefit local people and their environments.

My faith in this project fluctuated somewhat over time, however, largely because it is so easy to identify obstacles to effective and equitable tourism development. In addition, it somehow seemed less scholarly to focus on positive aspects of tourism. As Robert Chambers has noted, 'academics get more points for writing about failure than about success' (1983, cited in Adams and Megaw 1997: 218). I was reminded of the legitimacy of this project when I had the opportunity to talk with two graduate students at Victoria University, Wellington, where I was presenting a seminar. Both had recently returned from conducting fieldwork on tourism, one in Sarawak and the other in Tonga, and they were in the process of writing up their findings. As I talked with them about their research one thing kept bothering me: they both seemed to have found very little that was 'bad' about the projects in question, despite my grilling. Me: 'So, the locals now have restricted access to the protected area and only some of them can earn an income from selling goods to tourists who come to visit – aren't they resentful?' Student: 'No, they are just very proud of the protected area and that visitors come from far and wide to visit it. I was surprised too.' Similarly, the second student said that although the local community did not have direct control over the ecotourism initiative she was studying, they had developed an excellent relationship with an ecotourism operator and were pleased with the way this outside company was managing the project.

Further motivation for continuing with this project came from the realisation that Third World governments and communities alike were struggling to find effective means to promote economic growth and to enhance the well-being of their people: 'Most LDCs cannot hope to create acceptable living conditions for the majority of their people without continued economic growth, and for many of them . . . tourism represents one of the few apparently viable routes for such growth' (de Kadt 1990: 33).

Please note that while this book has a Third World focus, many of the issues raised are also relevant to indigenous communities who are pursuing tourism within Western societies. Occasional reference is therefore made to Maori people in New Zealand and Australian Aboriginals.

Before launching into Chapter 1, I would like to acknowledge the support of various individuals and institutions that helped to bring this book to fruition. Thanks to Stephen Page for asking me to write a book in this series, and to Matthew Smith of Pearson Education who has been so friendly and patient throughout. My appreciation also goes to Massey University which granted me study leave and provided funding so that I could conduct fieldwork in southern Africa. To all of those individuals who agreed to be interviewed in South Africa, Zimbabwe, and Zambia, and to villagers, conservation staff and development workers who showed me around your projects, I am very grateful. In addition, the Department of Human Geography at the Australian National University and the School of Tourism and Hotel Management at Griffith University were generous in offering me academic hospitality during the final stages of writing when I needed space away from my normal teaching duties. Staff at both of these universities were most welcoming and great to work with. Special thanks also are due to John Overton and Dave Weaver who provided feedback on specific parts of my book.

I am very grateful to those friends who have allowed me to include photographs from their travels. Thanks to Helen Leslie for Figure 7.1, John Morrell for Figure 8.1, and Henry Scheyvens for Figures 2.5 and 9.3. All other photos were taken by the author.

Finally, thank you to my parents who instilled in me the importance of education and have always encouraged me in my work and study, and to other family members and friends for their humour, friendship, and ongoing support. Craig, thanks especially for being house Dad for several months so I could complete this book. Thanks also to my wee girls, Sophie and Jessie, who helped me to keep my work in perspective by providing me with frequent distractions which I thoroughly enjoyed.

Publisher's acknowledgements

We are grateful to the following for permission to reproduce copyright material:

Table 1.2 from *World Tourism Organisation 2020 Vision-Executive Summary Updated*, p. 10 (WTO, 1998); Figure 2.6 from *New Internationalist Magazine* (Polyp, 2000) © Paul Fitzgerald, c/o New Internationalist Magazine; Table 4.1 from *Tourism Management* 20(2), Scheyvens, 'Ecotourism and the empowerment of local communities,' 245–9, copyright 1999 (Scheyvens, 1999a), Table 10.2 from *Annals of Tourism Research* 26(2), Burns, 'Paradoxes in planning: tourism elitism or brutalism?' 329–48 copyright 1999 (Burns, 1999b), Figure 5.1 from *Annals of Tourism Research* 21(3), Buckley, 'A frame work for ecotourism,' pp. 661–9 copyright 1994 (Buckley, 1994), with permission from Elsevier Science; Table 6.1 from *Tourism Ecotourism and Protected Areas: The state of nature-based tourism around the world and guidelines for its development*, IUCN, Gland. Switzerland and Cambridge xiv + 301pp, pp. 40–1 (Cebballos-Lascuráin, 1996); Table 6.2 from *Social Conceptions of the Roles and Benefits of National Parks*. Occasional Paper 119, p. 2, reprinted with permission of the Institute of Natural Resources (Breen *et al.*, 1992); Tables 10.3 and 11.1 from *Enhancing Community Involvement in Wildlife Tourism: Issues and Challenges* (Ashley and Roe, 1998); Figure 12.1 from Action for Southern Africa (for more information on their campaigns see their website: www.actsa.org), photo: Henner Frankenfeld/picturenet.africa.com

Elsevier Science Limited for material used in Chapter 9 from the article 'Backpacker tourism and Third World development' by Regina Scheyvens published in *Annals of Tourism Research* Vol. 29 No. 1, pp. 144–64, 2002, © 2001; and Multilingual Matters Limited for material used in Chapter 8 from the article 'Promoting women's empowerment through involvement in ecotourism: experiences from the Third World' by Regina Scheyvens published in *Journal of Sustainable Tourism* Vol. 8 No. 3 2000, © R. Scheyvens 2000.

In some instances we have been unable to trace the owners of copyright material, and we would appreciate any information that would enable us to do so.

PART I

Tourism and development: a contentious relationship

Introduction: what is tourism *for* development?

CHAPTER 1

Introduction

This book looks at tourism and development. Its primary aim is to consider appropriate ways in which tourism can facilitate rather than impede development, particularly from the perspective of Third World peoples. Thus while recognising the well-documented problems that tourism can bring to Third World societies, the focus of this book is unashamedly positive. Rather than labelling Third World peoples simply as 'victims' of poorly planned tourism development, it seeks to learn from past mistakes and to highlight examples of positive engagement of Third World communities in tourism development. Outright condemnation of tourism in the Third World seems inappropriate when many communities are struggling to find means of improving their well-being and as such, they have identified tourism as a key strategy for development (Figure 1.1). While tourism should not be seen as a panacea for the myriad of development problems facing Third World countries, it can bring definite benefits and help to reduce inequality between the rich and poor (Cater 1995: 214). It is thus seen as more constructive to search for examples of good practice which demonstrate ways in which communities are effectively securing significant benefits from tourism while also retaining some control over tourism as a process, than to search relentlessly for negative impacts.

Essentially this book attempts to show that tourism can work *for* development. Development in this context does not simply refer to an economic process, as commonly perceived. Rather, development is a multidimensional process leading to what can be described succinctly as 'good change' (Chambers 1997: xiv). In recognition of the dependency and lack of power of many Third World states in the global arena, and the marginalised position of many communities within Third World states, development herein is seen as embracing values of self-sufficiency, self-determination and empowerment, as well as improving people's living standards (Friedmann 1992; Mowforth and Munt 1998).

Figure 1.1   Zulu boys try to earn money after school by performing for tourists at the entrance to the Hluhluwe-Umfolozi Park, South Africa.

Thus this book supports the view that '. . . it may be possible to reconstruct the modernist project of development in a more accountable, diverse, and just way' (Blaikie 2000: 1047).

This chapter now presents an overview of issues relating to the growth of tourism in the Third World, which is followed by a discussion of the need to consider tourism from the perspective of local communities. Next, mass tourism and alternative tourism are compared in order to ascertain whether these forms of tourism can both have something positive to offer in terms of local level development. To conclude, there is an explanation of the key terms used in this book, including complex terms raised in this chapter such as 'community' and 'alternative tourism', and an overview of the book's structure.

Tourism in the Third World

Tourism is said to be the largest industry in the world and as the figures below attest, it is growing rapidly. Table 1.1 shows the increasing importance of Third World destinations as a market for international tourists. Growth rates for the traditionally strong tourist destinations of Europe and the Americas

Table 1.1 Growth in tourist arrivals by region, actual and forecast, 1990–2020

Region	Average growth rate p.a. (%)	
	1990–95 (actual)	1995–2020 (forecast)
Middle East	8.6	6.7
East Asia/Pacific	8.3	7
Africa	6	5.5
South Asia	5.9	6.2
Europe	3.4	3.1
Americas	3.4	3.8

Source: Adapted from WTO (1998: 5, 10).

Table 1.2 Forecast inbound tourism by region, 2000 and 2020

Region	International tourist arrivals (millions)	
	2000	2020
Europe	386	717
East Asia/Pacific	105	438
Americas	131	284
Africa	26	75
Middle East	14	69
South Asia	4	19

Source: After WTO (1998: 10).

over the next 20 years look small by comparison. However, when we consider overall arrivals in Table 1.2, it is clear that Europe is still likely to receive the greatest volume of tourists by the year 2020, but the Americas will be edged out from second place by the East Asia/Pacific region. The other Third World regions show very high rates of growth, although they account for relatively small volumes of tourists overall.

While tourism to the Third World may seem small compared with tourism to Europe and North America, it is extremely important to the economic development of many Third World countries. For example, tourism is a significant economic sector in 11 of the 12 countries that contain 80 per cent of the world's poor (WTO 1998, cited in Ashley *et al.* 2000). The fact that it is growing strongly is of some concern precisely because in going to the Third World for their holidays, many tourists are seeking the 'untouched' (read 'pristine environments') and/or the 'exotic' (read 'tribal peoples in ethnic dress'), both environments and peoples which are particularly vulnerable to exploitation (Albuquerque and McElroy 1995). Other factors contributing to a growth in tourism to Third World destinations include tourists' increasing amounts of disposable income, improved airline schedules, and the introduction by tour companies of holiday packages which minimise the uncertainties of travel to the Third World and can reduce costs considerably (Akama 1999; Cater 1995).

According to the World Tourism Organization (WTO), continued growth in tourism will be partly stimulated by 'push' factors, such as growing congestion in both Western and Third World cities, and by increased socio-environmental awareness of consumers due to greater international media attention to global issues (WTO 1998). These factors, along with the change from a 'service' to an 'experience' economy, which focuses on 'delivering unique experiences that personally engage the consumer' (WTO 1998: 9), are likely to lead to greater development of niche markets, such as ecotourism and cultural tourism. The WTO believes that in an environment characterised by increasing volumes of tourists, improved transport technology, removal of barriers to international travel, and consumers interested in socially and environmentally responsible travel, 'both large scale, "mainstream" and smaller volume "individualised" tourism will prosper' (WTO 1998: 9). This once again suggests why both of these types of tourism should be considered in this book in terms of their potential to promote community development.

It is important to draw attention also to the likely growth in domestic tourism, which constitutes approximately 80 per cent of world tourism flows (Boniface and Cooper 1994: 56), and accounts for three to four times as much spending as international tourism (WTO 1998: 4). Third World governments tend to place little emphasis on domestic tourism, which is seen as less glamorous than the international market, despite the huge increase in this market in countries with a growing middle class (Richter 1989: 106). Growth of domestic tourism in the next 20 years is expected to be particularly strong in Third World countries, as is growth of intraregional tourism within Asia and Africa (WTO 1998: 4, 11), thus it would seem timely for Third World policy makers to look at what benefits such forms of tourism could bring to their countries.

While there has been considerable growth in tourism, it is a very fickle industry in practice. For example, although the average growth rate of international tourist arrivals in the East Asia/Pacific region reached 9.6 per cent in 1995–96, the Asian financial crisis led to an average growth rate of −0.01 per cent for this region in the 1996–97 period (WTO 1998: 6). Meanwhile the terrorist attacks on the USA on 11 September led tourist arrivals worldwide to drop by 11 per cent in the last four months of 2001, with particularly strong drops in some regions – Middle East (−30%) and South Asia (−24%) (www.world-tourism.org/newsroom/Release/more_releases/january2002/numbers_2001.htm).

Despite such anomalies, the WTO suggests that there is much potential for growth even beyond their projections for 2020 because this will only involve 7 per cent of the world's population travelling internationally (WTO 1998: 3). We need to consider, however, whether such levels of growth in tourism should actually be encouraged. Noting negative social and environmental implications of tourism, for example, Wheeller (1997) argues that a decrease in the volume of tourism is needed. Still in many cases growth in tourism is being aggressively pursued by Third World governments based on the assumption that the economic benefits – such as foreign exchange earnings, employment opportunities and external investment – will outweigh any costs of tourism development. Supporting the concerns of some Third World governments, a number of detailed academic studies have drawn attention to the pitfalls of Third World tourism (for example, Britton and Clarke 1987; de Kadt 1979; Harrison 1992; Lea 1988). When Ron O'Grady wrote *Third World Stopover: The Tourism Debate* in 1981, tourism was already the biggest industry in many Third World countries. His book, and many since, have sought to temper enthusiasm for this growth with concern for the social, economic and environmental consequences of tourism, especially as it affects Third World communities.

However, in some cases tourism has been blamed for a multitude of ills for which it bears little responsibility. Tourism is susceptible to taking the blame for negative changes simply because it is such a visible industry (Crick 1989, cited in Brunt and Courtney 1999). Environmental damage may result from a combination of factors including overpopulation, poor resource conservation and inappropriate agricultural practices, rather than being solely attributed to tourism development (Hall and Page 1999: 134). Also, alternatives to tourism development such as cash cropping could be worse for local well-being: '. . . the alternative to tourism development may be starvation and disease and, for many, a permanently damaged environment incapable of sustaining the existing communities' (Middleton and Hawkins 1998: 77). Clearly we need to move beyond using tourism as a scapegoat for environmental and social problems emerging in Third World countries and develop a more nuanced understanding of the ways in which tourism affects Third World states, peoples and their environments.

A focus on negative impacts of tourism development has led some to reject the notion that tourism could be an agent of development. Marchand and Parpart (1995: 1) suggest that postmodern and poststructuralist critiques of development which follow such logic are little more than 'a "First World" preoccupation, if not indulgence, with little practical application for Third World . . . development problems'. It seems particularly inappropriate to reject all notions of tourism as a strategy for development when it has been identified by communities as a potential means of improving their well-being. Instead we should be listening to the voices of Third World peoples regarding both their concerns about tourism and what they hope to achieve through tourism, before carefully considering if there are appropriate means of pursuing tourism, and appropriate types of tourism, which will readily meet the needs and desires of local communities:

> It seems ironic that contemporary scholarly debates should clamour for a 'post-development' era, just when voices from the margins – so celebrated in discourses of difference and alternative culture – are demanding their rights to greater access to a more generous idea of development (Rangan 1996: 222).

For example, even in locations like Goa, where there is a well-developed anti-tourism lobby, protests in the past targeting tourism have been aimed primarily at mass rather than independent tourists, despite the fact that it is the latter group which have given the area its 'hippy haven' reputation. Wilson (1997) cites a well-publicised case of Goan people throwing rotten fish and cow dung at tourist buses. Rather than an attack against all forms of tourism, he explains, this incident was instigated by small-scale local entrepreneurs who felt that charter-package tourism was putting them out of business by providing for all of the needs of tourists (accommodation, transport and food) in a single outlet. Wilson argues that, in general, Goans welcome international backpackers and domestic tourists because they can easily service their needs, and this has resulted in a tourism industry characterised by '. . . wide local ownership of resources and the broad distribution of benefits throughout the local community' (1997: 63).

Thus it is simplistic, if not erroneous, to cast Third World peoples as victims of globalising forces such as tourism:

> Tourism is part of the process of modernization, and globalization, but local actors are agents in this process, and not just the recipients of modernization processes. They attempt to develop strategies by which encounters with tourists can be beneficial to them (Erb 2000: 710).

Having established that despite concerns about the growth of tourism in the Third World it is still perceived as a viable development option by many countries, it is important to explore what tourism can mean for those at the coal face, that is, communities facing tourism development.

Tourism and local communities

Much of the focus of this book will be on communities most affected by tourism development. It is not a book about how governments can extract the greatest economic benefits from encouraging foreign investment in tourism. Nor does it use narrow measures of the potential benefits of tourism, such as the number of jobs created. If job creation transforms a community of self-sufficient farmers and traders into a community of employees reliant on a resort for menial, seasonal jobs as cleaners and service personnel, it would be difficult to argue that 'good change' had occurred. Rather, the interests of local communities in tourism development are placed foremost. Such an approach is supported by Ashley *et al.* (2000), who advocate the need for 'pro-poor tourism', that is, tourism development which explicitly takes the concerns and needs of the poor into account. Tourism which supports sustainable livelihoods and aims to minimise negative effects and maximise positive effects for local people has also been referred to as 'fair trade in tourism' (Shah and Gupta 2000). Meanwhile Hitchcock *et al.* (1993) and Butler (1990) support forms of tourism which provide poor, often peripheral peoples with a more equitable share of the benefits. In the main, however, involvement of the poorer classes has been ignored in tourism policy except in cases where it is asserted they will benefit from job creation or the assumed 'trickle-down' of any economic benefits which occur. In fact Brown (1998a: 237) argues that few academics '. . . have proposed alternative forms of tourism set in transitional, non-industrial, village economies . . . where rural producers can acquire cash incomes'.

While using tourism to promote community development sounds like a wonderful concept in principle, in practice it is fraught with difficulties. One problem relates to the heterogeneous nature of communities. Often communities are split into various factions based on a complex interplay of class, gender and ethnic factors, and certain families or individuals are likely to lay claim to privileges because of their apparent status. In such circumstances, it is unlikely that community members will have equitable access to involvement in tourism development and the benefits this can bring. Elites often co-opt and come to dominate community-based development efforts and monopolise the benefits of tourism (Akama 1996; Mansperger 1995; Mowforth and Munt 1998; Rudkin and Hall 1996; Sindiga 1995; Stonich et al. 1995). Hitchcock and Brandenburgh (1990), for example, discuss how among an indigenous group of people in the Kalahari Desert, adult, multilingual males are much more likely to benefit from tourist enterprises than other members of the community. It seems, therefore, that the assumption that communities can share unproblematically in the production of the tourism product and the benefits deriving from this is excessively romantic (Taylor 1995). We should consider equitable participation as a key issue of concern when promoting community involvement in tourism (France 1997b), and realise that issues of class, gender and ethnicity need to be considered when planning for and analysing tourism development.

A second problem with identifying tourism as a strategy for community development is that communities typically lack information, resources and power in relation to other stakeholders in the tourism process, thus they are vulnerable to exploitation (McLaren 1998). For example, when finance is not available locally, there is generally a loss of control to outside interests (Woodley 1993). This is not to suggest that communities have no power: in fact, if they own land in a highly desirable location, such as a picturesque setting just outside a national park, they may be in a good position to bargain with private sector interests wishing to develop an ecotourism lodge. However, in general communities are not as experienced in the business sector nor as knowledgeable about legal and financial processes as are other tourism stakeholders. A key challenge for this book will thus be to consider how to ensure that communities in Third World tourism destinations have access to information, skills and resources that they need to make informed decisions about *whether* to engage in tourism development, and if their answer is positive, *how* to engage in tourism development.

There are various depths to which communities are involved in tourism, from indirect involvement such as collecting lease money from a tour operator who brings tourists on to tribal land, to community-based ventures. Community-based tourism ventures are those in which members of local communities have a high degree of control over the activities taking place, and a significant proportion of the economic benefits accrue to them. They may also be characterised by local ownership and a low level of leakage (Cater 1993; Woodley 1993). While this might be seen as an ideal situation, in practice many communities lack the skills, experience or networks – as mentioned above – to successfully engage in tourism in such ways and they may prefer to work in partnership with other stakeholders. In addition, because of negative experiences with outsiders in the past, some indigenous communities are wary that dealing directly with tourists and the tourism industry may undermine their cultural integrity and sense of self-esteem, thus they would prefer to be involved indirectly in tourism. Altman and Finlayson (1993) for example, note that some Aboriginal groups in Australia would rather produce crafts which are sold by others, or receive a percentage of gate takings for a protected area, than have direct contact with tourists.

While it is important not to romanticise the opportunities which tourism may provide for economic development within local communities, it is nevertheless clear that there is great potential in this area (Box 1.1). For this potential to be actualised, however, there is a need for cooperation with a range of other stakeholders in tourism development. It is a fact that communities rarely initiate tourism development without input from an external source, whether a local non-governmental organisation promoting sustainable livelihoods, an international conservation agency, a donor, a government small business officer, a park ranger or a private tourism operator. It is vital that equitable ways of communities working with these other stakeholders are developed, which is why Part III of this book will concentrate on roles other stakeholders can play in supporting community involvement in tourism.

BOX 1.1

Tourism as a tool for economic development among poorer communities

- brings consumers to the destination area thus providing local people with a potential market for additional goods and services
- provides opportunities for small-scale, informal sector workers to earn an income
- places a value on natural and cultural resources
- brings economic opportunities to remote and/or marginal areas
- provides opportunities for the involvement of economically marginalised groups, such as women.

Source: Based on Ashley *et al.* (2000); Macleod (1998).

Mass versus alternative tourism?

Often community involvement in tourism is only mentioned as part of so-called 'alternative' development strategies. Indeed, criticism of mass tourism is particularly evident from those who have a strong commitment to the interests of local communities. Thus, for example, Shah and Gupta's (2000: 40) careful analysis of tourism case studies from around Asia concludes that '. . . mass tourism, especially that associated with luxury hotels and resorts, does not always bring the best returns and has significant negative social impacts on local communities'. In response to such critiques over the social, economic and environmental impacts of conventional, mass tourism, tourism providers have established a growing selection of alternative tourism products. Such products go by a range of names, including the following: ecotourism, responsible tourism, green tourism, cultural tourism, soft tourism, ethnic tourism, alternative tourism and sustainable tourism. The question is, are these just new names for old products which have ultimately been repackaged to appear more attractive to consumers, or do they indicate a fundamental change in approach to tourism?

Alternative tourism entered into academic debates following Dernoi's (1981) publication entitled 'Alternative tourism: towards a new style in North–South relations'. Support for alternative tourism was 'driven by "a sense of outrage" over the misuse of nature, the costs of materialism and the loss of culture' in tourism destinations (de Kadt 1990: abstract). Instead, alternative tourism supports forms of tourism which are small scale, minimise environmental and cultural interference, and which prioritise community needs, community involvement and community interests, rather than being based on an agenda of economic growth which is often of primary benefit to interests based in Western countries. Such an approach is evident in the following statement by Khan (1997: 990), who makes strong claims about the benefits of ecotourism:

> Ecodevelopment promotes the use of indigenous knowledge, material, and labour. Use of local expertise and labour is financially beneficial to the community and creates a stronger multiplier effect as opposed to leakage due to import of expertise and labor. Moreover, this resists unlimited foreign investments and puts a cap on economic, sociocultural, and environmental carrying capacity. By emphasizing local lifestyles, values, and economic well-being of the local community, ecotourism promotes local identity, pride, and self-accomplishment. By empowering the community through local participation, ecotourism also creates an opportunity for self-generating tourism as opposed to capitalistic control of mass tourism.

According to Medlik (1993), alternative tourism indicates a new type of tourism which is socially and environmentally rather than profit-driven, and which seeks to minimise harm to the peoples and environments of destination area. Alternative tourism also purportedly attempts to develop more meaningful relationships between 'hosts' and 'guests' (Eadington and Smith 1992: 3). It has been suggested that alternative tourists are preferable to mass tourists because they adopt a specific approach to travel which is more sensitive to local peoples and environments (Loker-Murphy and Pearce 1995; Macleod 1998). Thus, 'While mass tourism has attracted trenchant criticism as a shallow and degrading experience for Third World host nations and peoples, new tourism practices have been viewed benevolently and few critiques have emerged' (Munt 1994: 50).

It is certainly timely to reflect on the concept of alternative tourism, which Brohman (1996a: 63) identifies as 'one of the most widely used (and abused) phrases in the tourism literature'. It is not only the tourism industry which has espoused support for alternative tourism, as noted by Hall: '. . . many governmental agencies and tourism academics have been caught up in the "sexy", supposedly "new", forms of tourism such as ecotourism and cultural tourism'. However, he goes on to note, we should be wary of uncritically embracing such alternative tourism: 'There is . . . a somewhat mistaken belief that these forms of tourism are somehow ethically superior' (Hall, in Hall and Butler 1995: 105). A number of writers are therefore sceptical about the supposed benefits of alternative tourism (Butler 1990; Macleod 1998; Mowforth and Munt 1998), suggesting that it may merely provide a more socially and environmentally friendly façade for continuing exploitation of Third World peoples and environments: ' "Alternative" travel . . . works as a reassuring front for continued extension of the logistics of the commodity system, even as it masquerades as a (liberal) project of cultural concern, and despite the best intentions of its advocates' (Hutnyk 1996: 215).

Some query the contention that alternative tourists will have fewer negative effects on the host community and destination than mass tourists. In fact, as Butler notes, alternative tourism may be more invasive because: '. . . alternative forms of tourism penetrate further into the personal space of residents . . . [and] expose often fragile resources to greater visitation . . .' (Butler 1990: 41). Others question the assumption that alternative types of tourism are always beneficial and will be well supported by local communities. For example, in their research on indigenous homestay accommodation in Bali, Wall and Long (1996) found that tensions had developed between neighbours, with those not involved in homestays complaining of noise associated with the visitors while homestay operators complained of noise made by chickens and dogs. Homestays also resulted in heavier workloads for women and children as it was their responsibility to clean, cook, shop and do the laundry for the business. Such factors led Wall and Long to conclude that 'small-scale, indigenous, tourism development, which is advocated by many proponents of "appropriate" tourism, is not without associated problems and will require compromises and trade-offs to be made' (1996: 45).

Alternative tourism will not always be regarded by communities as more beneficial to them than mass tourism either (Weaver and Oppermann 2000). Mass tourism, for example, may be preferred if it brings in more money to local communities. Local communities may also favour larger-scale tourism enterprises if they feel these are more likely to be competitive. Thus, for example, while '. . . small is beautiful in the context of ecotourism . . . small is also vulnerable' (Thomlinson and Getz 1996: 197). Mass tourism could actually be perceived as less culturally invasive by a local community if it involves busloads of tourists coming to them once a day for a cultural performance and to buy and then returning to their hotels, rather than cultural tourism whereby outsiders stay in their homes for a few days. There is also the 'glamour' element of mass tourism, with many communities seeing the trappings which go along with mass tourism, such as five-star hotels and luxury resorts, as signifiers of true development. This is despite the fact that in practice local people may be banned from entering these establishments unless they have a lot of money.

Nevertheless there is still evidence to support the claim that alternative tourism can be more beneficial to local communities than mass tourism. If conforming with ideal definitions, alternative tourism initiatives would provide significant opportunities for local involvement and benefits, mutual education of tourists and those in destination areas, and be carried out at a scale and at a pace which suited local interests. It would also be small or medium in scale, organised by families or cooperatives at the local level, and heavily reliant on local labour, materials and management (Brown 1998a).

This does not suggest that alternative tourism can, or should, take over completely from mass tourism. Regardless of the allure of alternative forms of tourism, we cannot divorce ourselves from the reality that 'much of third world tourism today is not small-scale, ecologically oriented, or even broadly participatory' (Clancy 1999: 5). Thus there is a need to examine mass tourism and how it might be reformed.[1] Wood and House (1991: 57) point out that with the increasing demand for travel experiences, there is definitely a place for mass tourism and that this can be catered for adequately at specialist sites like Disneyland which are set up to deal with a high turnover of visitors. Not everyone can be, or wants to be, an alternative tourist:

> . . . a sufficient number of people just want to go and escape for 'sun, sea and sand'. It doesn't really matter where and if these people go to the holiday clubs and on the cruise ships, a lot of pressure is taken off the other more sensitive areas. This is basically an honest formula for a holiday and may ultimately have the least negative consequences for the host country and its population (Wood and House 1991: 58).

It has been further suggested that alternative forms of tourism can readily develop into mass tourism, and that therefore it is useful to conceptualise distinctions between alternative and mass tourism as occurring along a continuum, rather than being polar opposites (France 1997b; Macleod 1998). For example, backpacking tourism has been regarded as an alternative form of 'off the beaten track' tourism in the Third World, but recently 'backpacker ghettos' where Western music, food and culture play a strong role have emerged in some parts of the Third World, providing evidence of an institutionalisation of this form of supposedly 'alternative' tourism (Aziz 1999; Cohen 1987). Similarly, it is apparent that blurring of the distinction between alternative and mass tourism occurs when mass tourists are motivated by alternative forms of tourism, such as ecotourism, and this influences their attitudes to travel and their behaviour while travelling. Weaver (1999: 809) thus distinguishes between 'hardcore' ecotourists and 'passive and casual' ecotourists, essentially mass tourists with an interest in nature. He notes that it is the latter group which, because of sheer numbers, has the greatest potential impact on local economies and may provide the greatest incentive for protection of natural areas.

Such examples support de Kadt's (1990) argument that if truly sustainable tourism is the goal, a dichotomous understanding of differences between mass and alternative tourism is not particularly helpful. Alternative tourism is not inherently 'good' and nor is mass tourism inherently 'bad' for local communities, and there is a great deal of overlap between the two types of tourism in practice. Furthermore, even with rapid growth of the alternative tourism market, Third World communities will continue to bear many of the costs of tourism development and share in few of the benefits unless some fundamental changes take place within mass tourism. It is not sufficient just to support small-scale alternatives which only involve a small percentage of the tourism market. Rather, we should explore further the idea that 'mass tourism itself can be practised in ways that minimize and mitigate its obvious disbenefits' (Husbands and Harrison 1996: 1). This quote is instructive: it is the *way in which tourism is practised* which must change, not just the rhetoric the industry uses to promote itself.

The above discussion has supported the need for both change within mass tourism, especially towards more social and environmental responsibility, and for alternative tourism to remain true to its meaning rather than merely being applied as a marketing label by profit-hungry tourism operators. It is thus apt that in its search for appropriate forms of tourism which promote community development, this book identifies both initiatives towards the mass and alternative tourism ends of the spectrum. While many of the examples of good practice in tourism which will be highlighted in the second part of this book could be seen as alternative ventures, an effort will be made throughout to identify strategies which can, or are, transforming mass tourism into a more socially and environmentally friendly prospect as well.

Terminology

Some of the key terms used in this book need to be clarified before the main discussion commences. Undoubtedly the most problematic term referred to is 'Third World'. The term 'Third World' was coined in 1952 by Alfred Sauvy, a French economist and demographer who used the word 'third' to suggest that it was 'excluded from its proper role in the world by two other worlds', not to suggest that it was inferior (Hadjor 1993: 11).[2] While the term 'Third World' lumps together a diverse range of countries into one category and thus is in danger of oversimplifying their socio-economic circumstances, there are also undeniable similarities among many Third World countries. These similarities stem largely from their histories of colonialism and imperialism, and are represented in their current economic dependency and in their disadvantaged political position in the world. The term 'Third World' thus draws attention to inequities in the world; it '. . . helps to emphasise the ways in which power, resources and development are unequally and unevenly shared globally' (Mowforth and Munt 1998: 6).

While the term 'Third World' is thus used in preference to a term such as 'less developed world' which implicitly infers inferiority, 'First World' is not used because of the notions of superiority it implies. Similarly, the increasingly popular use of 'North' versus 'South' in writing on development issues is rejected as this makes a geographical division out of what is really a social, economic and political division (Hadjor 1993: 11). Instead 'Western' will be used as the alternative to 'Third World' countries as this term has come to represent those societies exhibiting the economic systems, consumer culture and individualism characteristic of North American, Australasian and European countries.

The terms mass tourism and 'conventional tourism' will be used interchangeably in this text along with their supposed antithesis, alternative tourism. Brown (1998a: 237) defines 'conventional tourism' as 'capitalist multinational enterprises operating under the dictates of market competition and technological efficiency'. Meanwhile alternative tourism is

> [a] term generally used to refer to forms of tourism which seek to avoid adverse and enhance positive social, cultural and environmental impacts. Usually characterized by: small scale; individual, independent or small group activity; slow, controlled and regulated development; as well as emphasis on travel as experience of host cultures and on maintenance of traditional values and societies (Medlik 1993: 10).

As discussed above, however, while alternative tourism theoretically aims to distinguish itself from mass tourism by adopting a more sustainable and equitable approach, this is not what always happens in practice. While we can still use these terms, therefore, it should not be assumed that alternative tourism is ethically superior to mass tourism, nor that they are polar opposites. Examples of both forms of tourism need to be carefully scrutinized when considering ways of promoting the development of local communities.

This book is particularly concerned with ways in which communities can be beneficially involved in tourism but we cannot take the term 'communities' for granted. Problems in defining the 'community' are as much about scale as diversity. For example, would 'the community' include only people from a village adjacent to a new tourism attraction, or villagers from the surrounding area who may also want to benefit from the attraction? Does it include just 'locals', or migrant workers? Does it include only the poorer classes, or also the minority of elites (de Beer and Elliffe 1997)? In a very broad sense a community can be defined as 'A social network of interacting individuals, usually concentrated into a defined territory' (Johnston 2000: 101). This definition could include many different types of communities, from relatively self-sufficient villages in the Pacific with minimal engagement in the global economy to communities of sex workers in Bangkok with intricate ties to tourists around the globe. Milne (1998: 40) takes Johnston's definition a step further, noting that communities can 'provide identity, meaning and a sense of self-worth to their members'. Note that neither of these definitions claims that communities are homogeneous entities characterised by shared aims and the desire of all members for mutual well-being.

It is also worth reflecting on the term 'tourism' itself. As both a global industry and an agent of development, tourism embodies complex economic, social and political relationships (Butler 1990). While many studies have focused on how tourism *impacts*, usually in negative ways, on destination peoples and environments, this is mainly based on analysis of tourism as an industry. This book, by contrast, mainly focuses on tourism as a form of development: tourism and development are not necessarily independent entities (Clancy 1999). If practised in an equitable and sustainable manner, therefore, tourism should be able to bring considerable benefits to people living in Third World communities. This is a presumption which will be tested throughout this book.

Structure of this book

This book is divided into three main parts. To begin, Part I considers the contentious relationship between tourism and development. Chapter 1 has contributed to this aim by raising concerns about the nature of tourism growth, by explaining why it is vital that local communities are considered central to debates over appropriate forms of tourism development, and by exploring hypothetical and actual differences between mass and alternative tourism. Chapters 2, 3 and 4 all examine how development theory helps us to understand tourism processes and explore ways of overcoming some of the problems which tourism can cause. In Chapter 2 the focus is on critically assessing how tourism has been understood by proponents of modernisation and dependency theories, while Chapter 3 draws on postmodern theory in considering how the tourist gaze is constructed with respect to the peoples and places of the Third World. To conclude Part I, Chapter 4 examines what the neopopulist and sustainable development literature relating to empowerment and participation can contribute to our understanding of effective strategies for community involvement in tourism.

While it is important to look critically at the tourism industry, equally challenging, and of more practical relevance from the perspective of communities seeking constructive, equitable engagement with tourism, is to look at ways in which tourism can lead to development. Thus it is that Part II, 'The search for appropriate forms of tourism', explores positive examples of tourism in practice in the Third World. The chapters in this section are organised as follows: ecotourism (Chapter 5); tourism and protected areas (Chapter 6); justice tourism (Chapter 7); gender-sensitive tourism (Chapter 8); and budget tourism (Chapter 9). In each chapter, the meaning of these forms of tourism development is discussed and their potential for supporting the well-being of local communities is considered. While recognising their limitations, examples and case studies which demonstrate positive aspects of each form of tourism development are then purposefully sought out.

Taking the practical focus of this book a step further, Part III, 'Promoting development through tourism', comprises three chapters which consider ways in which governments, actors from civil society (non-governmental organisations and local action groups) and private interests in the tourism industry, can facilitate appropriate tourism development. The latter group is particularly important to consider, as strategies to promote benefits to local communities from involvement in tourism must be commercially viable (Ashley *et al.* 2000). A concluding chapter summarises the main ideas presented throughout the book and suggests principles to guide those attempting to ensure that tourism contributes to both development and empowerment of Third World communities in the future.

At the end of each chapter questions which can help readers to review the main issues are presented, along with suggestions for further reading and a list of useful websites for those who wish to explore the topics in greater depth.

Questions

1. Which Third World regions have seen the most rapid growth of tourism in recent years? List possible pros and cons of such growth.

2. Apart from bringing economic benefits, do you think tourism can contribute to the well-being of Third World communities?

3. Does alternative tourism necessarily provide a positive change from conventional mass tourism?

Suggestions for further reading

Butler, R. 1990 'Alternative tourism: pious hope or trojan horse?' *Journal of Travel Research*, 28(3): 40–5.

Cater, E. 1995 'Consuming spaces: global tourism', pp. 183–231 in J. Allen and C. Hamnett (eds), *A Shrinking World? Global Unevenness and Inequality*, Oxford University Press, Oxford, in association with the Open University, Milton Keynes.

Mowforth, M. and Munt, I. 1998 *Tourism and Sustainability: New tourism in the Third World*, Routledge, London (Chapter 4: Tourism and Sustainability).

Useful websites

World Tourism Organization – information on meetings, publications and statistics:
www.world-tourism.org

Information on the Department for International Development's pro-poor tourism strategy, including background papers:
www.propoortourism.org.uk/index.html

Notes

1. See Weaver's interesting discussion of the difference between 'Sustainable mass tourism' (SMT) and 'Unsustainable mass tourism' (UMT) (2001: 165–8).
2. These other two worlds were the Western capitalist countries and the Eastern communist countries.

Modernisation, dependency and globalisation

CHAPTER 2

Introduction

This chapter raises key theoretical issues surrounding the contentious relationship between tourism and development. Chapter 1 noted that there is a great deal of negative literature about Third World tourism and this chapter will show that much of this derives from dependency theory thinking which emerged in response to the overwhelmingly positive, modernist ideas about tourism espoused before it. Discourse surrounding globalisation is also considered, as this has also focused on problems with the way in which Third World countries are economically, socially and politically marginalised, which makes it difficult for them to exert an influence over global tourism and secure significant benefits from it. Chapters 3 and 4, to follow, will address contemporary theories on development in relation to tourism in order to show how ideas have progressed with the help of postmodern, sustainable development and neopopulist perspectives. The various theories presented in Part I of this book can help us to recognise problems with tourism as well as inspiring insights into the context within which Third World communities can benefit from engaging with the tourism industry.

Changing perspectives on tourism

In order to provide an overview of how perspectives on tourism have changed over the last few decades, this chapter starts with a discussion of two time lines. This is intended to help readers grasp the diversity of attitudes to tourism in Third World contexts, as well as different conceptual approaches which can be used to understand tourism development. The time line in Figure 2.1 presents viewpoints on tourism from a variety of Third World stakeholders, including governments, business interests and civil society actors. This is distinct from Figure 2.2 which demonstrates how perspectives on Third World tourism from academics, both those from the Third World and the West, have evolved over time. Obviously there is some overlap as, for example, protests over the impacts of tourism by Third World action groups certainly stimulated debates among academics concerning the form and function of tourism development. These figures are intended to provide a very broad overview of perspectives on Third World tourism, rather than to offer a comprehensive framework covering every viewpoint and theory.[1]

Both Figures 2.1 and 2.2 clearly demonstrate how tourism in the Third World was traditionally seen primarily as a means of promoting economic growth and thus of achieving the goal of modernisation:

> Up to twenty years ago all studies tended to assume that the extension of the industry in the Third World was a good thing, though it was acknowledged that there were a number of associated problems to be overcome in time (Lea 1988: 1).

Such thinking was ousted in the 1970s by perspectives on tourism informed by social theory and the environmental movement, with pressure coming from both academics and Third World protest groups. While initially academic works on tourism had a tendency to be descriptive in nature, often using models to depict tourist flows or the development of destination areas over time, this period witnessed '. . . a maturing depth in the theoretical works and conceptual treatment of the tourism phenomenon' (Teo and Chang 1998: 120). Thus academic writing on tourism has come to be characterised by a stronger role of critical perspectives which make a concerted effort to understand the workings of tourism as a process. For example, those writing from a political economy perspective have highlighted how tourism is representative of the uneven power relations inherent in the capitalist system (Britton and Clarke 1987; Mowforth and Munt 1998). There are also postmodern reflections on the tourism industry (Urry 1990; Ringer 1998) which consider issues such as the ways in which Third World destinations and peoples have been (re)created and (re)presented in order to attract tourists. Meanwhile the burgeoning literature on sustainable development has targeted problems associated with growth-oriented perspectives on tourism development which do not recognise the finite nature of many of the earth's resources. Finally, a combination of both people's movements in Third World countries and a shift in academic thinking have contributed to neopopulist perspectives on tourism which suggest that Third World communities need to have more control over tourism processes if they are to experience the full range of benefits that tourism can bring.

Concurrently, however, there has been a resurgence in support for modernisation thinking under the guise of neoliberalism. Neoliberalism is strongly supported

1950s/1960s	1970s to mid-1980s	Mid-1980s to late 1990s	2000+
• Many newly independent governments embraced growth in tourism as a means of internationalising their economies and earning income for meeting national development goals • Advent of commercial jets allowed Third World destinations to promote themselves to Western markets • Resort-style development often favoured • Incentives provided to encourage foreign investment in tourism • Limited examples of Third World governments which sought to reject tourism or to control the spread of tourism and its impacts (e.g. Bhutan)	• Tourism became the leading economic sector, or a close contender, in many small Third World countries • Concern from some governments about the rapid, unplanned growth of tourism, the development of tourist ghettos and the negative social and environmental impacts of tourism in specific locations • Most governments favoured luxury tourism development while hoping other sectors, such as the 'hippy market' would disappear • Little attention paid to allowing the needs and interests of people in the destination area to shape tourism development. Rather, it was assumed they would automatically benefit from income-generation opportunities and employment in tourist enterprises • Growth of NGOs and people's organisations which monitored the impacts of tourism and criticised foreign tourism (e.g. Consumers' Association of Penang in Malaysia; protest groups in Goa, India)	• Many governments sought to increase tourist arrivals to pay off foreign debts • A small number of governments opted for alternative models of tourism development, such as a focus on nature tourism (e.g. Belize), or low-volume, high-value tourism (e.g. Botswana) • Efforts to 'clean up' forms of tourism seen as less desirable, such as sex tourism • Continued monitoring and lobbying by anti-tourism groups in selected countries and increasing networking among them, facilitated by the internet • Recognition among pro-development NGOs that tourism could be a strategy for community development, thus efforts made to assist communities to gain benefits from tourism • Asian economic crisis of the late 1990s serves as a warning to governments of the dangers of relying too heavily on the tourism sector	• Growth of the middle classes in many Third World countries – their interest in tourism forces governments to respond to the needs and concerns of this sector of the tourism market • Greater development of niche markets in response to tourist demand for environmentally and ethically responsible tourism, e.g. strong interest from an increasingly urbanised population in the West to visit protected areas in the Third World • Increasing conflicts between environmentalists wishing to protect the world's last remaining pristine areas (often using local organisations as conduits to push their agendas) and poverty-stricken indigenous people who rely on natural resources to meet their livelihood needs • Increasing recognition of the marketability of 'culture' in response to interest from consumers disillusioned with cultural homogenisation resulting from globalisation • Lobby groups sceptical of mainstream support for supposedly 'alternative' forms of tourism, e.g. there has been a backlash against 2002 being named by the United Nations as the 'International Year of Ecotourism' • Terrorist attacks on the USA on 11 September 2001 deter many would-be long-haul travellers and lead Third World governments to tighten security at gateways and important attractions

Figure 2.1 Time line – tourism development in the Third World: perspectives from within.

1950s/1960s	1970s to mid-1980s	Mid-1980s to late 1990s	2000+
• Academic interest in tourism dominated by economists convinced that growth of tourism in the Third World was a 'good thing', integral to the modernisation of Third World economies and cultures through the spread of Western-style development • Efforts to quantify the movement of tourists across space began	• Criticism of tourism's impacts on local people and their environments often headed by sociologists, anthropologists and geographers. This was mainly descriptive at first, followed by efforts to conceptualise the forces at work (e.g. dependency theory suggested that companies based in 'core' Western countries were exploiting the resources and people of Third World countries) • Recognition that many of the supposed economic benefits of tourism were lost to the Third World (e.g. large hotel chains repatriating their profits) • 'Small is beautiful' philosophy stimulated debates over finding alternative development strategies which could bring greater local benefits • Beginnings of interest in 'green', more sustainable tourism, due to concern over environmental damage in some tourist sites, and the understanding that environmental degradation actually undermines tourism potential	• Neo-liberal stance sees tourism as a good way to earn foreign exchange to balance payments and pay off foreign debt • Also strong growth of critical perspectives on tourism, as reflected in the following three approaches: • Sustainable development perspectives: advocates of tourism take a 'weak sustainability' perspective which allows for economic growth through responsible use of natural resources. Support for environmentally friendly tourism and the idea of 'ecotourism'. Recognition that local people need to benefit from tourism if they are to support conservation efforts • Postmodern stance: exposes the way in which Third World peoples and landscapes have been positioned as the 'Other' to be consumed by tourists. Recognises also local people's agency and the fact that they can negotiate the way in which tourism develops and resist tourism in specific places. • Neopopulist stance: recognition of problems which arise when there is only passive participation of local people in tourism development, and support for strategies which aim to empower local communities to have some control over tourism development and ensure they share equitably in the benefits of tourism. Recognition of ethical issues regarding distribution of the benefits of tourism and the rights of communities to resist tourism development	• Debates rage over 'alternative' forms of tourism – e.g. are 'ecotourism' and 'responsible tourism' just fancy labels to attract clients? • Increasing recognition that 'mass' and 'alternative' forms of tourism are not necessarily at opposite ends of the spectrum – there is much overlap in practice and alternative forms of tourism are not necessarily ethically superior e.g. 'Neo-dependency' writers argue that both conventional, mass tourism and new forms of tourism (such as revolutionary and ethnic tourism) create dependency and perpetuate unequal power relations between Western and Third World countries • Academic critique leads to growth of 'corporate responsibility' among tourism providers, mainly demonstrated in terms of environmental (rather than social or economic) measures • Postmodern perspectives continue to offer insights especially into areas in which there has been limited development of ideas previously, e.g. the way in which tourism influences gender roles and relations and vice versa, and the means by which communities in destination areas negotiate their cultural identity

Figure 2.2 Time line – academic perspectives on tourism in the Third World.

by multilateral institutions such as the World Bank and International Monetary Fund (IMF), which are keen to find ways in which Third World countries can earn foreign exchange to pay off their foreign debts. To follow, the bulk of this chapter comprises an elaboration of modernisation theory and neoliberalism, which generally see tourism in a very positive light by focusing on its economic potential, and a discussion of critiques of modernisation thinking and concerns over globalisation inspired by political economy perspectives. Other theories raised in Figure 2.2 will be elaborated upon in the two chapters to follow.

Modernisation theory and neoliberalism

From the 1950s through to the 1970s, development discourse was dominated by strategies and approaches which arose from modernisation theory. Modernisation theory was based on the assumption of a dualism between the 'undeveloped' Third World and the 'developed' Western world, with the latter supposedly occupying superior status to which the former should aspire. It further espoused that inputs of capital, technology and knowledge were needed from Western countries to kick-start development in the Third World (Rostow 1960). Once economic growth started to occur, it was assumed that any benefits would 'trickle down' to improve the quality of life of the majority of a country's population.

While industrialisation was seen as the main means of economic growth under modernisation theory, the 'soft' industry of tourism was also identified as an important tool for economic development. Tourism was assessed as having great growth potential and it was also seen as a means of providing employment in the formal economy (Clancy 1999). There was little mention of the potential links between tourism and the informal sector, as this sector was positioned as being of limited importance in a modern economy. Proponents of modernisation also felt that tourism development could encourage social development through the spread of new skills and technology and that growth of tourism would go hand in hand with infrastructural improvements in areas such as transport and communications. Encouraging tourism was further seen as a way of diversifying the economies of countries otherwise dependent on the export of a few primary products, such as sugar and bananas. The agriculture sector was not seen as playing a dominant role in a modern economy.

Thus some governments pursued tourism development with a passion, and by the 1970s tourism had become the major economic sector in a number of small Third World countries (Lea 1993). It soon became clear, however, that a modernisation approach to tourism development had some serious negative spin-offs: '. . . an earlier simple faith in the merits of economic growth as such has given way to questions about the balance of that growth and the distribution of material benefits' (de Kadt 1979: xi). Many of the benefits accrued to foreign investors and multinational corporations, while local benefits were cornered by a minority of elites. Furthermore, government money was invested in establishing infrastructure for tourism while the basic infrastructural needs of citizens for water and electricity, for example, were pushed aside. A number of social and cultural problems also came to be associated with tourism in the Third World (Harrison 1992), including drug abuse, crime and prostitution among the local population in destination areas, denigration of important spiritual or cultural sites by tourists, and a rapid undermining of the values and norms of societies in the destination area. Environmentalists meanwhile started to raise serious concerns about the pressure on unique ecosystems of rapid tourism development, and problems associated with the inadequate disposal of waste from tourists.

While diversification of economies occurred in some contexts, in other cases tourism simply took over from forms of agricultural production. Thus some countries have become heavily dependent on tourist dollars such that if demand suddenly declines, as happened in Fiji for example during military coups, their entire economy is thrown into crisis (Australian Department of Foreign Affairs and Trade 2000). Small countries are particularly vulnerable to international fluctuations in demand by tourists, for while they only constitute 0.3 per cent of the world's population they receive 4.6 per cent of international visitors (Weaver 1998a: 293).

While such critiques gave modernisation theory a battering in the 1970s, the 1980s saw a rapid growth in support for a revamped form of modernisation theory known as neoliberalism. The neoliberal paradigm currently dominates thinking on development (Blaikie 2000). In a similar way to modernisation theory, neoliberalism was based on a belief in market-led growth and economic liberalisation; thus removing barriers to trade and encouraging foreign investment become key government policies. This is despite the fact that, as Holder (1996: 145) argues:

> There are some cases where regulation is required, some protection is desirable, and some limits to privatisation and other processes must be set, either to protect the weak or because the benefits of particular processes have produced greater negative effects than positive results.

Under the neoliberal paradigm scant attention is paid to principles of self-sufficiency and self-determination, which had been important catchphrases of Third World development in the 1970s.

Brohman (1996a) asserts that a key problem with tourism in the Third World is that it continues to be pursued as an outward-oriented development strategy, in line with a neoliberal rationale for development. Rather than encouraging domestic tourism or promoting tourism as a means for developing cross-cultural awareness, for example, for most Third World countries tourism is explicitly being pursued as a means of earning foreign exchange. This is why, he suggests, tourism in the Third World has often left an unpleasant legacy, including dependence on foreign investment and skills, environmental problems, cultural decay and spatial inequality. There is little interest in this brand of thinking about forms of development which build upon the skills and knowledge of local people (Blaikie 2000).

A neoliberal model supposedly offers opportunities for both foreign and local operators to engage in tourism enterprises; however, this fails to recognise the power relations at play. Specifically, tour operators based in the West have inherent advantages over their Third World counterparts as the majority of the world's tourists derive from Western countries:

> It follows that such companies have become predominant in the control of international tourist movements. . . . In addition, their expertise, marketing connections and capital resources give them an overwhelming competitive advantage over local tourism operators (Cater 1995: 200).

Support for neoliberalism continues to be strong, based largely on a desire by multinational companies to secure markets for their products and to have unimpeded access to resources and investments around the world, and multilateral financial institutions' interest in securing the repayment of foreign debts. However, many Third World governments are also supportive of neoliberalism and in this regard they see the growing international tourism industry as offering them a great economic opportunity. Tourism is being embraced partly because they have experienced a slump in the price of their major commodity exports with, for example, returns for rice falling by 51 per cent and returns for coffee falling by 64 per cent between 1980 and 1997 (*New Internationalist* 1999: 16). Indebted countries subject to IMF and World Bank-sponsored structural adjustment programmes (SAPs), in particular, have felt pressure to earn foreign exchange through growth of tourism as is the case in India:

> It is no coincidence that the increase in tourist arrivals in India provoked by the 'Visit India 1991' advertising campaign coincides with the period in which International Monetary Fund (IMF) and World Bank directed 'market internationalization' also rises. Debates over tariff protection, the (re)introduction of transnational food and drink chains – Pepsi and Pizza Hut – and massive development of tourism infrastructure in India can be fitted into much wider, but nevertheless crucial, international processes of global economic 'readjustment' and 'restructuring', often brutal (Hutnyk 1996: 10).

Brohman (1996a) is concerned about the narrow perspective taken by governments who encourage more visitors to a country to increase foreign exchange, without linking this specifically to wider development goals such as poverty alleviation or balanced regional development. More visitors could just mean more money for elite businesspeople who have invested in resort development in key areas. Also of concern is the fact that neoliberalism asserts that market-led development is the ideal way of meeting not only economic, but social and political goals as well (Watts 2000b). However, these wide-ranging goals are often undermined in the face of tourism development in practice:

> if mass tourism promotes economic growth and development, then how come many
> tourist-receiving Third World countries . . . are suffering from foreign dependence
> along with persistent poverty, economic inequality, and destruction of cultures
> and communities in the name of tourism development (Khan 1997: 989).

It is furthermore asserted that the market is the best mechanism for valuing the
environment. There is a blatant contradiction, however, apparent in the notion
that tourism to the Third World will help to place a value on, and thus preserve,
natural areas which are otherwise under threat from human habitation. Basically,
as long as Third World countries continue to struggle with crippling debts they
will feel pressure to exploit their natural resources in order to pay off their debts.

Political economy perspectives

Political economy is a branch of the social sciences which examines the interrelationships between political and economic institutions and processes: 'The
political economy of tourism encompasses the ways in which the industry
manifests the division of labour, class relations, ideological content, and social
distributions specific to a social formation . . .' (Britton 1987b: 171). Thus
researchers adopting a political economy approach to tourism might be interested in the historical development of tourism in a particular area, considering
which social actors (private companies, state interests, local elites) have controlled tourism development, who is employed by tourism enterprises and on
what terms, and how the benefits of tourism have been distributed.

The major challenge to modernisation theory's promotion of tourism was
launched from a political economy perspective, which demonstrated that the
benefits of tourism in the Third World were often felt more by the West, whose
companies made profits from their investments in hotels and resorts in the
Third World, and whose airlines and travel agents secured the majority of revenue from those travelling to the Third World: '. . . Third World countries
especially are sub-ordinated to the touristic currents that flow from and to the
advanced capitalist economies' (Munt 1994: 54). Academics writing from a
political economy perspective are thus wary of the way in which Third World
countries have been incorporated into the global economy (Pleumarom 1994):

> The growth of tourism to developing societies has not come without controversy.
> . . . When developing countries promote this trade – the provision of tourism-
> related goods and services to foreign visitors – they are, in effect, embracing
> greater integration into the world economy. It is the terms of this integration, and
> the direct economic and political effects stemming from them, that invite this con-
> troversy (Clancy 1999: 2).

De Kadt's (1979) book, *Tourism: Passport to development?*, made an important contribution in this field, providing a thorough analysis of the relationship
between tourism and development in the Third World, concentrating on social

and cultural effects. Drawing on political economy theory, de Kadt stated that the case studies and issues presented in this book demonstrate that:

> no development strategy can hope to be successful without restructuring of North–South economic relations . . . major institutional and structural adjustments will be needed in the industrialized countries if the poor nations are to achieve their development goals (1979: xii–xiii).

This is an interesting challenge to the neoliberal stance which insists it is the Third World economies which need restructuring.

Krippendorf (1987) furthered the arguments against tourism by lending a political angle to debates which rested on economic dependency, claiming that tourism was colonialist in nature and that this undermined the autonomous decision-making power of local people. Such views are endorsed both by dependency theorists and by activists within Third World countries, such as Rohan Seon who wrote the calypso song 'Alien', an extract of which appears in Box 2.1.

BOX 2.1

Extract from the calypso song 'Alien'

All inclusive tax exclusives
And truth is
They're sucking up we juices
Buying up every strip of beach
Every treasured spot they reach . . .

For Lucians to enter
For lunch or dinner
We need reservations, passport and visa
And if you sell near the hotel
I wish you well
They will yell and kick you out to hell.

Chorus:
Like an alien
In we own land
I feel like a stranger
And I sensing danger
We can't sell out whole country
To please the foreign lobby
What's the point of progress
Is it really success
If we gain ten billion
But lose the land we live on?

Source: Pattullo (1996: 80–1).

Figure 2.3 Cartoon depicting the enclavic, exclusive nature of many tourism resorts in the Third World.

This song expresses the outrage of St Lucian people over resorts which buy up beautiful stretches of coastline and then forbid Caribbean people from entering unless they can buy an expensive day pass. Dependency theory positions tourism as a new form of imperialism (Figure 2.3), just another way in which the West is exploiting the physical and human resources of the Third World. Thus Third World countries were not 'undeveloped' but 'underdeveloped', suggesting that they had missed out on development opportunities because of the way in which they were tied to Western capitalist countries (Clancy 1999). Development of the 'core' capitalist countries was seen as occurring at the expense of 'peripheral' Third World societies.[2]

Britton (1982) used dependency theory to show how small island states which had pursued tourism development were particularly vulnerable in a global economy dominated by multinational corporations which controlled a range of tourism products and services, from transport to accommodation.

His work inspired wide application of dependency theory to research on Third World tourism, as demonstrated in the following quote by Akama (1999: 7–8):

> . . . the establishment and development of tourism in most Third World countries is usually externally oriented and controlled, and mainly responds to external market demands. In consequence, the nature of international tourism as a 'luxury and pleasure seeking industry' usually entails rich tourists from the metropolis (mainly from developed Northern countries) visiting and coming to enjoy tourist attractions in the periphery (mainly the poor and resource scarce countries in the South). These forms of tourism development accentuate the economic structure of dependency on external market demand, and also lead to 'alien' development (i.e. the establishment of tourism resorts in Third World countries) to which local people cannot relate and respond, both socially and economically.

Both Weaver (1998a) and Akama (1999) argue that core–periphery relations not only occur between Western and Third World countries, rather, they can exist within a state: 'Internally induced core–periphery dynamics . . . have been neglected as a framework for the analysis of Third World tourism, as if domestic involvement in the national tourism sector were somehow assumed to be either implicitly benign, or negligible' (Weaver 1998a: 292). In Kenya, the spatial concentration of tourism facilities and infrastructure increases the likelihood of negative impacts in tourism areas, and also precludes other areas from sharing in the benefits that tourism may bring (Akama 1999).

Dependency theorists have often drawn attention to the leakage of tourist dollars which occurs, for example, when multinational tourism companies follow centralised purchasing procedures which impede local managers from buying supplies locally (Brown 1998a). Overall, leakages can be as high as 70 per cent (Milne 1990, cited in Khan 1997: 989). This direct loss of the economic benefits of tourism to a host country is particularly evident when individuals book their travel through Western travel agencies, use Western airlines, stay in accommodation that is part of a multinational hotel chain, and eat mainly imported food and drink. Thus, for example, transnational companies based in the West dominate the international transport sector because of superior technology, sophisticated marketing strategies and established links with tour operators, making it difficult for Third World carriers to compete (Cater 1995). It is estimated that Kenya Airways transports less than 10 per cent of visitors to Kenya. In this respect it is useful to consider which contributes more to the local economy, the cruise ship shown in Figure 2.4 or the individuals whose boats are shown in Figure 2.5?

Figure 2.4   Cruise ship in Tahiti, French Polynesia.

Figure 2.5   Boat owners ply for tourist custom on the Buriganga River, Bangladesh. (*Source*: Henry Scheyvens)

Tourism in a globalising world

Literature on globalisation draws our attention to the fact that peoples, places and countries in our world are increasingly interdependent. Through the 'shrinking of space', distant and unfamiliar lands are now no longer seen as so out of reach or so unfamiliar (Teo and Chang 1998: 123). Countries once considered inaccessible to Western tourists because of geographical barriers such as distance or remote locations, transport and communication barriers such as a lack of airstrips and electronic booking mechanisms, or because of warfare or major cultural differences, are now not only becoming accessible – their very remoteness in the past has made them increasingly popular choices for travel today. Third World countries are also targeted by so many travellers because they offer something 'different' and they can be cheap (de Kadt 1979; Harrison 1992). This makes Third World peoples and environments vulnerable to exploitation by international tourism:

> Tourism seeks consciously and specifically to capitalise on differences between places and when these include differences in levels of economic development then tourism becomes imbued with all the elements of domination, exploitation and manipulation characteristic of colonialism (Momsen 1994: 106).

Globalisation has cultural, political and economic dimensions (Potter *et al.* 1999: 94). Cultural globalisation is said to be characterised by cultural homogenisation as Western consumption and lifestyle patterns spread around the world, a process certainly facilitated by the flow of travellers from the West to the Third World. Through the demonstration effect, for example, we can see trekking guides in Nepal wearing Levi jeans and Rayban sunglasses. Political globalisation involves the undermining of the roles and importance of nation states as borders are opened up to free trade and investment. Economic globalisation, meanwhile, is multifaceted. A key aspect of economic globalisation has been the increasing power in the hands of a small number of travel and tourism companies with a high degree of vertical integration, leading to oligopolistic control within the industry (Brown 1998a; Cater 1995). These large companies can, for example, shift thousands of clients from one destination to another if the conditions in a particular country are seen as unsuitable (Akama 1999). This is what happened in The Gambia, a country which recently reversed its ban on all-inclusive holidays because of a large decline in the number of tourists. In this case, tourist agencies simply directed their clients to all-inclusive resorts in other countries.[3] This may result in the collapse of a small Third World economy while the profit margins of the tour company are maintained. Thus the espousal of free trade inherent in globalisation discourse effectively limits the ability of individual countries to place conditions upon investment by outside companies, conditions which could protect the country and its people from exploitation. Trade liberalisation has further undermined the enterprises of small-scale local producers (Badger *et al.* 1996).

An issue of grave concern with relation to increasing global interconnectedness, is that the players are not meeting on a level playing field: 'Countries, cities and individuals having the wherewithal to move with globalization have much to gain, but many others not having the infrastructure or investment to be tuned in are bypassed and marginalized' (Yeung 1998: 476). Thus while there are positive aspects to globalisation such as opportunities for sharing information or technology and promoting cultural exchange, concerns have been raised that the power hierarchies at play may see Third World economies and societies being undermined. For example, Cater notes that relationships between local people and other tourism stakeholders are 'markedly skewed' in favour of the latter (1995: 207). Thus while globalisation brings increasing opportunities for, say, fisherpeople in the Philippines to enhance their livelihood options through tourism enterprises, it also increases the chance of their being exploited by a multinational hotel chain which wishes to build a five-star complex adjacent to their fishing beach. Economic rewards which may be earned from such a venture by the community in the short term may soon be overshadowed by the social dislocation and disharmony which the community faces when local elites in collusion with the hotel company gain the rewards of tourism while the rest of the people find that their primary livelihood activity, fishing, is threatened. This is why Ringer suggests that tourism is 'an industry that satisfies the commercial imperatives of an international business, yet rarely addresses local development needs' (Ringer 1998: 9).

Similarly, Hutnyk (1996: 211) reveals some of the contradictions which signify the inequality between travellers and local people in Third World destinations such as Calcutta: 'The ISD stall near the Modern Lodge offers instant phone connections home – it is run by an Orissa man who has not seen his family in four months.' Hutnyk (1996: 10) is particularly critical of backpackers who, he suggests, think they are involved in an ethical form of travel when in fact they are exploiting the fact that exchange rates allow them to live 'like Rajas in Indian towns' (Figure 2.6):

> Budget travellers can visit the 'Third World' because it is cheap; because there are developed systems of transnational transportation and communication; and because they have the ability – even, perhaps, the need – to leave their usual domestic circumstances in order to travel and 'see the world' (Hutnyk 1996: 214).[4]

Such examples of the relative lack of power of local communities compared to tourists and outside companies whom they come into contact with show that while 'Globalisation opens new doors of opportunity and affluence . . . its pernicious effects have to be fully tackled before it can be accepted as a benign influence that propels the world and its peoples forward' (Yeung 1998: 477). Furthermore, there are concerns that global trading agreements which epitomise the sorts of economic relationships globalisation seeks to establish, may undermine the ability of states to protect the interests of local people involved in tourism

Figure 2.6 Cartoon on tourism and poverty. (*Source: New Internationalist*, **324**, June 2000)

development. Concern has recently been expressed about the General Agreement on Trade in Services (GATS) which is administered by the World Trade Organisation. The GATS seeks to liberalise the trade in services so that member countries would have to allow foreign-owned companies free access to their markets, and no favouritism could be shown to domestic investors. Such a policy is more likely to benefit large companies and investors, while thwarting the opportunities open to small investors and informal sector actors which require support to be able to compete with larger interests and protection from the state to avoid being bought out by larger companies (Kalisch 2000).

Beyond dependency theory

This chapter has highlighted the very important contribution of dependency theory to discussions of tourism and development, that is, to show the uneven balance of power which accords large private organisations, usually Western-based, an unfair influence over tourism development and control over the economic rewards of tourism. It has also shown how modernist and neoliberal discourse is primarily preoccupied with macro-level improvements to economies rather than with enhancing the self-determination of Third World countries or a broader concern for increasing the well-being of the majority of a country's population. There is thus considerable evidence to support the contention that tourism reinforces global inequalities.

Dependency theory has, however, been criticised for displaying a 'crude sense of political economy' (Watts 2000a: 171), in that it typically offers sweeping statements about the ills that the capitalist system has wrought on Third World countries through exploitative core–periphery relationships (de Kadt 1990). Studies of the global–local nexus have shown that power is not unidirectional, and that it is simplistic to see forms of development such as tourism as being uniformly exploitative of local peoples and places. For example, while larger hotels may be foreign owned and guilty of repatriating a large proportion of their profits, they may be preferable to smaller, locally owned accommodation in some cases because they offer training, job security, better working conditions and higher rates of pay. Parnwell (1998) further questions dependency theory logic which suggests that expansion of tourism necessarily undermines the economic and political sovereignty of Third World countries. Rather, he urges us not to assume that globalisation is an upstoppable, uncontrollable force because 'The way that global processes and forces are negotiated, regulated and interpreted at the local level may be just as important as the nature and extent of globalisation itself' (Parnwell 1998: 214). Thus we should not overlook the agency of local actors (Cheong and Miller 2000): 'although tourism is an important manifestation of the globalisation phenomenon, its impact on host societies is very much dependent upon the influence of local institutions and actors' (Parnwell 1998: 212).

The time lines in Figures 2.1 and 2.2 showed that theories and perceptions of tourism development in the Third World have both built upon and diverged from the early theories presented in this chapter. It is thus appropriate that we move on to reveal the application of more recent theories to tourism processes in Chapters 3 and 4.

Questions

1. In what ways has modernisation theory encouraged Third World governments to support tourism growth and development?
2. Why is it of concern that Third World countries pursuing development through tourism have followed paths directed by exogenous forces?
3. What (a) opportunities and (b) threats does economic globalisation offer small tourism operators in Third World countries?

Suggestions for further reading

Britton, S. 1982 'The political economy of tourism in the Third World', *Annals of Tourism Research*, 9(3): 331–58.

Khan, M. 1997 'Tourism development and dependency theory: mass tourism vs. eco-tourism', *Annals of Tourism Research*, 24(4): 988–91.

Mowforth, M. and Munt, I. 1998 *Tourism and Sustainability: New Tourism in the Third World*, Routledge, London (Chapter 3: Power and Tourism).

Pleumarom, A. 1994 'The political economy of tourism', *The Ecologist*, 24(4): 142–8.

Seifert-Granzin, J. and Jesupatham, S. 1999 *Tourism at the Crossroads: Challenges to Developing Countries by the New World Trade Order*, Equations, Bangalore and Tourism Watch, Leinfelden-Echterdingen, Germany.

Useful websites

Reference list for research on the impacts of tourism:
www.geocities.com/Paris/9842/impref1.html

Third World Network site which contains articles on tourism and globalisation:
www.twnside.org.sg/title/focus6-cn.htm

Rethinking Tourism Project's 1999 publication entitled *Globalisation, Tourism and Indigenous Peoples: What You Should Know About the World's Largest Industry*:
www2.planeta.com/mader/ecotravel/resources/rtp/globalization.htm

Notes

1. The changes signalled in the two figures correspond somewhat with the first three stages of Jafari's (1989) discussion of four 'tourism platforms' which, he suggests, have dominated thinking on tourism at different stages. As Weaver and Oppermann (2000: 8–9) note, the early enthusiasm for tourism under the advocacy platform was curbed by concerns over the negative impacts of tourism, as seen in the cautionary platform which emerged in the late 1960s. By the 1980s, attempts were being made to identify how tourism could be more beneficial to host communities through alternative approaches, under an adaptancy platform. There is less support in Figures 2.1 and 2.2, however, for Jafari's fourth 'knowledge-based' platform, which is said to be characterised by a heavier reliance on objective studies to inform planning discussions.

2. Two of the key contributors to development of this brand of thinking were Andre Gunder Frank (1975) who devised a metropolis–satellite model, and Immanuel Wallerstein (1974), whose world systems theory proposed a four-part model: core, semi-periphery, periphery and external.

3. See Box 10.1.

4. The case of backpackers is considered further in Chapter 9, which looks at budget tourism.

Gazing at 'the Other'

Introduction

Chapter 3 is concerned with postmodern theory and how it can help us to gain a deeper understanding of tourists, of tourism as a process, and of the way in which tourism and destination communities interact. It enables us to see, for example, the very real way in which people and places are constructed as objects of interest to be consumed by tourists. This is no more true than in the Third World where the imagery surrounding the 'exotic Other' is a major drawcard for tourists from the Western world, particularly those who see themselves as 'real travellers', as opposed to tourists: 'Tourism is promoted today as an industry that can turn poor countries' very poverty into a magnet for sorely needed foreign currency. For to be a poor society in the late twentieth century is to be "unspoilt"' (Enloe 1990: 31).

Tourism researchers engaging with postmodernism have moved debates away from questions about the costs or benefits of tourism to a particular area and drawn attention to other issues which have been somewhat marginalised in the literature. Thus postmodernists ask questions about representation of peoples and places (Morgan and Pritchard 1998), the production of tourist landscapes (Ringer 1998), social relations between tourists and those living in destination areas (Urry 1990) and commodification of culture and authenticity (Cohen 1988). They are also concerned with cultural identity and cultural politics, considering for example how people have manipulated or adapted aspects of their own culture in the face of tourism development (Potter *et al.* 1999).

In addressing such issues, postmodern analysis differs significantly from grand theories such as modernisation and dependency considered in Chapter 2. Rather, both the postmodern paradigm and the neopopulist paradigm (to be discussed in Chapter 4) have the following attributes in common:

- reject modernisation;
- embrace diversity;

- support local action and respect local voice;
- recognise that power relations inform the construction of knowledge and the establishment of research agendas and development priorities;
- reject the notion of a single truth;
- accept that the meaning of development is contested, and subjective (Blaikie 2000: 1045).

Postmodernism is particularly concerned with searching for the complexity of ways in which the tourism process works and interacts with local peoples and environments, thus rejecting simple dualisms, such as the suggestion that mass tourism is inherently bad for local communities while alternative forms of tourism are inherently good:

> unlike the polemic, authoritative, and homogenizing discourse of modern tourism, the discourse of postmodern tourism consists of compromising statements and stresses the multiplicity of tourist experiences . . . postmodern systems of knowledge are less authoritative, less conclusive, and more pluralized than modernist systems of knowledge (Uriely 1997: 982, 983–4).

Postmodernism questions the impacts approach to tourism studies in the Third World, which tends to assume that tourism is an external force which erodes local cultures and undermines local economies and societies (Wood 1998). Picard (1993) explains that tourism and culture are not independent of each other in many contexts. Instead, Third World peoples respond to and interact with tourists and the tourism process in complex ways. Claims that tourism has 'destroyed indigenous culture' in a particular locality thus need to be examined carefully, as cultures are constantly evolving: 'The implicit notion of a pristine pre-tourist cultural baseline against which to measure tourism's "negative" impact is exposed as obfuscating at best and in a profound sense, meaningless' (Wood 1993: 63). Furthermore, 'traditional cultures and societies do not dissolve in the face of tourism' (Teo and Chang 1998: 124).

Thus postmodern analysis of tourism revels in demonstrating the myriad of ways in which local people have responded to, and sometimes resisted, tourism development, rather than assuming that they are victims of a burgeoning, unstoppable industry. This alternative approach recognises that while the engagement of local people with tourism is not always positive, they are nevertheless active agents who may be able to adapt tourism processes to suit their own circumstances (Cheong and Miller 2000; Parnwell 1998). Arguing that tourism is 'a negotiated process', Pagdin (1995: 195) states that '. . . locally-affected people are not shaped passively by outside forces but react as well, at times even changing the conditions of the larger system'.

This chapter highlights the contribution of postmodern scholars to tourism research by starting with a discussion of John Urry's (1990) much cited concept of the tourist gaze. It also considers ways in which Third World places and peoples are constructed and commodified as objects which can be experienced and enjoyed by tourists, and the role of tourism literature in this process. A case study explains the way in which women, in particular, have been constructed as the 'exotic Other'. Finally the chapter considers the issue of 'authenticity' of tourism experiences, questioning whether groups of tourists pursuing alternative travel experiences are engaging in ethically superior forms of travel.

The tourist gaze

The idea of the tourist gaze was introduced by Urry (1990) who used this concept to express the curiosity we have about other peoples and places, which is part of our motivation for taking holidays. Thus we go to gaze upon new and interesting landscapes. The suggestion is that in seeking out 'exotic' or 'out of the way' destinations such as those in the Third World, we are seeking encounters with 'the Other'. Thus the 'Otherness' of hill tribe peoples wearing ethnic dress in Thailand can be packaged and sold to tourists: 'For the vast majority of people, otherness makes the destination attractive for consumption by establishing its distinctiveness' (Hall 1998b: 140). This 'exotic Other' is becoming much more accessible to tourists thanks to new technologies which result in time–space contraction, as mentioned in Chapter 2. Thus, for example, West Africa need no longer be perceived as out of reach by city dwellers in London; in fact it would be much quicker to fly to The Gambia than to Los Angeles.

As shown in Table 3.1, the character and object of 'the gaze', as well as other factors such as the overall number of tourists in an area, also influence the nature of interaction between tourists and local communities.

Urry (1990) explains that our holiday experience begins even before we leave home in terms of the anticipation of what we will encounter. This anticipation is largely fuelled by tourism imagery as presented to us by tourist brochures, television and magazines, but also through other sites of advertising such as the internet, and through travel writing in the guide books, newspaper articles and novels about our destinations: 'The tourism phenomenon . . . perhaps more than any other business, is based on the production, reproduction and reinforcement of images' (Hall 1998b: 140). The way in which the industry chooses to represent 'the Other' as an interesting and attractive destination has only recently become an important area of academic research and this is connected to the concept of the 'geographical imagination'.

Geographical imagination refers to the 'way in which we understand the geographical world, and the way in which we represent it, to ourselves and to others' (Massey 1995: 41). There is no neutral means of understanding the geographical world. For example, while images of destinations are critical to the success of the tourism industry, these images are highly selective and biased towards beauty and exoticism. This causes Cater (1995: 189) to speculate about how genuine tourism promotion is:

Table 3.1 Factors influencing the nature of social relations between tourists and people living in destination areas

Determinants of social relations	Examples
The *number* of tourists visiting a place in relationship to the size of the host population	A small Pacific island with limited fresh water and 500 residents could find even 40 tourists per week (> 2000 tourists per year) highly invasive
The predominant *object* of the tourist gaze	Objects can, for example, include landscapes (the Himalayas), ethnic groups (hill tribes in Thailand) and nature (wild animals in Africa). It is more intrusive when people are the object of the tourist gaze, particularly when tourism impinges on their private lives (therefore village visits will produce more social stress than cultural performances in a hotel)
The *character* of the gaze	For example, tourists may get instant gratification from seeing and photographing the Taj Mahal, but they may require several days or more on safari if their dream is to experience 'wild Africa'
The *organisation* of the industry	For example, is the industry completely foreign owned and run by expatriates, offering only casual, servile positions to local people, or do small-scale operators who encourage local partnerships dominate the industry in the area in question?
How tourism affects other *livelihood activities*	While some activities may be undermined by tourism (e.g. fishing in an Indian village may become impossible because of the pressure for beach front land for resorts), others, such as growing coconut trees, may be preserved because they, and the activity of scaling coconut trees to collect the fruit, become objects of the tourist gaze
The extent of *economic and social differences* between tourists and people in the destination area	While in most Third World countries the economic differences are likely to be extreme, the social inequalities may be broken down somewhat by tourists who choose to stay in local bed and breakfast types of accommodation rather than lavish resorts or hotels
Demand from visitors for certain *standards* of accommodation, service and security	Those visiting The Gambia on an all-inclusive tour are likely to be reluctant to leave 'the security of the Western tourist bubble' created by their resorts, which deliver Western-style accommodation and service. More independent travellers may actually seek more 'out of the way' destinations in which they have the chance to experience more of the local lifestyle
The role of the *state* in planning for and promoting tourism	While many Third World governments see tourism as the key to earning foreign exchange and thus foreign investment in this sector is unreservedly encouraged, in other cases (such as Bhutan and the Maldives), tourists are limited to certain spaces or in terms of their total numbers, in order to protect the local people and their culture

Source: 'Determinants of social relations' from Urry (1990: 57–9); examples are author's own.

> How real is the image of a destination that is gleaned by whatever means? In pro-
> motional literature it is undoubtedly superficial and idealized. The place has
> become a commodity to sell and so nothing to detract from the image and reduce
> its value will be presented.

Cater goes on to explain that visual images are especially superficial, failing to
show the complexity of life in destination areas. Idealised representations can be
easily set in our imaginations due to the development of communications technology, such as satellite television and the internet, which are '. . . the means by
which simplified, inaccurate or downright misleading images and representations can be propagated' (Potter *et al.* 1999: 101). Thus 'Otherness' is framed by
the geographical imagination in a particular way which obscures certain truths:

> the popular misconception of the entire Caribbean as a 'beach replete with sway-
> ing coconut palms' is the direct outcome of tourist advertising / and promotional
> campaigns . . . the daily realities of urban concentration, poverty and poor housing
> in the Caribbean are selectively weeded out from the stereotype. . . . In a similar
> vein, the local population is also represented as a group of smiling, servile natives
> ready to respond to the bidding of predominantly White tourists (Potter *et al.*
> 1999: 102–3).

The following section moves on to consider how specific destinations, such as
the Caribbean, and the people living there have been packaged for consumption by tourists (Cloke 2000).

Social construction of Third World peoples and places

Particular destinations have been socially constructed in ways deemed to attract
certain types of tourists. While the packaging of Mediterranean and West African
landscapes for charter tourists as sun, sea and sex destinations is apparent to many
people, we may be less familiar with the packaging of other tourist destinations. Calcutta, for example, epitomizes a charity tourism landscape. Tourists are
lured to Calcutta based largely on the public image of the good works of Mother
Teresa and her predecessors, as well as images from the film *City of Joy*, which
starred Hollywood's Patrick Swayze (Hutnyk 1996: 207). Thus those who
travel to Calcutta tend to see themselves as independent travellers and they
often stay for several weeks or months to assist with street-side medical clinics.

Tourists to Africa and Asia, more broadly, are similarly influenced by stereotypes implanted in their minds prior to travel, as exposed by Carter (1998). He
summed up British travellers' perceptions about these continents under the
banners 'Appalling Africa' and 'Amazing Asia'. Thus the notion of difference was
construed in terms of exoticism where Asia was concerned, while difference
was equated with danger when Africa was the travel destination. This is perhaps
not surprising when the 'Africa' implanted in the minds of most Westerners is

based on images gleaned from television news and documentary features, with wild animals, famine and civil strife all featuring strongly. In terms of tourism appeal, Africa has been marketed as a wild paradise, with the key drawcard being Africa's rich endowment of unique and charismatic – to the Western mind at least – species (Anderson and Grove 1987):

> When we see an elephant or a rhino, a lion or a leopard, a giraffe or a zebra . . . we think 'priceless heritage'. When an African sees one of these animals, he [or she] is more likely to think of a source of meat . . . [or] about the devastation that a rampaging elephant can wreak on his [or her] crops or the death that a lion or leopard can bring to his [or her] children (Bonner 1993: 7–8).[1]

Like Asia, Polynesia has been exoticised and feminised to some extent (as discussed in the case study to follow). Figure 3.1 exposes the irony of present-day advertising based on scantily clan Polynesian people when in fact many Polynesians now dress very conservatively and they are offended by the scantily clad tourists. Meanwhile Melanesia has been constructed as a primitive, adventurous site. Tourist stereotypes of Melanesia are highlighted both by Douglas (1994) who titled her thesis on the history of tourism to Melanesian countries, *They Came for Savages*, and O'Rourke (*c*.1987), whose film on the

Figure 3.1 Cartoon on changing Pacific islands dress codes.

interaction between European tourists and people living along the remote Sepik River was named *Cannibal Tours*.

The way in which Third World destinations are socially constructed essentially reveals important power asymmetries (Pritchard and Morgan 2000). Thus, for example, when 'imagining' a tropical holiday destination such as Bali, we are more strongly influenced by tourism advertising images of sandy beaches and blue seas than we are by the interests or concerns of local people. Wall (1998) explains how the same features of the landscape in Bali, be they paddy fields, beach vistas or temples, are embedded with vastly different meanings depending on whether one is a local or a tourist. This leads to landscapes being contested and negotiated by different users: landscapes '. . . are continually (re)created, modified and shared, at a price, by, among others, the Balinese, their gods, the tourism industry and the tourists' (Wall 1998: 61). 'Reading the landscape' to see who has control over the beach, for example, investors and tourists or local people who use the beach for livelihood, ceremonial and recreational purposes, can reveal much about the extent to which local interests determine the nature and extent of tourism development (Ringer 1998).

The following case study details how women in many Third World destinations have been socially constructed as the 'exotic Other' and indeed, whole landscapes have been feminised.

Case study: Women as the 'exotic Other' and feminised landscapes

In many cases, the 'Otherness' which is sought by travellers is that of the exotic female, because 'Signs and symbols, myths and fantasies are often male oriented' (Kinnaird *et al.* 1994: 14). Thus cultural performances in regions where women as 'exotic Other' are used to attract tourists may manipulate the image of women which is presented to tourists. In Hawaii, for example, particular emphasis has been placed on exoticising the 'hula' and drawing on the supposed charms of the welcoming 'native' women with their lei: 'Without beautiful Hawaiian women dancing, there would be no tourism' (Trask and Trask 1992: 50).

In addition to being positioned as 'exotic', women in certain Third World destination are represented as 'erotic', leading male travellers, in particular, to have certain preconceptions about the possibilities their travel experiences will open up to them:

> . . . representations of gender and heterosexuality [in tourism marketing materials] have led to women being represented as exoticized commodities which are there to be experienced – and Western male tourists have been socialized into seeing women of colour as somehow more willing and available (Pritchard and Morgan 2000: 125).

Asian women, in particular, have been exoticised in tourism literature and promotional material. Thus in Carter's interviews he found that '. . . the subject of sexuality was a predominant theme in many of the male travellers' accounts of Asia' (1998: 356); 'Asia, for these travellers, is a place where different sexual norms apply and where women are "exotic" and "dangerous" ' (1998: 357). This simply confirms Truong's finding from an extensive examination of links between prostitution and tourism in South-east Asia. She believes that a discourse representing Eastern women as the 'exotic Other' has dual purposes: '(1) creating a distinct national identity to attract consumers; and (2) legitimizing oppressive practices by relegating them to the culture of a particular ethnic group and thereby helping to ease the conscience of the consumers' (Truong 1990: 199–200). Urry (1990: 141) expands on this point:

> ... the combination of relations of gender and ethnic subordination had colluded to help construct very young Asian women as objects of a tourist/sexual gaze for male visitors from other societies which are in a sense ethnically dominant. The resulting tourist patterns cannot be analysed separately from relations of gender and racial subordination.

It is not just women, however, but the landscapes which they inhabit, which have been exoticised. Thus 'the Orient' can be seen as more of a Western construct than a geographical space and one which is based on binary oppositions of the West versus the Orient (Said 1977). 'The Orient' is 'the Other' to Westerners, in a very hierarchical sense which implies superiority of the West and incorporates suggestions of the allure and exoticism of Asian women.

Pritchard and Morgan argue that landscapes of Third World countries are often construed as 'passive, seductive and feminine' (2000: 129). There is evidence of this in tourism imagery of both the Caribbean and the Pacific regions:

> the language and atmosphere of seduction is never far away when the destination is Jamaica. Terms laden with feminine sexuality are used to describe Jamaica – a destination which is 'tempting' and 'innocent', 'sinful', 'sensuous', 'seductive', 'teasing' and 'hypnotic' (Pritchard and Morgan 2000: 126).

> In the minds of many Western tourists the idea of the Pacific conjures up impressions of swaying tropical palm trees, white sand beaches, warm, crystal-clear water and, possibly, dusky maidens in grass skirts or sarongs. This stereotypical and highly gendered image of 'paradise' has been consistently portrayed over many years, not only in tourist advertising but also in many other forms of image making, such as film, newspapers and magazines, novels and even academic works (Hall 1998b: 140).

The stereotypical Pacific Islands woman wears flowers and has long black hair flowing over her bare shoulders. Paul Gauguin's paintings of women in Tahiti, and the novels of Somerset Maugham and Robert Louis Stevenson, helped to perpetuate this stereotype. Thus 'Much of what constitutes the desirability of the South Pacific is in fact its place in popular fiction, travelogues and films' (Sturma 1999: 714). This image of Polynesia as a place and of Polynesian womanhood essentially ignores indigenous history and distorts indigenous culture. It seems a strange irony that it is Western intruders (such as the painters and writers mentioned above) who have created this image of the South Pacific as an 'untouched paradise' when their very presence obviously touched the Pacific, and their work established the images which are used to lure so many tourists to these islands today (Sturma 1999).

Deconstruction of tourism literature

Postmodernists have provided valuable insights into the subjective and biased nature by which images of destinations are created in the minds of tourists by deconstructing tourism literature: 'deconstruction . . . seeks to demonstrate how the (multiple) positioning of an author (or reader) in terms of class, culture, race, gender, etc. has influenced the writing (and reading) of a text (Ley 2000: 621). Thus the way in which other societies are represented in travel writing reveals how we see our own and others' identities (Allen and Massey 1995), and this can reveal important power asymmetries:

> Exploration, travel writing, tourism, and so on, are means of representation. But they are ways of representing the world that also amount to, and maintain, a 'formidable structure of cultural domination'; a system of truths, as Said argues, that has 'rarely offered the individual anything but imperialism, racism and ethnocentrism for dealing with "other" cultures (1991: 18)' (Mowforth and Munt 1998: 78).

Tourism brochures have been singled out for deconstructive analysis by a number of academics (Dann 1996; Marshment 1997; Selwyn 1993). Marshment (1997: 27) suggests that local people together with their geographical and cultural landscapes are 'offered up to the tourist gaze' through the photographs in brochures, in which '. . . exoticism is signified by an absence of the modern'. Thus we see ethnic dress, not T-shirts and jeans, we see bamboo and leaf houses, not city apartments, and we are shown images of women carrying water jars on their heads, not people turning on a tap inside their homes.

Table 3.2 provides an analysis of the images of women and men used in tourism brochures for Third World destinations, showing that apart from the African brochure, a region which seems to be marketed as wild and primitive, many more images are provided of women than of men. In all of the brochures, women are more often clothed in ethnic or exotic dress, and are shown as placid objects of interest and beauty. When men are attired in ethnic dress, they are typically portrayed as 'wise, old men' or 'warriors'. In the Acacia brochure for Africa, for example, there are photos of female and male groups from the Samburu tribe in ethnic attire, but while the former are named 'Samburu *girls*' under the photo, the latter are named 'Samburu *warriors*'. According to Marshment (1997: 31), 'The ideologies which associate women with physical beauty and docility are employed in taming the disturbing potential of the "other" embodied in these images of "primitive" manhood.' Women are also shown working in traditional roles, such as fetching water in large urns or crushing grains manually, thus '. . . the poverty of people is transformed into the picturesque' (Marshment 1997: 28). Meanwhile men are shown to engage in a much wider variety of roles, both in the subsistence and the monetary economy. Also interesting is that while there are images of women with children,

Table 3.2 Images of women and men in tourism brochures for Third World destinations

Brochure	Images of women	Images of men
India Suntravel Experience India 2000 Overall emphasis of brochure: Exotic, colourful India	Groups of women in colourful dress; engaging in traditional work (e.g. carrying water urns on their heads, tending crops)	Mainly older men in ethnic dress – especially with turbans; engaging in a variety of work both traditional (e.g. markets) and contemporary (e.g. hotel bar, taxis)
Africa Acacia Adventure Holidays and Camping Safaris 2000/2001 Overall emphasis of brochure: Wild, primitive Africa	Relatively few images of women: groups in ethnic dress, posing for camera or dancing; selling crafts; engaging in traditional tasks, e.g. crushing grain; with children	Many more images of men: mainly either groups of men in ethnic dress – labelled as 'warriors', or working as guides; very few photos of men engaging in traditional tasks, e.g. fishing
Latin America Tucan South and Central America and the Caribbean 2000–2001 Overall emphasis of brochure: Adventurous, scenic South America	Numerous photos of small groups or individual women in colourful ethnic dress; women mostly working in markets	Very few photos of men – only two of individual men in ethnic attire and a few of men working

it is very difficult to find images of mixed groups: 'What this fails to suggest, therefore, is the existence in the host culture of a home life, or of familial or sexual relations . . . this host culture is offered up in segments to the tourist gaze . . .' (Marshment 1997: 29).

Similarly, guidebooks have gained attention from tourism researchers concerned that those reading them think they are learning 'the facts' about a country and its culture (Bhattacharyya 1997). Aziz (1999/2000: 4) suggests that guidebooks provide only rudimentary insights into local culture: 'When mention of local traditions are made they often take the form of warnings, depicting local traditions as nuisances that need to be worked around.' Guidebooks also often reflect a colonial mentality on travel to the Third World, as reflected in the inclusion of Morocco in a guidebook on Europe (Aziz 1999/2000).

Searching for 'authentic' experiences

Recognition of issues surrounding the typically biased representation of Third World peoples and places in tourism literature leads on well to debates over the authenticity of tourism experiences. While some commentators have focused on how traditions have been 'bastardised' as a result of tourism, postmodernists have often cast a different interpretation on issues of authenticity, stressing that many tourists enjoy attractions even when they know they are contrived. They also note that this may protect the private lives of performers from the tourist gaze (Urry 1990), and that it is much less taxing for hosts to fit a stereotype (Boniface 1998). In any case, Cohen (1988) is adamant that authenticity is negotiable: 'genuineness or authenticity of a tourism setting is not a real property or tangible asset, but instead is a judgment or value placed on the setting by the observer' (Moscardo and Pearce 1999: 418). This would be supported by those who see culture as something constantly evolving, rather than fixed in time and space.

Postmodern analysis has criticised new forms of tourism which supposedly search out more authentic experiences, showing that they are not necessarily ethically superior (Boxes 3.1 and 3.2). Thus Munt (1994) discusses how it has become trendy for the middle class of the West to pursue 'eco-friendly' holidays, which may say more about the 'ego' of the visitors than anything else. Citing the example of the growing popularity of colonial-style luxury safaris, he suggests that such trips are based upon racism and class subordination. He claims, for example, that such eco-safaris exude a 'neo-colonial aura':

> This is symbolically reproduced by J & C Voyageurs. In the single black and white photograph offered in its brochure . . . a trail of porters (thirty-five, they tell us) are shown tramping through an eco-colonial landscape, carrying the supplies for the group of six, 'most of the comforts of home – iced drinks, spacious sleeping tents, loos and showers'. It is an image and ambience that is recreated by many new, independent tour operators, whether it be luxury safaris or treks and expeditions for the young and adventurous; an army of global porters trot behind or ahead . . . to ensure that these new ethical tourists are regularly refreshed (Munt 1994: 55).

Munt further speaks of the 'water-thin disguise' of this type of tourism 'as a more ethical and moral pastime of the new bourgeoisie' (Munt 1994: 59). Urry (1990: 95) adds that tourists who pursue 'real holidays' which involve avoiding mass tourism destinations are merely extending the concept of the 'pleasure periphery' to more remote areas of the globe. Yet they remain part of the same tourism process which brings charter planes full of tourists to Bali or Goa.

Others have questioned whether backpackers, who generally prefer to be known as 'travellers' not 'tourists', are really seeking authentic experiences (Figure 3.2). While they often claim they are searching for interaction with the host population, many seem to be attracted to accommodation outlets, such as the Modern Lodge in Calcutta, which have a strict 'foreigners only' policy (Hutnyk 1996). In worst-case scenarios, backpackers may travel from one backpacker ghetto to another, seeking further doses of backpacker culture in the form of sex, drugs and banana pancakes (Aziz 1999). Box 3.1 provides an

---

BOX 3.1

South-east Asian backpacker's mantra

In times of trial, tribulation and doubt – as I lose all feeling in my legs in the 14th hour of an 8-hour local bus ride … when I can't sleep for the noise of a thousand rats scurrying through the ceiling and floor of my $2/night room … as vomit and diarrhea spew simultaneously from my salmonella saturated body – I will repeat this mantra unto myself …

I am not a tourist
I am not a tourist
I am not a tourist
I am not a tourist
I am not a tourist …

… until the doubt passes and I am ready for more authentic Asian experiences.

Source: Kampuchea Gadfly –
http://thorntree.lonelyplanet.com/thorn/repliesflat.pl?Cat=&Topic=243499

Figure 3.2   Backpacker heading off on the road less travelled, Malaysia.

amusing reflection on backpacker culture and the backpacker's questionable search for authenticity, referring specifically to the South-east Asian backpacker trail.

If we are the 'trendies' or other travellers seeking authentic experiences, our range of options may seem to be diminishing because 'Every niched pack-

---

BOX 3.2

Tourism advertising slogans emphasising unique/authentic experiences

Zambia – the real Africa . . .
Malaysia – *truly* Asia
Cook Islands – a special place, a special people, a special magic
Tahiti – islands beyond the ordinary
Papua New Guinea – paradise live . . . the last great adventure destination!

Source: Official government internet sites for each country.

Figure 3.3   Hilltribe boys from northern Thailand.

aging of adventurous or exotic place-experience has the effect of narrowing the scope of tourisms which are yet to be encountered' (Cloke 2000: 842). We are attracted by the exotic Other yet the exotic Other changes in response to contact with Western tourists (Figure 3.3). What Thailand offered ten years ago, Vietnam may offer today. Thus our tourist gaze shifts over time, reflecting cultural change. This has implications for Third World countries wishing to sustain a certain level of tourism interest. Box 3.2 provides examples of countries specifically trying to trade on uniqueness and/or authenticity in their tourism slogans.

Conclusion

Postmodern analysis has made a number of contributions to deepening our understanding of tourism processes. It has introduced concepts such as the 'tourist gaze' and 'geographical imagination' which help to reveal how subjective our impressions of this world and its people are, particularly with regard to popular tourism destinations. Postmodernists have further deconstructed representations of Third World peoples and places in tourism literature and advertising to show how shallow, inaccurate or harmful they may be. Nevertheless Third World governments often choose to market themselves based on such representations of difference in order to tap into the desire of Western tourists to experience the authentic 'exotic Other'. One other important contribution of postmodernism has been to show that grand theories such as dependency theory often oversimplify issues, such as suggesting that tourism is wholly controlled by Western interests and that it is inherently exploitative of Third World peoples and resources. Instead postmodernism emphasises that local people have agency and they can modify or negotiate their position.

Postmodern analysis also has weaknesses, however, which need to be overcome if it is to move beyond academic critique and contribute to finding more appropriate paths to tourism development. It has been criticised for a fixation with discourse, as evidenced by '. . . a disinclination to undertake detailed research into development processes and policy, [and] a preoccupation with texts and representations by the development industry . . .' (Blaikie 2000: 1033). In essence, postmodern analysis of development issues in general has provided insightful critiques but has not focused on conceptualising what could be done to improve development practice in light of these criticisms, instead sometimes opting to take an anti-development stance (Simon 1997). This is not particularly helpful to those Third World people who have identified tourism as a means of improving their livelihoods and bringing about local development. This is why Blaikie (2000: 1033) suggests many postmodernists have perpetuated '. . . an indulgent and agenda-less academic cul-de-sac'. This need not be the case, however. Rather, '. . . an alternative imaginary of development [such as postmodernism] can, and in my view should, lead to reflection about what the audience as well as the author can actually do about it' (Blaikie 2000).

The following chapter is concerned with neopopulist thought which is more specifically directed at finding strategies which will help Third World communities engage with tourism in rewarding ways.

Questions

1. Think of a tourist 'place' you have visited. What were some of the features of the tourist landscape and who was responsible for creating this landscape? Do you think local communities had some control over the creation of this landscape or the way in which their culture was represented (if it was represented at all)?

2. How are ethnic and sexual stereotypes established or perpetuated through tourism advertising?

3. Provide examples of ways in which people in destination areas can show themselves to be agents, not victims, of tourism development.

Suggestions for further reading

Cohen, E. 1988 'Authenticity and commoditization in tourism', *Annals of Tourism Research*, **15**(3): 371–86.
Pritchard, A. and Morgan, N. 2000 'Constructing tourism landscapes: gender, sexuality and space', *Tourism Geographies*, **2**(2): 115–39.
Ringer, G. 1998 'Introduction', pp. 1–16 in G. Ringer (ed.), *Destinations: Cultural Landscapes of Tourism*, Routledge, London.
Urry, J. 1990 *The Tourist Gaze: Leisure and Travel in Contemporary Societies*, Sage, London.

Note

1. See also Figure 6.1.

Participation, empowerment and sustainable development

CHAPTER 4

Introduction

Pick up any recent text within the broad realm of development studies and it should not be long before you come across the words 'participation', 'empowerment' and 'sustainable development'. These undeniably popular terms are part of the current discourse on development, even though their meanings have been rigorously contested. Some suggest that because they have been used by so many different organisations and individuals in varying contexts they have become part of the seductive, yet meaningless, language of development (Goldsmith 1991). This chapter takes an alternative view, arguing that the dialogue surrounding participation, empowerment and sustainable development can contribute significantly to our understanding of how local communities can gain benefits from, and control over, tourism in their surrounding area.

The terms 'participation', 'empowerment' and 'sustainable development' are strongly associated with neopopulist and sustainable development perspectives, which are discussed in the first part of this chapter. Neopopulist perspectives focus on people in local contexts and on small-scale, bottom-up strategies for their development. While sustainable development is informed by a wide variety of perspectives, they all suggest that 'the environment' should be central to debates on development. The latter part of the chapter explores the concepts of participation and empowerment in more detail, and an 'empowerment framework' is presented as a means of determining whether or not communities are engaging in tourism in ways which are ultimately beneficial to them.

Overall the aim of this chapter is to show that tourism can present opportunities for communities to enhance their social, economic and environmental well-being. However, romantic notions about tourism providing a panacea for the long-standing development problems facing Third World communities countries are unhelpful because it is not always possible for communities to determine the form(s) of tourism which will be dominant in their area or to have any control over tourism development. Furthermore, there may be a myriad of contextual issues, including government plans to focus on resort-based tourism as a means of maximising foreign exchange earnings, or power plays between local elites and outsiders, which determine whether or not communities can benefit from tourism. In the final instance, most communities will require some forms of support from outside interests to be able to engage in tourism enterprises in an effective and equitable manner.

Neopopulist perspectives

The neopopulist approach to development emerged due to a number of converging factors at work in the late 1970s, including critiques by social scientists of the technocentric, top-down nature of the modernisation approach, the 'reassertion of populist sentiments' in terms of people's protest and grass-roots development movements, and the participatory research style being advocated by institutes for agricultural research (Blaikie 2000: 1043). Neopopulists advocate that development is about empowering disenfranchised groups, providing them with opportunities to have greater control over their own lives and well-being. They value indigenous knowledge and skills, and attempt to build upon local resources, both cultural and physical (Friedmann 1992). Thus when considering strategies for facilitating development of local communities through tourism, neopopulist thought is an obvious starting point.

As discussed in the previous chapter, both neopopulist and postmodern thought reject mainstream development paradigms which seek a universal truth, preferring to seek out diverse voices and arguing that the meaning of development is contested (Blaikie 2000: 1045). However, rather than putting all of their energies into deconstructing and critiquing the notion that tourism can be seen as a means to development, neopopulists are more likely to search for appropriate forms of tourism which can enhance the well-being of local communities. Such sentiments are expressed by Brohman (1996a: 60):

> Community-based tourism development would seek to strengthen institutions designed to enhance local participation and promote the economic, social, and cultural well-being of the popular majority. It would also seek to strike a balanced and harmonious approach to development that would stress considerations such as the compatibility of various forms of tourism with other components of the local economy; the quality of development, both culturally and environmentally; and the divergent needs, interests, and potentials of the community and its inhabitants.

Thus under neopopulism, tourism *for* development means tourism for development of Third World peoples, not tourism for the development of the industry itself.

Perhaps the major contribution of neopopulism to thinking on tourism issues is the way in which it highlights the importance of civil society, rather than assuming that tourism should be led by the market and variously controlled or supported by the state: 'renewed concern with civil society – with communities, popular movements, and social networks . . . [provides] the possibility of alternative (grassroots, participatory, subaltern) visions of development outside of the horizon of both state and market' (Watts 2000a: 170). Neopopulists argue that the 'people power' implicit in civil society is integral to a self-determined form of development, and thus their strategies often focus on working with non-governmental organisations (NGOs) and voluntary organisations. Thus in this book, three key groups of players are considered in Part III which looks at supporting appropriate tourism development in the Third World: the state (Chapter 10), the market (Chapter 11) and NGOs and local action groups (Chapter 12).

Neopopulist theory suggests that local communities should be central to tourism planning and management, and it encourages the voices of those most affected by tourism to be heard. This may be in the shape of formalised systems of local level planning which actively involve local communities or, at the other extreme, protests by community groups dissatisfied with the way tourism is impacting on their society and environment. Thus, for example, through the actions of tourism protest groups in Goa (to be discussed in Chapter 12),

> we are witnessing an increase in the political practice of multiple identities, loyalties and conflicting sovereignties associated with localised politics and development in particular places. These alternative political arrangements challenge the hegemonic role of the nation state to define people's political identities (Kindon 1999: 200).

Sustainable development perspectives

Sustainable development perspectives began to be applied in tourism studies as part of the 1970s critique of the impacts of tourism, particularly impacts on the natural environment. The environmental consequences of the large-scale resort approach to tourism in many Third World countries were highlighted with numerous cases of destruction of ecosystems (for example, the draining of mangrove swamps to allow construction of buildings), overuse of finite resources (for example, so much water needed for golf course irrigation that local agricultural yields were diminished), and pollution (for example, raw sewage flowing from hotels into waterways). The potential for a positive relationship between tourism and conservation has also been noted (Hall 1998a), as tourists are clearly attracted by pristine and attractive natural environments.

The more specific term 'sustainable tourism' was eventually coined and generally regarded as a subset of alternative tourism. This term:

has come to represent and encompass a set of principles, policy prescriptions, and management methods which chart a path for tourism development such that a destination area's environmental resource base (including natural, built, and cultural features) is protected for future development (Hunter 1997: 850).

There are debates within sustainable development perspectives on tourism depending on whether or not one takes a strong sustainability position. At one end of the spectrum of perspectives on sustainable development are mild, reformist policies (corresponding with a weak sustainability position) which argue that development, through responsible use of resources, can go hand in hand with conservation. Meanwhile the other end of the spectrum is dominated by viewpoints which stress the need for preservation of resources and zero growth (corresponding with a strong sustainability position) (Lélé 1991; Rees 1990). Such theoretical ideas have also been applied to specific forms of tourism, as seen in Acott et al.'s (1998) analysis of the difference between 'deep' and 'shallow' ecotourism.

In general, the tourism literature adopts the weak sustainability position because this assumes that a win–win situation which allows for economic growth *and* environmental protection, can occur. This causes Hunter (1997) to argue that the sustainable tourism literature is too 'tourism-centric'. Others agree, suggesting that the influence of sustainable development on tourism is superficial, as evidenced by the way in which tourism has rebranded and promoted itself and its products as being environmentally sensitive (Pleumarom 1994). Thus, it is argued, the term 'sustainable tourism' as it is now used needs to be more environment-led and have more of a development focus (Burns 1999b; Hunter 1997).

A development focus is apparent when local concerns become a priority of tourism development. Too many efforts at implementing environmentally sensitive tourism have focused on conservation of resources and failed to embrace the development imperative, thus neglecting the livelihood needs of local communities. A concern for livelihoods should be integral to development efforts (Chambers and Conway 1992), based on the recognition that local people need to benefit from the existence of natural resources in their area, rather than suggesting that these resources all be diverted to enhancing tourist experiences. Political ecology perspectives are of relevance here as they have helped draw attention to the roles of power in relationships between tourism stakeholders and how this influences the way in which stakeholders have access to, and manage, the environment (Stonich 1998). For example, Thrupp (1990, cited in Stonich et al. 1995) questions the creation of large parks as conservation estates in Costa Rica for the benefit of tourists and the tourism industry, when there is increasing landlessness within the country. A livelihoods approach also calls for attention to be paid to a diversity of livelihood strategies, rather than encouraging communities to embrace tourism at the expense of other subsistence and economic opportunities. One of the most effective ways in which tourism can both conserve nature and improve local livelihoods is through community approaches to natural resource management (Ashley 2000). Under such a regime a community may identify tourism as just one strategy for development utilising their natural resources, while agriculture, craft production and hunting are concurrently pursued in a sustainable manner.

Both livelihoods and political ecology perspectives provide useful insights into issues concerning the creation of protected areas. Protected areas were generally intended to both protect unique, pristine environments while also providing enjoyment for people (Hall 1998a). The interests of local people displaced so that protected areas could be created are clearly missing from this equation, as will be discussed in Chapter 6. In the Third World, not only do protected areas represent a preoccupation and prioritisation of the needs of nature/wildlife over people, but a preoccupation often supported by Western environmental organisations whose own countries no longer have numerous areas of ecological significance to protect (Dasmann 1988).

The reliance of Third World communities on natural resources to meet their basic livelihood needs leads Hunter to suggest that '. . . different interpretations of sustainable tourism may be appropriate for developed and developing countries' (1997: 858). While Western countries may adopt a strong sustainability position, for the Third World it may be necessary to take a softer position which allows imperatives such as income generation to take priority (Munt 1992, cited in Hunter 1997: 859).

The sections to follow consider how the terms 'participation' and 'empowerment' encompass principles that could help to determine a more equitable, sustainable path to tourism development in the Third World, as well as drawing attention to possible weaknesses with neopopulist logic.

The challenge of participation

It is not participation per se but the nature of this participation which has become critical in dialogue concerning community involvement in tourism planning or tourism ventures (Cater 1995):

> The debate is currently not one of whether local communities should be involved in the development of tourism to their areas, but how they should be involved and whether 'involvement' means 'control'. This struggle for power and control over the tourist activities and financial benefits is at its sharpest at the destination end (Mowforth and Munt, 1998: 103–4).

A useful tool for ascertaining the nature of participation in tourism ventures is Pretty's (1995) 'typology of participation' in which he identifies seven levels of participation, with manipulative participation at one end of the spectrum and self-mobilisation at the other. A simplified dichotomy arising from Pretty's typology is passive versus active participation. When communities are passive participants in a tourism process they may merely receive a few menial jobs at a tourist resort or have a percentage of gate takings from a national park disbursed to them, while exerting no control over the nature of tourism development or their involvement in it. Active participation, alternatively, should mean that communities have access to information on the pros and cons of tourism development, and are directly involved in planning for and managing tourism in line with their own interests and resources.

This does not mean, however, that only involvement that is initiated by local communities offers opportunities for active participation. Milne (1998: 42), for example, discerns a difference between *sanctioned participation*, in which governments establish and direct a process encouraging local involvement in decision-making (see for example the CAMPFIRE scheme, discussed in Chapter 5), and *independent political organisation,* whereby separate groups attempt to exert control over tourism, sometimes through non-confrontational means but other times through direct protest (see Chapter 12 for a discussion of anti-tourism groups in Goa, India). These are very different scenarios but in both cases local agency can be asserted. Similarly, while there are greater opportunities for active participation in small-scale forms of tourism, such as homestay accommodation and cultural experiences offered in a Solomon Islands village (Figure 4.1), active participation can also occur in more up-scale forms of tourism such as luxury resorts (Figure 4.2) if local people share ownership and management of the resort. While active participation is an ideal, putting this

Figure 4.1   Village in Malaita, Solomon Islands.

Figure 4.2   Exclusive resort in Moorea, French Polynesia.

BOX 4.1

Constraints to the active participation of communities in tourism ventures

1. Communities often lack proprietorship over land and natural resources, thus participation in tourism is limited to co-option in ventures controlled by outsiders.
2. Appropriate skills, knowledge and resources for developing tourism ventures are often lacking at the community level.
3. Poor communities find it difficult to accumulate or attract the capital necessary to develop tourism facilities or attractions.
4. Communities are typically heterogeneous, comprising a range of different interest groups which may come into competition regarding the development of a potentially lucrative tourism venture.

Source: Based on Koch (1997).

---

into practice is by no means a simple process. Koch (1997) has identified a number of constraints to participation of local communities in tourism ventures in South Africa (Box 4.1), and his points are applicable to a broad range of contexts.

As highlighted by Koch's first point, communities can only be expected to participate actively in a tourism project if they have a sense of ownership of the project (Guevara 1996). This is why moves by the governments of Zimbabwe and Namibia to allow communities to manage the wildlife on their communal lands offers them an excellent opportunity to find ways of engaging equitably in tourism ventures. With relation to the second point, de Beer and Elliffe (1997) are concerned that many strategies for tourism development *assume* there will be opportunities for active involvement of local communities without actually planning for this or putting in place support programmes which acknowledge the relative lack of experience and resources of local people. This suggests that neopopulist approaches aimed at awareness-raising and capacity-building could work if implemented at an early stage of planning for tourism development rather than tagged on to a project at a later date. Koch's third point draws attention to the lack of financial resources communities can harness to invest in tourism development. Certainly local control is more difficult to achieve when communities become indebted to moneylenders or are involved in partnerships with more powerful outside interests in order to gain finance to initiate tourism ventures.[1] Koch's fourth point specifies that communities are comprised of diverse interest groups, suggesting that marginalised groups within communities will find it particularly difficult to be active participants in tourism processes. This point was also raised in Chapter 1. As de Kadt (1990: 30) warns, '. . . calls for community participation gloss over the well-known tendency for local elites to "appropriate" the organs of participation for their own benefit'. Elites within communities often become more wealthy than others simply because they have the power and confidence to deal with outsiders and ensure that development opportunities offer particular gains for themselves and their families (de Kadt 1990). Thus:

> Unless specific measures are taken to encourage meaningful participation in community decision making by members of the popular sectors, including traditionally disadvantaged groups, increased local participation may simply transfer control over development from one elite group to another (Brohman 1996a: 60).

As France (1997c: 150) notes, however, 'Scale . . . will affect the intensity and nature of participation.' Thus it is much easier for communities to take a controlling role in small-scale ventures than in large, capital-intensive enterprises. Similarly, less powerful groups in society will have more chance of participating in small-scale enterprises: '. . . the ability of women to influence the sustainability of tourism development increases as one moves *down* the global–local nexus towards the community and household/firm levels' (Milne 1998: 41).

The critical factor concerning active participation in tourism is community control, which should mean that communities have the power to decide whether or not tourism is an appropriate development avenue for them to pursue and in what form it should be pursued. As active participants in tourism, they should be able to fight to put a stop to tourism development which threatens their well-being. Parnwell (1998: 217) identifies NGOs and advocacy groups as local actors which can support communities in resisting tourism in cases such as Burma where it is seen as supporting an oppressive military regime, or in transforming tourism into a more positive process in other circumstances: 'the process of tourism development is neither unidirectional nor static, nor is it entirely conditional upon or contributing to negative circumstances'. At the same time, he notes, 'the effectiveness of such organisations and actors is also heavily circumscribed by the prevailing socio-political context' (Parnwell 1998: 217). Third World governments, for example, may use their agency to facilitate penetration by international capital in the self-interest of national level elites, rather than to serve the interests of the majority of citizens (Parnwell 1998). For all the noble sentiment of neopopulism, local agency will not always be sufficient to challenge prevailing tourism models advocated by powerful state and market actors and to turn tourism into a more equitable activity (France 1997b).

The following section is more hopeful, however, and offers insights for those who wish to identify specific ways in which empowerment can result from community involvement in tourism.

Empowerment framework

The discussion to follow introduces an empowerment framework which can be used to analyse the actual or potential impacts of various forms of tourism on local communities (Table 4.1). For the purposes of this book empowerment is understood as a process 'through which individuals, households, local groups, communities, regions and nations shape their own lives and the kind of society in which they live' (France 1997c: 149). Four dimensions of empowerment – economic, social, psychological and political – are utilised in this framework in recognition of the multidimensional nature of development (Scheyvens 1999a).

When considering whether or not a community has been economically empowered by a tourism venture, it is necessary to consider opportunities which have arisen in terms of both formal and informal sector employment and business opportunities. While some economic gains are usually experienced by a community involved in tourism, concerns may arise over inequity in the spread of economic benefits (Wilkinson and Pratiwi 1995). As discussed above, typically it is elites who manage to secure most of the economic benefits arising from tourism development in a community, and it is particularly hard for some groups, such as women and youths, to take advantage of such economic opportunities.

A local community which is optimistic about the future, has faith in the abilities of its residents, is relatively self-reliant and demonstrates pride in traditions and culture, can be said to be psychologically powerful. In many small-scale, less industrialised societies, preservation of aspects of tradition is extremely important in terms of maintaining a group's sense of self-esteem and well-being (Mansperger 1995). Tourism initiatives which respect and show interest in aspects

Table 4.1   Framework for assessing extent of empowerment of communities involved in tourism

	Signs of empowerment	Signs of disempowerment
Economic empowerment	Tourism brings lasting economic gains to a local community. Cash earned is shared between many households in the community. There are visible signs of improvements from the cash that is earned (e.g. houses are made of more permanent materials; more children are able to attend school)	Tourism merely results in small, spasmodic cash gains for a local community. Most profits go to local elites, outside operators, government agencies, etc. Only a few individuals or families gain direct financial benefits from tourism, while others cannot find a way to share in these economic benefits because they lack capital, experience and/or appropriate skills
Psychological empowerment	Self-esteem of many community members is enhanced because of outside recognition of the uniqueness and value of their culture, their natural resources and their traditional knowledge. Access to employment and cash leads to an increase in status for traditionally low-status sectors of society, e.g. youths, the poor	Those who interact with tourists are left feeling that their culture and way of life are inferior. Many people do not share in the benefits of tourism and are thus confused, frustrated, uninterested or disillusioned with the initiative
Social empowerment	Tourism maintains or enhances the local community's equilibrium. Community cohesion is improved as individuals and families work together to build a successful tourism venture. Some funds raised are used for community development purposes, e.g. to build schools or improve water supplies	Disharmony and social decay. Many in the community take on outside values and lose respect for traditional culture and for their elders. Disadvantaged groups (e.g. women) bear the brunt of problems associated with the tourism initiative and fail to share equitably in its benefits. Rather than cooperating, families/ethnic or socio-economic groups compete with each other for the perceived benefits of tourism. Resentment and jealousy are commonplace
Political empowerment	The community's political structure fairly represents the needs and interests of all community groups. Agencies initiating or implementing the tourism venture seek out the opinions of a variety of community groups (including special interest groups of women, youths and other socially disadvantaged groups) and provide opportunities for them to be represented on decision-making bodies, e.g. the Wildlife Park Board or the regional tourism association	The community has an autocratic and/or self-interested leadership. Agencies initiating or implementing the tourism venture fail to involve the local community in decision-making so the majority of community members feel they have little or no say over *whether* the tourism initiative operates or *the way* in which it operates

Sources: Scheyvens (1999a); structure based partly on Friedmann (1992).

of traditional culture can, therefore, be empowering for local people. This is exemplified in a photo in Krippendorf's book *The Holiday Makers* (1987) which shows a girl standing tall with bunches of flowers to sell to tourists, and the caption states 'Relaxed self-confidence and a consistent commitment to one's own culture are the most effective weapons against "touristification" '. Psychological disempowerment can also occur, however, if the tourism development makes local people feel that they are somehow inadequate or inferior, as in situations where they service the needs of tourists for a minimal wage, and when they feel they have no control over the pace and direction of development. According to Norberg-Hodge (1991: 81) whose work with the Ladakhi people in the Himalayan region is well known, the 'psychological pressure to modernize' which comes from exposure to tourists and other aspects of Western society, can undermine the self-esteem of indigenous peoples. Evidence of psychological disempowerment emerged from research by Berno (1999: 668) who quotes a resident from an outer island in the Cook Islands:

> we still get a few people who come here who go to an outer island and feel that . . . [it] should be possible to get very cheap accommodation here with a local family . . . they might get one or two [tourists] that are good, that they enjoy, and suddenly they get one that is so much bad news for them, and they lose a lot of self-esteem . . . because they just open their mouth and say 'I'm not going to do that, you expect me to go into that toilet' or 'I can't eat that food' and so on and it just destroys their desire to have people in their home again.

It is very important, therefore, that communities feel empowered prior to engaging in tourism initiatives, both so they can choose whether or not tourism is an appropriate activity to pursue, and so that they can exert control over any tourism which does develop.

Social empowerment refers to a situation in which a community's sense of cohesion and integrity has been confirmed or strengthened by involvement in tourism.[2] Strong community groups, including youth groups, savings clubs, church groups and women's groups, and good participation in community meetings, may all be signs of an empowered community. On the other hand, social disempowerment may occur if tourist activity results in crime, begging, displacement from traditional lands, loss of access to resources, cultural decay or prostitution (Mansperger 1995). In an examination of community-based wildlife management, including ecotourism initiatives, in South Africa, Lesotho and Swaziland, Mander and Steytler (1997: 15) found that 64 per cent of respondents from the 38 initiatives studied thought that community dynamics had a big influence on project success. They concluded, 'It may therefore be desirable to design initiatives in such a way where benefits and costs are equitably distributed throughout the community from the outset to promote community cohesion' (1997: 15).

If a community is to be politically empowered by tourism, their voices and their concerns should guide the development of any tourism project from the feasibility stage through to its implementation, and they should receive ongoing education relevant to the project (Guevara 1996). They should also be involved in monitoring and evaluating tourism projects over time, and diverse interest groups within a community, including women and youths, need to have representation on community and broader decision-making bodies. Such political empowerment is closely tied to psychological empowerment, as demonstrated in the case of local people engaging in tourism in Yogyakarta, Indonesia, who expressed 'a sense of inadequacy among themselves, in terms of touristic knowledge, for participating in decision making' (Timothy 1999: 386). A lack of experience with formal decision-making forums or dissatisfaction with the structure and function of these forums may mean that not all communities seek participation in them, however. Rather than nominating a representative to sit on a tourism development board initiated by the local council, for example, a community may decide that it is more politically empowering for them to sit down as a group and discuss their development priorities, and then to invite the tourism development board to a community meeting to hear their views. Thus Hunter (1997: 864) argues that 'It may well be that different levels of community involvement in tourism development decision-making are appropriate for different pathways of sustainable tourism.'

Conclusion

The final chapter in this introductory section on theories relating to the contentious relationship between tourism and development has engaged with ideas stemming from sustainable development and neopopulist agendas. It has been particularly concerned with how local communities might participate in tourism in an equitable manner and be empowered by their experiences. While these communities are clearly not on a level playing field when attempting to ensure that their concerns are addressed by the burgeoning international tourism industry, this chapter joins Parnwell (1998) in rejecting the view that tourism is an unstoppable global phenomenon impinging on Third World countries and communities in a completely uncontrollable fashion. Tourism is a process open to negotiation which can be framed by national and local needs. Local agency can play an important role when, for example, communities say 'no' to powerful investors who want to build a resort on their land and choose instead to build homestay accommodation over which they can retain control.

Much of the discussion on tourism and development to date has considered the roles of Third World governments and the responsibilities of the tourism industry. These actors are seen as bearing responsibility for the form in which tourism develops and therefore the way in which it impacts on local communities. The neopopulist perspective, however, has drawn attention to the roles that civil society actors such as NGOs and advocacy groups can play in facilitating community level development through tourism.

Neopopulist theories stress that it is the nature of participation in tourism by communities that is of vital concern in terms of whether they are likely to see benefits to their well-being and livelihoods. Active participation, whereby communities have some degree of control over, as well as sharing equitably in the benefits of, tourism, was seen as more likely to lead to empowerment than passive forms of participation. It seems more likely that communities will be able to be actively involved in alternative tourism ventures which are small scale and based around local skills and resources.

Writers such as Mowforth and Munt (1998), however, are somewhat wary of the neopopulist fervour regarding the potential of alternative approaches. Instead, they suggest that such new forms of tourism are just as likely as conventional tourism to create dependency and perpetuate unequal power relations between Western and Third World countries. It is thus important that we reflect carefully on issues of control and benefits surrounding any tourism initiative which is proposed, whether it conforms more to the mass or alternative tourism mould. As Chapter 1 showed, it is not helpful to simply dismiss mass forms of tourism which will continue to dominate the market and which can provide benefits to local communities. The empowerment framework presented herein is a tool which could be applied to a wide variety of tourism scenarios in order to help us to understand conditions under which communities can be empowered from participation in tourism.

The chapters to follow in Part II of this book offer some ideas of ways forward to ensure that, rather than overwhelming local communities, tourism occurs in ways which are sensitive to the needs and interests of Third World peoples.

Questions

1. Consider different ways in which local voices can influence tourism planning and management.

2. Explain how a strong sustainability position could undermine the well-being of people living in areas which are attractive to tourists.

3. What is the difference between passive and active participation in a tourism venture?

4. Provide four signs that a community has been (a) empowered, or (b) disempowered by involvement in a tourism venture.

Suggestions for further reading

Brohman, J. 1996 'New directions in tourism for the Third World', *Annals of Tourism Research*, **23**: 331–58.

De Kadt, E. 1990 *Making the Alternative Sustainable: Lessons from Development for Tourism*, DP 272, Institute of Development Studies, Sussex.

McLaren, D. 1998 *Rethinking Tourism and Ecotravel: The Paving of Paradise and What You Can Do to Stop it*, Kumarian Press, West Hartford.

Useful websites

Retour is an organisation based in the Netherlands which conducts consultancy work on tourism and sustainable development. The following page explains critical issues to consider regarding empowerment through tourism:

www.do.nl/retour/CriticalIissues.html

This site provides a number of links on sustainable and community-based tourism:

www.ftsl.demon.co.uk/

United Nations' pages on sustainable tourism:

www.un.org/esa/sustdev/tourism.htm

Notes

1. This does not preclude the possibility of equitable partnerships being formed between communities and the private sector, as will be shown in Chapter 11.

2. Note that Harrison (2001: 38) suggests that community cohesion may be a prerequisite to effective involvement in tourism, especially in terms of collaboration with outside stakeholders.

PART II

The search for appropriate forms of tourism

CHAPTER 5

Ecotourism

Introduction

This chapter addresses one of the most popular, and rapidly growing, forms of tourism in the Third World: ecotourism. After a general discussion about the popularity of ecotourism, the need to carefully define this concept, and the importance of approaching ecotourism from the perspective of local communities, the issue of empowerment is discussed. Empowerment of communities through ecotourism, so that they not only share equitably in the benefits of ecotourism but they actually have some control over ecotourism activities in their area, is an ideal towards which those encouraging community involvement in ecotourism should be aiming.

In the case of the CAMPFIRE programme in Zimbabwe, there are examples of communities which have secured control over ecotourism through gaining the right to manage natural resources, including wildlife, on their communal lands. While supporters cite this as an ideal example of ecotourism because it can also result in enormous revenue for local community development projects, others argue that it is not 'true' ecotourism because it is consumptive, that is, the communities make their revenue through leasing out hunting rights to safari companies. Can hunting wildlife be seen as a form of ecotourism? This controversial issue is raised in the final section of the chapter.

The popularity of ecotourism

Ecotourism is currently a 'hot' topic. The fury is predictable. It is a movement that potentially involves billions of dollars, high-level politics, the survival of threatened cultures, and the preservation of rapidly disappearing wildlands (Ziffer 1989: 1).

Ziffer's comments from over 10 years ago still ring true today: the 'heat' or fervour associated with ecotourism has not abated. The demands of increasingly affluent Western consumers for 'remote', 'natural' and 'exotic' environments have seen an upsurge in ecotourism ventures, particularly in Third World countries. The Ecotourism Society (1998) cites studies which indicate the rate of growth of ecotourism in Third World countries: the number of trekkers in Nepal increased 255 per cent between 1980 and 1991; visitors to Kenya increased by 45 per cent between 1983 and 1993, with approximately 80 per cent of them drawn by wildlife; and nature tourists to Honduras increased by 15 per cent in 1995 alone. Overall, it has been estimated that from 1996, ecotourism will grow by up to 25 per cent each year until 2005 (Herliczek 1996: 31). Concurrently, there has been a dramatic rise in the number of local communities seeking to benefit from the booming ecotourism trade. Ecotourism is being embraced as a potential economic saviour by many rural communities which are motivated by the promise of jobs, new business opportunities and skill development, as well as the chance to secure greater control over natural resource utilisation in their areas (Ashley and Roe 1997).

A number of authors caution us from uncritically accepting ecotourism as a common good, however, especially where vulnerable peoples and environments of Third World countries are involved (Ziffer 1989; Boo 1990; Cater and Lowman 1994): 'there is a very real danger of viewing ecotourism as the universal panacea, and the ecotourist as some magic breed, mitigating all tourism's ills' (Cater 1993: 85). Of concern is the fact that it is precisely the more remote, less developed tourism areas that ecotourists seek which are most vulnerable to cultural disruption and environmental degradation (Cater 1993: 89).

In many cases the 'ecotourism' label has simply worked as an attractive marketing tool (Thomlinson and Getz 1996; Ziffer 1989), drawing in punters from a range of different backgrounds and with varied motives for travel, as shown in Box 5.1. Woodwood (1997: 167), commenting on an ecotourism conference in Johannesburg in 1996, noted that for most of the 400 delegates, 'Ecotourism . . . is represented by well-off first-world visitors staying in luxury game parks and spending their time between game drives and *braai* (barbecues).' Other writers, however, suggest that the ecotourist is becoming increasingly aware of environmental, cultural and developmental issues relating to the areas they are visiting (Lew 1998a).

It has been claimed that 'True ecotourism can . . . be one of the most powerful tools for protecting the environment' (Ceballos-Lascuráin 1996: 24). It is essential, therefore, that ecotourism is clearly defined in order that we can distinguish between the initiatives espoused by responsible operators with a concern for ethical environmental and social development and the operations of 'eco-pirates', whom Lew (1996: 723) describes as '. . . people who copy existing responsible tourism products, but in a non-responsible manner – typically offering lower prices, inferior experiences, and detrimental environmental and social impacts'.

BOX 5.1

Who are ecotourists?

Whoopies (wealthy, healthy, older people)

Professional people, perhaps retired or on extended periods of leave, from rich, industrialised countries. Aged between 44 and 64 years. Are bored with traditional mass tourism destinations and search out unique, pristine destinations.

Sensitive souls

Members of the liberal middle classes in the West: donate to charities, are eco-friendly and perhaps, vegetarian. They prefer to book their travel with operators which promise an appreciation of natural attractions in an exotic location, but in ways which ensure local communities benefit from tourism.

Ego-tourists

Young Western travellers who are financially less well endowed than the previous two categories, and who seek 'alternative' travel in the Third World as part of an extended vacation. They may travel independently or with an overland truck company, and are often more environmentally aware than other types of tourists. Interested in curriculum-vitae building, they feel that as travellers (as opposed to tourists) they will gain certain personal attributes from their experience (see Munt 1994).

Affluent southerners

Members of the growing middle class in Third World countries who may not be able to afford to travel abroad, especially to Western countries (unless they work for an aid organisation which funds this), but who have an interest in the cultural and natural heritage of their own and neighbouring countries.

Source: After Panos (1995).

Definitions of ecotourism

Various authors have come up with ways to distinguish between different forms of ecotourism (Blamey 1997; Hvenegaard 1994). For example, some draw on the literature of sustainable development in their assessments, speaking of 'deep' and 'shallow' ecotourism (Acott *et al.* 1998). Such categorisations seek to expose the difference between a genuine, environmentally and socially responsible form of ecotourism and situations in which ecotourism is simply used as a tool to market nature. A broad definition of ecotourism embraces all tourism which focuses on appreciation of natural phenomena: nature-based tourism. As shown in Figure 5.1, however, a natural setting alone is not sufficient for more restrictive definitions of ecotourism, which assert that

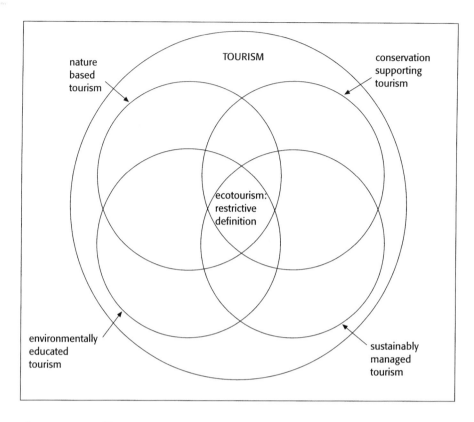

Figure 5.1   Buckley's ecotourism framework. (*Source*: Redrawn from Buckley 1994)

ecotourism should be sustainably managed, include environmental education and support conservation (Buckley 1994: 661). While Buckley's framework helps us to understand that ecotourism is much more than just a product, nature, it omits issues of local livelihoods and empowerment of local people, and thus from a development perspective Buckley's framework is flawed.

Some authors have clearly adopted a livelihoods perspective embracing development and conservation when providing definitions of ecotourism. Lindberg *et al.* (1996), for example, examine ecotourism case studies from Belize in terms of the extent to which they generate economic benefits for the local community. However, this does not account for how the greater amount of money entering the community might be distributed, or how a community is being affected socially and culturally by ecotourism initiatives. Wight (cited in Thomlinson and Getz 1996: 186) provides a more holistic approach, stressing the need for social, environmental and economic goals to be considered in ecotourism initiatives. Cater (1993: 85–6), further, states that to be sustainable, tourism development should '. . . meet the needs of the host population in terms of improved living standards both in the short and long term'.

The following definition of ecotourism, proposed by the man often credited with coining the term in 1983,[1] incorporates both the nature of the tourism as well as the impacts of this on local environments and populations:

> Ecotourism is environmentally responsible, enlightening travel and visitation to relatively undisturbed natural areas in order to enjoy and appreciate nature (and any accompanying cultural features both past and present) that promotes conservation, has low visitor impact, and provides for beneficially active socio-economic involvement of local populations (Ceballos-Lascuráin 1996).

It is clear from the above discussion that ideally, in addition to supporting conservation and increasing people's appreciation of natural phenomena, ecotourism initiatives in the Third World must provide opportunities for beneficial involvement of local communities and enhance local livelihoods. It could also be argued that ecotourism should be empowering for local participants. While the issue of livelihoods will be discussed further in Chapter 6, community involvement and empowerment are considered in detail below.

Community-based ecotourism

Community-based ecotourism (CBET) ventures aim to ensure that members of local communities have a high degree of control over the activities taking place, and a significant proportion of the economic benefits accrue to them (Liu 1994; Cater 1993). This is in contrast to a large number of ecotourism ventures which are controlled wholly by outside operators whose primary motivation is making profits. It is also distinct from contexts in which most of the economic benefits of tourism accrue to the national government (Akama 1996: 572). Thus, for example, while the slogan for East Africa that 'wildlife pays so wildlife stays' is apt (Ziffer 1989: 2), to date it has mainly 'paid' for governments, foreign tourism companies and local entrepreneurs. This problem is exemplified in the case study on Zambia.

Case study: Locals miss out on benefits of nature-based tourism in Zambia

In the Chiawa communal lands of Zambia which border the Zambezi River, the Chieftainess granted around 20 tourism operators the rights to lease land both along the river banks and bordering the Lower Zambezi National Park. Her decision was based on the hope that this would bring much wanted investment and jobs to the region. The government, not the community, collects lease money from these operators. Most of the guests are higher-spending tourists who engage in fishing expeditions, canoe safaris, game drives and other nature-tourism activities.

The local benefits from these ventures to date have been extremely limited. While some young men have received work at the lodges which have been established, and some lodge owners have paid individuals for providing thatching grass or gravel, there have been few other economic opportunities for the local community. Meanwhile, their access to certain prime sites along the river bank has been impeded, fishing activities have been interrupted by speedboats and crop damage by wild animals – the major drawcard for tourists – continues to severely impinge on the well-being of these largely impoverished people. As local women walk several kilometres to collect water or to take their 20 kilogram sack of maize to be ground, smart four-wheel-drive vehicles carrying tourists and provisions from the city drive past, leaving nothing in their wake but a cloud of red dust.

Source: Author's fieldwork, July 1998.

While the rhetoric suggests that there is much support for CBET ventures, in practice it is difficult to find good examples of this. Woodwood (1997) found that even the most enlightened South African operators seemed only to recognise the need to involve local communities in ecotourism in terms of their public relations value. There was little commitment to supporting the rights of indigenous peoples to benefit from their traditional lands and wildlife. It is important that local communities have the opportunity to be fully and actively involved in ecotourism, as would happen if they were involved in all four levels on the following scale of community participation:

1.   Information sharing – 'project designers and managers share information with the public in order to facilitate collective or individual action'.
2.   Consultation – 'the public is not only informed, but consulted on key issues at some or all stages in a project cycle'.
3.   Decision-making – 'the public is involved in making decisions about project design and implementation'.
4.   Initiating action – 'the public takes the initiative in terms of actions and decisions pertaining to the project' (Paul 1987, cited in Drake 1991: 133–4).

One way of analysing existing ecotourism ventures, and planning for future ventures that will be good examples of CBET, is to view them from the perspective of community empowerment.

Ecotourism and empowerment

From the above discussion, it should be clear that the way in which ecotourism is approached is critical to its success in terms of promoting the well-being of both local peoples and their environments. It has only been in the last few years that an empowerment approach has attracted the interest of those writing on ecotourism; however, those who do discuss it fervently support the concept (Hawkins and Khan 1998; Scheyvens 1999a; Theopile 1995). In order that local peoples benefit more and have some control over ecotourism occurring in their regions, Akama (1996: 573) has suggested that:

> ... there is a need for the initiation of alternative wildlife conservation and tourism programmes aimed at the social and economic empowerment of rural peasants ... the local community need to be empowered to decide what forms of tourism facilities and wildlife conservation programmes they want to be developed in their respective communities, and how the tourism costs and benefits are to be shared among different stakeholders.

Gauthier (1993: 105) goes even further, claiming that 'Empowerment of local people within the context of environmental protection is one of the tenets of ecotourism.' Theopile (1995: 27) would seem to agree, noting the need to empower local people so they can decide how to 'strike a balance' between economic and environmental concerns facing them. Thus an empowerment perspective suggests that it is not sufficient to ensure that local communities gain direct benefits from ecotourism activities, although this would be a great improvement on the status quo in many areas. What is also necessary is that they have some measure of control over ecotourism initiatives. These two criteria, benefits and control, appear to have been met in the CAMPFIRE programme in Zimbabwe, which is examined in the second part of this chapter.

The CAMPFIRE programme in Zimbabwe

Gibson and Marks (1995: 942) assert that not only do local communities need to gain economic benefits from ecotourism if they are to support conservation, rather '. . . conservation will be more successful at the local level when rural residents possess significant *legal claims* over wildlife resources and its management'. This is the logic behind the CAMPFIRE (Communal Area Management Programme for Indigenous Resources) scheme in Zimbabwe.

CAMPFIRE provides one of the best-known examples of the community-based natural resource management (CBNRM) approach. CBNRM aims to provide a way of ensuring that conservation efforts promote rural development by encouraging management of natural resources by local communities (Wainwright and Wehrmeyer 1998). Typically it is applied to programmes on communal lands, that is, land owned by a large number of people with common affiliations (e.g. a tribe or clan), rather than programmes associated with state-protected land such as national parks. Many CBNRM approaches are essentially based on sharing with communities the economic benefits of controlled exploitation of wildlife resources (Gibson and Marks 1995).

The CAMPFIRE programme in Zimbabwe aims to empower local communities by enabling them to manage wildlife resources on their communal lands and to determine how they can benefit economically from this wildlife. Officially launched in 1986, CAMPFIRE is legally supported by a 1982 amendment to the Parks and Wildlife Act (1972) which delegates appropriate authority for the management of wildlife resources to district councils. Under CAMPFIRE, these councils then devolve this management responsibility to local communities, who have the power to decide how they wish to utilise resources on communal lands for their own benefit. Their options include sales of live animals, use of animals for their own consumption, non-consumptive ecotourism and consumptive ecotourism.

CAMPFIRE communities in wildlife-rich areas have generally chosen to pursue consumptive forms of ecotourism (Hasler 1996). The concept of consumptive ecotourism has only entered the literature on CBNRM since the 1990s, and it remains an ill-defined concept. One can assume, however, that consumptive ecotourism refers to ecotourism which relies upon the direct use, or consumption, of natural resources. Thus while activities such as birdwatching and photographic safaris are clearly non-consumptive, fishing and using local fuelwood are consumptive. In the natural resource management literature, however, the term 'consumptive ecotourism' is most commonly applied to activities involving safari hunting. This form of ecotourism has raised controversy, based partly on the fact that some ecotourism proponents believe that ecotourism is about *preservation* rather than *conservation* (Duffus and Dearden 1990; Whelan 1991). There is a subtle, but important, difference between conservation and preservation, as the latter implies that the resources which are the subject of ecotourism activity or experience should not be consumed in any form. Consumptive tourism inherently rejects such a stance, arguing that allowing restricted consumption of some elements of the natural ecological system can actually lead to greater support among local populations for conservation.

While so far readers may feel benign towards the concept of consumptive ecotourism, most people judge CAMPFIRE quite harshly at first once they realise that essentially, it proposes that the shooting of elephants (and other wildlife) can be seen as ecotourism. In the book *1001 Ways to Save the Planet* (Vallely 1990), one of the things specifically to avoid is hunting. Before passing judgement, however, it is important to understand the philosophy behind and workings of the CAMPFIRE programme in more detail.

In CAMPFIRE, the Zimbabwe branch of the Worldwide Fund for Nature (WWF) works with communities to propose a sustainable hunting quota based on existing wildlife numbers. The community then strikes a deal with a safari company to bring trophy hunters onto their land to hunt on a sustained yield basis (Hasler 1996). This can bring in good money to local communities, including payment for the hunting concession as well as for any trophies taken. A single elephant trophy is valued at up to US$12,000. Depending on what negotiations have taken place with the safari company operating their concession, the community may also get other benefits such as meat from the animals

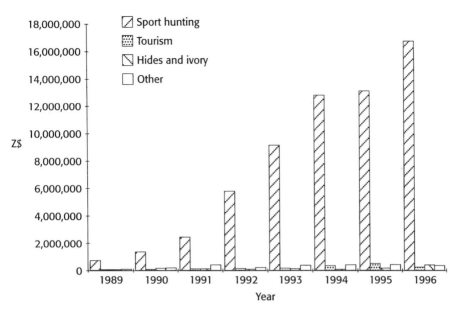

Figure 5.2 CAMPFIRE income, 1989–96. (*Source*: Based on information from the WWF, Harare)

which are shot. This meat is an important source of protein in impoverished rural communities.

The economic gains made from safari hunting in CAMPFIRE areas are large. Figure 5.2 reveals that the earnings for non-consumptive forms of eco-tourism, such as community campsites, under the CAMPFIRE programme pale in comparison to revenue from sport hunting, which generates over 90 per cent of all CAMPFIRE earnings. Thus far communities have chosen to spend their money in a variety of ways, often opting for household dividends to be paid in years of drought but at other times investing the money in community development initiatives such as school or clinic buildings, maize-grinding mills or road improvement. In Masoka, for example, the community invested US$30,000 of hunting revenue into building a tarred road, the first in their area, which helped to alleviate their isolation and gave better access to markets and services. Some villagers had previously walked up to 50 kilometres to catch a public bus. Safari hunting has brought revenue for infrastructural improvements in Masoka as well: 'You see all this infrastructure? We have built it all ourselves, this clinic, the boreholes and the teachers' houses and more. None of this was put up by government' (Masoka headman, cited by Koro 1999a: 3). Clearly the local people are proud of what they have achieved based on their own priorities, not on the ideas of outside agencies.

But can the shooting of elephants, buffalo, impala and the like really be seen as a form of ecotourism? Those who say 'yes' cite the dramatic change in the attitudes of people living in CAMPFIRE areas in favour of conservation of wildlife. Rather than regarding the wildlife as a pest which threatens human lives and valuable crops, people have started to manage wildlife as an asset (Chalker 1994). For example, CAMPFIRE communities tend to be vigilant in controlling poaching on their land because each animal taken by poachers is potentially money (and meat) lost to the community: 'Our people have stopped poaching. They understand that a buffalo is worth much more if it is killed by a foreign hunter' (Champion Machaya, Dete wildlife committee, cited in CAMPFIRE Association *c*.1998a). In the past, these same communities often assisted poachers (Baker 1997).

While the shooting of elephants may seem abhorrent to Western minds saturated with images from wildlife documentaries, elephant numbers have actually increased in areas where controlled hunting (for example under CAMPFIRE) takes place, whereas in other areas numbers have often drastically decreased due to poaching. Elephant numbers recovered from a low of 4,000 in Zimbabwe at the beginning of the twentieth century to 66,000 by the end of the century (Child *et al*. 1999). It is also important to recognise that elephants can cause enormous destruction to natural habitats and deplete water supplies, undermining the viability of other species: 'In one day, an adult eats 150–300 kg of vegetation, drinks 200 litres of water if available, and in forested areas destroys an average of three trees' (Child *et al*. 1999: 6). It is thus vital that in countries with growing populations of elephants, such as Zimbabwe, elephant numbers are controlled. Hunting quotas can assist with this aim (Baker 1997). Johnson (1998: 11) thus argues that '. . . it is time that we de-romanticise wildlife management in Africa, and recognise it as an important development tool alongside merely protecting biodiversity'.

Proponents of consumptive ecotourism go as far as to claim that hunting provides a more desirable form of ecotourism than photographic safaris, for reasons summarised by Baker (1997):

1. Hunters have few infrastructural demands – they are prepared to live in basic tents, for example, and they travel in very small groups, causing little environmental damage.

2. Hunters generally stay in a country for longer than other tourists, they spend a large amount of money per day, and a high proportion of the money they spend remains in the destination country: 'A former Director of Tanzania's Wildlife Department has commented that one hunter is worth 100 tourists to the local economy' (Baker 1997: 308). Non-consumptive ecotourism in southern Africa is still dominated by international and national tourism operators, with few benefits reaching local communities in most cases.

3. Sport hunting disperses tourism funds to remote areas where wildlife numbers and variety remain high, thus bringing valuable economic benefits to communities with tenuous livelihood options. These communities typically lack the infrastructure and experience to tap into the mainstream tourism market.

Does CAMPFIRE meet ecotourism criteria?

The evidence above suggests that CAMPFIRE does contribute to conservation of natural resources, but some may still doubt whether it complies with stricter definitions of ecotourism. Thus in Table 5.1 CAMPFIRE is assessed according to six characteristics which the Australian Conservation Foundation has specified as necessary components of ecotourism.

On the whole, CAMPFIRE meets certain criteria of an ecotourism project extremely well by being low-impact, encouraging conservation, and bringing tangible economic benefits to local communities. A little doubt, however, can be cast over CAMPFIRE's ability to meet the first two criteria. The first criterion, visitation to enjoy nature, wildlife, culture and archaeology, could be debated, as many people see hunting as the antithesis of enjoyment or appreciation of nature, but hunters themselves could disagree. According to one safari operator, many hunters are keen to support programmes such as CAMPFIRE which have a conservation focus: 'Most of our hunters are keen conservationists, so their aim is not to shoot as many as possible, but to bag a prime specimen. They come to us because they know we can provide the goods, but also because their money is going into supporting conservation' (Bill Bedford, Ingwe Safaris, cited in CAMPFIRE Association c.1998a). The second criterion calls for a high degree of interpretation, which can be provided by the professional hunters who accompany all hunting expeditions. However, the information they provide is likely to focus mostly on the tracking of animals.

How equitable and empowering is this form of ecotourism?

Clearly CAMPFIRE brings substantial economic benefits to some communities and has successfully promoted the conservation of resources. But is it empowering, and are the benefits of CAMPFIRE shared equitably among community members? Probably the most significant way in which CAMPFIRE has empowered local people is by making them aware of their right to control their land and the resources thereon and to yield tangible benefits from this: 'People feel that they are the managers of their own resources after almost a hundred years of alienation' (Kalén and Trägårdh 1998: iv). Secondly, CAMPFIRE has promoted grass-roots democracy by building the capacity of local community members to plan their own projects, manage their finances and run effective committees which allow for wide representation of community interests. They have formed democratic decision-making bodies, and the whole community meets annually to discuss revenue distribution.

One problem identified with CAMPFIRE, however, is that the authority to manage the wildlife resources is actually in the hands of rural district councils, which have a responsibility to devolve management authority to communities themselves. Not all councils have been willing, or have made sufficient effort, to devolve authority to these communities (Kalén and Trägårdh 1998). This

Table 5.1   Assessment of CAMPFIRE based on ecotourism criteria

Ecotourism criteria	CAMPFIRE's performance
Visitation to enjoy nature, wildlife, culture and archaeology	Some commentators would argue that hunting is destruction of wildlife rather than enjoyment of wildlife. However, some hunters have a deep appreciation of nature as evidenced by the fact that a lot of hunters book their tours in association with the CAMPFIRE scheme because of the conservation benefits this brings
A high degree of interpretation	All foreign trophy hunters have to be accompanied by a licensed professional hunter, who has had training in guiding and wildlife management. Professional hunters are usually highly skilled and knowledgeable, although their focus is likely to be more on understanding how to track a wild animal than appreciating the wider ecosystem in which they live. While local people may be employed as trackers, they are rarely qualified as professional hunters
High-quality, low-impact design in all infrastructure	Hunters have minimal infrastructure requirements. Safari operators usually provide all of their own portable equipment, such as tents and four-wheel-drive vehicles, and remove their rubbish
The provision of net benefits to environmental protection	In the past, district councils could retain up to 15% of the gross revenue generated from wildlife, using up to 35% for wildlife protection and management and returning at least 50% to local communities. Now they have been asked to return 80% of wildlife revenues to the communities. When communities spend their CAMPFIRE revenue on electric fences around their crops, this helps to minimise human–animal conflicts
Promotion of conservation knowledge and ethics	One of the greatest achievements of CAMPFIRE has been to foster support for wildlife conservation among the local population – wildlife is now an asset, not just a liability which endangers lives and destroys crops. This has led to a reduction in both poaching and complaints about problem animals. Some communities have been proactive in improving wildlife habitat, for example, providing drinking water sources for animals and banning grazing of cattle outside their community boundaries. Young people are trained to be game scouts to assist in wildlife management and prevent poaching. A national parks game scout must accompany the hunting party to ensure quotas are observed
The provision of net benefits to indigenous communities and other affected communities	This is the other major achievement of CAMPFIRE. Because of the significant revenues which can be raised (e.g. trophy fee of US$12,000 for one elephant) for community projects, infrastructure or household dividends, direct economic benefits are received by the communities managing the resources. Some members of communities have also been employed as game scouts

Criteria set by the Australian Conservation Foundation (cited in Beaumont 1998: 241).
Sources: Based on Kalén and Trägårdh (1998); CAMPFIRE Association (c.1998a).

BOX 5.2

The case of conservancies in Namibia

In 1996, legislation was passed in Namibia to enable communities to establish wildlife conservancies. This system of conservancies goes a step further than the CAMPFIRE programme, directly devolving power over natural resources to local communities, rather than using district councils as intermediaries. Thus the Ministry of Environment and Tourism will determine sustainable hunting quotas based largely on proposals from the conservancies themselves (Baker 1997).

In order to establish a conservancy, a community must form a committee which represents the interests of that community and has the responsibility of managing funds and equitably distributing any revenue generated by the conservancy. Their group must have a clearly defined membership, and definite boundaries for the conservancy. The people also need to draft a constitution which outlines, in particular, their objectives regarding sustainable utilisation of wildlife within the conservancy. Once registered, the conservancy has full rights to decide upon both consumptive and non-consumptive use of the resources within their area. The government will no longer deduct a proportion of the revenue from game which has been hunted: all such revenue will be in the hands of the community.

While Namibian communities on communal lands have been running a range of tourism ventures since 1995, including campsites, open air museums, craft centres and traditional villages, they are keen to embrace opportunities open to them through the conservancy scheme because safari hunting will allow them to generate more revenue. In Khoadhi Hoas conservancy, for example, the people have been granted a hunting quota valued at $28,000. This consists of 1 bull elephant, 50 springboks, 20 baboons, 2 duikers, 1 leopard, 4 kudus, 2 giraffes and 4 zebras. It was not surprising, therefore, that Khoadhi Hoas villagers chose to chase away a kudu cornered by local dogs rather than killing the animal. In all four conservancies which had been gazetted by 1999, including Khoadhi Hoas, there were examples of conservancy members apprehending poachers (Koro 1999b).

---

problem has been avoided in Namibia under their more recent conservancies regime which is explained in Box 5.2.

In some ways, the revenue from CAMPFIRE has enhanced equity, bringing benefits to traditionally disadvantaged groups in rural communities. For example, grain-grinding mills purchased with CAMPFIRE monies have had particular benefits in easing the workloads of women, while the construction of classrooms is likely to lead to increases in the numbers of girls attending school, because parents do not like to send their daughters to school if this necessitates travelling some distance from home. In other cases, however, projects intended to benefit an entire community have inadvertently disadvantaged women. Thus in Masoka village, a decision was made to erect a 20-kilometre electric fence around the settlement and cropping areas in order to control problem animals, whose numbers had increased under the CAMPFIRE scheme. However, the limited number of gates put in the fence meant women had to walk further to gain access to daily household requirements, specifically water and fuelwood (Nabane 1996). This is not surprising when considering the following observation about a game fence in another area of Zimbabwe: 'While the fence and its gates had been sited in painstaking consultation with villagers, only men had been involved in the formal consultations' (Fortmann and Bruce 1993: 3).

Where CAMPFIRE communities have chosen to divide up part of their earnings from wildlife as household dividends, some anomalies have arisen as well. This money is generally paid to the household head, usually assumed to be a man, so women do not necessarily gain any control over CAMPFIRE revenues (Nabane 1996). In some CAMPFIRE areas, however, local campaigners have managed to secure dividends for women. In Kanyuriria ward, women argued that because they have to deal with the consequences of greater numbers of wildlife as they work in fields which wildlife have destroyed, married women should be registered in their own right so they would be entitled to receive CAMPFIRE dividends (CAMPFIRE Association c.1998b). In another ward, women insisted that in a family of three wives, a common occurrence in the polygamous societies of southern Africa, each should be registered as a separate household. In another case, a divorced mother successfully convinced men and women in her area that divorced women with children should also share in the distribution of financial revenue from wildlife utilisation (Fortmann and Bruce 1993). Both men and women are users of natural resources and their lives are affected by ecotourism schemes, so both should gain benefits if they are to be expected to support the conservation aims of ecotourism projects.

Conclusion

This chapter has introduced the concept of ecotourism and shown why this term needs to be carefully defined. It is relatively easy for consumers to get carried away with support for products with an 'eco' label; however, many ecotourism operators are simply exploiting this label without having any commitment to ecotourism principles in practice. Ecotourism is not simply nature-based tourism. At its best, however, when sustainably managed, and when it involves environmental education, conservation of resources and empowerment of local people through direct benefits and control over ecotourism activities, ecotourism can provide an excellent example of sustainable development in practice. Some of Honey's (1999) examples support this contention.

Despite the continuing growth in this sector of the market, however, it would be unrealistic to expect that ecotourism could provide an alternative to mass tourism in many cases. With the ever growing number of tourists from both Western and Third World countries it would be dangerous to encourage a complete switch to ecotourism as this would put undue pressure on very fragile ecological areas.

This chapter provided an example of an ecotourism scheme which has worked towards the empowerment of local communities: CAMPFIRE. As discussed, CAMPFIRE is an example of consumptive ecotourism which raises revenue for local conservation and development projects mainly by leasing hunting rights to safari companies. Critics do not see this as ecotourism (Humane Society of the United States 1997), but CAMPFIRE has successfully met most criteria of ecotourism and in addition, it has built local capacity to set goals and plan for future development. Baker (1997), who has compared trophy hunting in several eastern and southern African countries, argues that it can be sustainable when certain provisos are followed: there must be scientific population estimates on which to base quotas and these quotas must be enforced; safari operators who are granted hunting concessions must be reputable and experienced; and finally, there must be a transparent system for returning revenue to local communities, and efforts to ensure equitable sharing of the benefits of the enterprise. This is an area which still requires attention under programmes such as CAMPFIRE, in which the difficulties in disbursing benefits to disadvantaged groups were not well appraised from the outset.

In the past it has been suggested that protected areas, to be examined in Chapter 6, offer the ideal site for ecotourism; however, both CAMPFIRE and the conservancies of Namibia show that there are successful examples of communities planning ecotourism initiatives on the communal lands as well. These CBNRM programmes thus seriously challenge the premise that it is necessary to separate human habitation from natural areas if conservation is to occur. This offers great hope for the future as it allows for conservation and development to occur on much wider areas of land than that covered by state-owned protected areas. It also shows that local communities can sustain viable livelihoods from the land and follow a self-determined development path by engaging with the tourism sector.

Questions

1. Ecotourism is not simply nature-based tourism. Provide a definition of ecotourism which expands upon this idea.

2. Explain the difference between consumptive and non-consumptive ecotourism.

3. How can the shooting of elephants lead to improved conservation practices?

4. Local empowerment is about communities (a) sharing the benefits of ecotourism and (b) having some control over ecotourism in their area. How is empowerment facilitated in the case of CAMPFIRE?

Suggestions for further reading

Dowling, R. 2002 *Ecotourism*, Pearson Education, Harlow.
Fennell, D. 1999 *Ecotourism: An Introduction*, Routledge, New York.
Weaver, D. 1998 *Ecotourism in the Less Developed World*, CAB International, Oxford.

Useful websites

The Green Tourism Association's resource centre provides links to some excellent eco-tourism and sustainable tourism sites:
   www.greentourism.on.ca/gt_resourcemain.html

An overview of debates surrounding the United Nations' declaration of 2002 as the International Year of Ecotourism:
   www.planeta.com/ecotravel/tour/year.html

A clearing house for articles debating the International Year of Ecotourism:
   www.twnside.org.sg/title/iye.htm

To find out more about the CAMPFIRE programme:
   www.campfire-zimbabwe.org/

To find out more about conservancies and the policy framework for CBNRM in Namibia:
   www.dea.met.gov.na/index.html

Note

1. Please note that Fennell's (1999: 31) book claims that, contrary to popular belief, the term 'ecotour' was actually used first by the Canadian Forest Service in 1976.

Tourism and protected areas

Introduction

Now that the concept of ecotourism has been thoroughly discussed in the previous chapter, Chapter 6 will examine a popular focus of conservation and development projects: tourism in association with protected areas. While such tourism could be seen as 'nature-based tourism', it should certainly not be assumed that tourism in association with protected areas automatically adheres to the principles of ecotourism, as explained in Chapter 5.

Many writers argue that conservation and tourism can benefit one another, as the latter provides funds for conservation as well as for local community development, leading to enhanced conservation practices among the local population. In an ideal situation, the conservation–tourism relationship can indeed be mutually supportive; however, there is a need for careful planning and management if this is to be the case. It is important to acknowledge that tourism is not likely to provide funds to conserve *all* ecologically significant sites around the globe. In some cases, for example mangrove swamps, the sites may simply not appeal to tourists. In the same way that the large, exotic beasts of Africa such as the elephant and rhinoceros hold more fascination in the Western imagination than the dung beetle, coral reefs are of more interest to most tourists than mudflats. There are also examples where environments are too fragile to sustain visitation by tourists, and sites which are too remote and inaccessible to be able to attract tourists.

The chapter begins with a discussion of local livelihoods, including a historical account of the way in which Western notions of conservation were imposed on Third World countries when parks and reserves were planned and the livelihoods of many people were thus undermined. This is followed by an examination of new approaches to conservation and development in the Third World which provide inspiration as to ways in which local people and parks staff can constructively work together and achieve mutual benefits. The chapter concludes with a discussion of critical planning issues for protected area managers.

Table 6.1   Protected area management categories

	Title	Description
Category Ia	Strict nature reserve	Protected area managed mainly for *science*
Category Ib	Wilderness area	Protected area managed mainly for *wilderness protection*
Category II	National park	Protected area managed mainly for *ecosystem protection* and *recreation*
Category III	Natural monument	Protected area managed mainly for *conservation* of specific natural features
Category IV	Habitat/species management area	Protected area managed mainly for *conservation* through management intervention
Category V	Protected landscape/seascape	Protected area managed mainly for landscape/seascape *conservation* and *recreation*
Category VI	Managed resource protected area	Protected area managed mainly for the *sustainable use* of natural ecosystems

Source: Ceballos-Lascuráin (1996: 40–1).

Protected areas and ecotourism

According to the International Union for the Conservation of Nature (IUCN), a protected area is '. . . an area dedicated primarily to the protection and enjoyment of natural or cultural heritage, to maintenance of biodiversity, and/or to maintenance of ecological life-support services' (Ceballos-Lascuráin 1996: 29). The IUCN has designated a number of different categories for protected areas. As shown in Table 6.1, most categories focus on conservation and wilderness protection, with only two categories (the national park and protected landscape/ seascape) intended for recreational purposes, such as tourism. Note also that it is only the last category (managed resource protected area) which allows for sustainable use of natural products from the protected area.

There are almost 7,000 legally protected areas around the globe and it is claimed that they provide the most ideal site for ecotourism because '. . . they offer the best guarantee for maintaining their attractions in the long term' (Ceballos-Lascuráin 1996: 32). Ziffer takes this argument a step further, claiming that successful ecotourism can only take place in conjunction with protected areas such as national parks: 'The supply of nature-travel destinations depends mainly on the establishment of protected areas and the manner in which protected areas are developed and managed' (1989: 11). While others do not necessarily agree with this statement, it is certainly true that in Western minds at least, protected areas are seen as epitomising conservation efforts. This is especially true for the national park: '. . . it encapsulated all that was "good" and "unselfish" in nature conservation' (Carruthers 1997: 125). But how do these protected areas affect the livelihoods of people living in areas where national parks and reserves are created?

Local livelihoods in and around protected areas

Under a livelihoods approach to development, both the quality of life of people *and* the conservation of resources are promoted (Chambers and Conway 1992). Thus a livelihoods approach argues that although resource conservation is an environmental imperative, continued resource use is also an essential aspect of human livelihood systems. This is especially important to remember in contexts in which many people rely on natural resource use and extraction for their survival. This is the case in much of the Third World, such as the Pacific islands:

> In Western industrial societies, where large amounts of land are privately or state-owned, and where legislation can be enacted to promote conservation and wild-life protection, and prohibit resource degradation, tourism and conservation verge on the symbiotic. This (idealised) view of ecotourism becomes problematic in the context of Pacific Island societies, where economic livelihoods (20%–80% of real incomes) and cultural integrity depend on the continued use of ecosystems on a sustainable basis, be they forests, the sea, rivers, beaches, reefs, or agricultural and village lands (Helu Thaman 1994: 188).

An integrated livelihoods approach recognises the need to secure, and develop, people's livelihoods capacities through a diversity of strategies, one of which may be tourism. A livelihoods approach assumes that when people's livelihoods are secure, they will be less likely to resort to practices which are detrimental to the integrity of the environment (Food 2000 1987; Thomlinson and Getz 1996). They may even have the inclination to put effort into conservation initiatives (Sindiga 1995: 50).

Conversely, if the establishment of conservation areas for tourism occurs but local people fail to share in the benefits of this tourism, they will be unlikely to support conservation. The creation of national parks in many African countries, for example, which has supported tourism initiatives, saw indigenous peoples pushed off land which they traditionally had access to, their livelihoods undermined. This issue is discussed in the following case study.

Case study: The implications of colonial-style conservation in Africa

The history of conservation efforts in southern Africa does not suggest sensitivity to the needs or interests of local communities (Adams and McShane 1992; Bonner 1993). Conservation spaces in which the Western values of species preservation and recreation were embedded were created out of areas which held both spiritual and livelihood values to indigenous Africans. Game reserves, for example, were established when colonial hunters realised that animal numbers had decreased drastically in parts of the continent (MacKenzie 1987). Much of this reduction in wildlife was due to overhunting by colonialists and increasing demands on land for commercial agriculture. It was this phenomenon that turned colonial hunters into conservationists, rather than a broader commitment to preserving ecosystem integrity and ensuring the existence of a sound natural resource base for future generations of Africans (MacKenzie 1988; Carruthers 1997; Adams and McShane 1992; Anderson and Grove 1987).

African peoples were often resettled on marginal land where they found it difficult to survive, thus they resorted to poaching wildlife and other resources, such as firewood, from the protected areas where they had once roamed freely. Conservation authorities were characterised by a law enforcement mentality which saw rangers spending much of their time hunting down and arresting poachers, for crimes as minimal as catching cane rats or chasing a lion from a kill, and those illegally harvesting products from protected areas (Carruthers 1997). Relationships between people in communities surrounding the parks and parks staff were characterised by hostility and mistrust.

Because most early conservation authorities adopted exclusionary approaches, a strident anti-conservation attitude developed among communities adjacent to protected areas (Davies 1997). This was ironic, considering that many tribes had previously practised highly effective means of preserving the soils, water, animals and plants upon which their livelihoods depended (Matowanyika *et al.* 1992): 'Conservation has long operated on the comfortable belief that Africa is a paradise to be defended, even against the people who have lived there for thousands of years' (Adams and McShane 1992: xviii).

From the perspective of local people their land had become merely a playground for rich, predominantly white, tourists. Meanwhile there were laws forbidding the people from killing the wild animals encroaching on their land from nearby parks and reserves, threatening both crops and people's lives. Eco-dollars generated by the creation of the protected areas have traditionally benefited tour operators and the national government, with small amounts invested in wildlife conservation but little spent on the development of impoverished communities (Boyd 1997). It is increasingly recognised that rural communities have borne the majority of the costs of wildlife conservation, while receiving few benefits (Wells 1994/5):

> The costs in terms of alienated land, restrictions on resource use and damage to life and property are mainly carried by rural populations, particularly those at the interface between settlement and conservation areas. The political and financial costs of administering conservation programmes are carried mainly by national governments. The benefits of aesthetic and recreational experiences and scientific

Figure 6.1   Elephants: magnificent beasts or dangerous pests?

opportunities are enjoyed mainly by foreigners. The benefits of national prestige are enjoyed mainly by national governments as, currently, are most of the
revenues from the use of wildlife resources (Bell 1987: 80).

The caption under Figure 6.1 draws attention to the different ways in which
elephants are often perceived by Westerners and Africans as a consequence of
this differential sharing of costs and benefits.

In summary, for many Third World peoples the creation of protected areas
– now the focus of major ecotourism activities in Africa, Asia and Latin
America – has led to forced, uncompensated resettlement, alienation from
resources and sacred sites, and damage to crops, livestock and humans by the
animals living within the protected area (Akama 1996). In the case of the
Cockscomb Basin Wildlife Sanctuary, of 21 households dealing with damage
to livestock, fish or crops by wildlife from the protected area, only 29 per cent
received direct economic benefits from ecotourism (Lindberg *et al.* 1996: 559).
They cannot be expected to support conservation under such circumstances.
Similarly, in Kenya, 20 out of 25 national parks could otherwise be used for
agricultural or pastoral activities. In such situations, local people 'pay a heavy
price for supporting wildlife protection areas' (Sindiga 1995: 50). Meanwhile

Table 6.2   Generalised comparison of the situations inside and outside traditional parks and reserves in southern Africa

Inside	Outside
Many resources (natural, infrastructural, trained people)	Few resources (natural, infrastructure, trained people)
High economic activity	Low economic activity
Many opportunities	Few opportunities
Increasing resources – immigration with skills	Declining resources – emigration with skills
Western conservation ethic followed	Western conservation ethic rejected (e.g. poaching from the park)
Economic growth	Impoverishment
Access to development capital	Little access to development capital
Wealth	Poverty
Sustainable land use	Unsustainable land use

Source: After Breen *et al.* (1992: 2)

in North Sulawesi, Indonesia, local communities living inside and around three protected areas are reliant on natural resource use for up to 85 per cent of their livelihood activities. There is no great incentive for them to support conservation, however, when the direct economic benefits of ecotourism associated with these protected areas are being captured by outside operators and parks staff who own homestays and run guided tours (Ross and Wall 1999). Cater argues that if they undermine local livelihoods, national parks '. . . cannot be regarded as truly sustainable practices because they pay little regard to the needs of the host population in either the short or long term' (1993: 88).

Table 6.2 exemplifies the problems for communities which have been pushed off land so that protected areas can be created. Expertise and resources are invested in the parks and reserves, where economic development thus occurs, while those surrounding the parks and reserves are faced with inadequate resources, impoverishment and few opportunities to change their situation.

Community conservation

Since the 1980s 'fortress conservation' of the type discussed in the above case study, whereby local people are locked out from conservation estates, has not been popularly espoused and it is increasingly the rhetoric of 'community conservation' that holds sway (IIED 1994; Adams and Hulme n.d.). Development practitioners and conservationists alike have demanded more participatory approaches to park management which aim to improve the livelihoods of communities surrounding protected areas through activities such as ecotourism. This is partly in recognition that the costs and benefits of conservation efforts have not been shared equally among different sectors of society, but also in response to the failure of the fortress conservation approach – for example poaching in Africa increased rapidly in the 1970s and 1980s (Barrett and Arcese 1995; Gibson and Marks 1995; Adams and Hulme n.d.). Clearly unless local people gain some benefits from the conservation of wildlife and other natural resources on their own or neighbouring land, they will have little incentive to sustainably manage these resources.

Community conservation recognises that the protectionist approach which had created national parks as islands of anti-development was not acceptable for Third World countries. Rather, conservation programmes needed to actively promote socio-economic development and furthermore, local people should be involved in processes of establishing such programmes (Wells and Brandon 1992; Hardie-Boys 1999). It is now internationally proclaimed that '. . . protected areas must serve human society' (Carruthers 1997: 134). One important way in which they can do this is through ensuring local communities share the benefits of tourism associated with protected areas:

> . . . the successful management of natural resources often depends on successfully meeting the needs of people living adjacent to these resources. . . . Tourism can be an important component of resource management because it can help meet these needs (Lindberg and Enriquez 1994: 91).

Consequently, in an effort to overcome what Wells calls a 'legacy of distrust and hostility' (1996: 40), many agencies, including conservation authorities, donors, NGOs and private sector interests, are actively facilitating greater involvement in tourism initiatives by communities adjoining protected areas. Ashley and Roe (1997) note that local people are motivated by community conservation because of the promise of jobs, new business opportunities and skill development, as well as the chance to secure greater control over natural resource management in their areas. Employment is a particularly strong incentive and it is not an unrealistic motivating force: in Africa, for example, tourism and travel provided one in every 10 jobs in 1993 (Ferrar et al. 1997: 18). Economic diversification is regarded as another incentive, as seen in the following comments by Senior Chief Mukuni, whose village is located near to the Victoria Falls in Zambia: 'There are three crops grown in my area: maize, cattle and tourism. Two of these are affected by drought but tourism is not' (Zambia National Tourism Board 1998: 3).

Box 6.1 shows well-planned and managed protected areas can bring significant benefits to the local level, not only the national and global levels.

BOX 6.1

Benefits of protected areas

Global benefits

- Biodiversity conservation leads to a healthier planet for all.
- Stimulates international understanding of the benefits of nature conservation.

National level benefits

- Earns funds for management of parks and reserves.
- Earns foreign exchange.
- Makes constructive use of land which is not ideal for cropping or livestock rearing.
- Leads to a positive image of the country.

Local level benefits

- Stimulates domestic enterprises such as accommodation and transport systems, handicraft stalls and guide services.
- Generates employment in tourism, associated services and resource management.
- Improves local infrastructure, including roads and telecommunications.
- Demand for agricultural produce for tourists stimulates the rural economy.
- Leads to diversification of the local economy, offering an alternative to employment in agriculture, for example in areas where this activity may be marginal.

Source: Adapted from McNeely *et al.* (1992).

Managers of protected areas have instituted specific programmes to facilitate the development of those people living on lands surrounding parks and reserves. For example, in Kenya, some cultivation, timber harvesting and pastoralism are conditionally allowed in areas designated as national reserves so that local communities can meet their subsistence needs (Sindiga 1995). In Kruger National Park, South Africa, their 'social ecology' programme goes further, focusing on building effective communication strategies with surrounding communities, providing opportunities for local people to sell products and services within the park and developing participatory decision-making structures. The Natal Parks Board in South Africa has instituted a policy with similar aims (see the following case study), which has been well received. This is not surprising considering the grim economic reality of KwaZulu Natal Province where they operate. Formal economic opportunities are so poor in KwaZulu Natal that 13 times more people are engaged in subsistence agriculture than in formal employment (Posel and May, cited by Wood 1996).

Case study: The Natal Parks Board (NPB)[1] and community conservation initiatives

KwaZulu Natal Province in South Africa is home to an extensive conservation estate, with proponents claiming it boasts some of the most well-managed protected areas in the world. Just over 8 per cent of the terrestrial area of 91,481 square kilometres is protected, along with 28 per cent of the coastline (Trevor Sandwith, NPB: Author's fieldwork, May 1998). Wildlife parks, marine reserves and wetlands provide key drawcards for tourists.

However, conservation agencies face a major challenge in preserving these protected area systems in the face of demands from the largely impoverished black communities which surround the parks (Koch 1994). These surrounding communities have rarely benefited from the tourist dollars and yet their access to plant and animal resources has been severely constrained by the existence of protected areas. As noted by Wells (1996: 5), 'The urgency of this problem is intensified by the high expectations among South Africa's black population for a more equitable distribution of resources and opportunities under the current [post-Apartheid] government.' A commitment to improving the livelihoods of impoverished rural communities is supported in current legislation, including the White Paper on the Conservation and Sustainable Use of South Africa's Biological Diversity, which aims '. . . to ensure that local communities, particularly previously disadvantaged communities, benefit through active participation in tourism associated with protected areas and sites' (Department of Environmental Affairs and Tourism 1997: 33).

Prior to the 1990s the NPB's response to community conservation was not ideal: 'We thought we knew what was best, and the communities had nothing so they would accept anything that we had to offer them. But now the power gradient has started to even out' (Paula Morrison, NPB: Author's fieldwork, May 1998). In the 1970s, for example, a law enforcement ideology which saw many NPB resources devoted to anti-poaching activities predominated. By the 1980s, programmes including extension and environmental education were being introduced, but it was only in the 1990s that participatory approaches really emerged (Sandwith *et al.* 1998).

In 1992 the NPB's Neighbour Relations Policy was adopted, based on the premise that it is in the interests of long-term conservation to work with local communities and to gain their support (Natal Parks Board 1996). The NPB now professes to manage one of the biggest conservation outreach programmes on the planet (Davies 1997). The range and number of community conservation projects they have been involved with are demonstrated in Figure 6.2. Their first initiatives for positive engagement with local communities included the establishment of 86 neighbour forums and environmental education programmes, which helped to develop better understanding between them and their neighbours. Under the Neighbour Relations Policy they have also attempted to introduce a range of practical development initiatives so that local people feel they really gain from the existence of NPB-protected areas and tourism therein. These projects have included controlled harvesting of park resources such as reeds, thatching grass and mussels. In Hluhluwe-Umfolozi Park, for example, they allow cutting of trees in areas which need to be thinned out because of bush

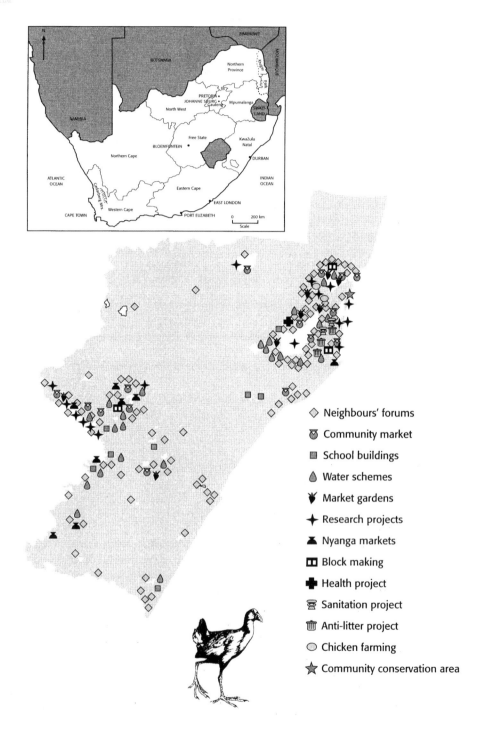

Figure 6.2 Natal Parks Board community conservation projects, 1996/97. (*Source:* NPB *Annual Report, 1996/1997*)

encroachment, and they provide free transport of the cut timber within a 10-kilometre radius of the park. They have also established a nursery for medicinal plants within the Hluhluwe-Umfolozi Park, with associated training for traditional healers about propagation of plants and means of harvesting which limit damage to the natural resource base. This has helped enormously in an area where high population densities outside the parks mean that many plants used in natural remedies have been severely depleted. A number of communities adjacent to NPB-protected areas have also benefited from sales of crafts to tourists, some informally spreading out their wares around park entrances while in other cases the NPB has assisted them in obtaining funding for more permanent structures.

Now the hostility that characterised relations between the NPB and surrounding communities has in many cases been overturned. A local *sangoma* (traditional healer) commenting on the growing trust between the NPB and the community, stated that, 'Before I thought the Natal Parks Board were cruel people – now they are friends who help us' (Author's fieldwork, May 1998).

In another initiative, community levies were introduced in 1998. Effectively this meant visitors to each NPB park or reserve paid an additional 5 rand in their entrance fee, which they were informed about via a brochure, to be placed in a community fund which rural groups could apply for. At the same time, the NPB was establishing a system for tribal representatives to sit on park management boards to decide on issues such as problem animal control and the disbursement of the community fund.

Source: Author's fieldwork, May 1998; see also Brennan and Allen (2001).

Valuing conservation

In Africa, the well-known catchphrase of tourism based around protected areas is 'Wildlife pays, so wildlife stays' (McNeely *et al.* 1992: 7). The willingness of tourists to pay good money to engage in activities centred on natural attractions, including game viewing, trekking and diving, can help both national governments and local communities see that there is a value to conserving natural resources. And in the case of protected areas which can charge significant fees to tourists because they offer a unique experience, a large amount of revenue can be raised for conservation purposes while concurrently restricting overall visitor numbers. In Rwanda, for example, visitors pay a fee of nearly $200 per day to trek to see the mountain gorillas (Box 6.2). In other cases, however, tourists are not charged an entrance fee sufficient to cover even basic park management operations. In Doi Inthanon National Park in Thailand, for example, the potential earnings from the park are enormous, with almost 1 million visitors in 1993. With entry fees of US$0.20 for Thai nationals and US$1.00 for foreigners, however, takings amounted to only US$252,000 that year. A survey revealed meanwhile that 83.4 per cent of foreign visitors

BOX 6.2

Gorillas in the Mist

The rainforest-covered slopes of central Africa's highlands (Rwanda, Zaire and Uganda) are home to the endangered mountain gorilla, as popularised in the Hollywood film *Gorillas in the Mist* which followed Dian Fossey's long-term study of these primates.

From 1935, some of the Rwandan gorillas led a relatively protected existence within the bounds of Africa's first national park, Parc National des Volcans, but a combination of poaching and the Rwandan government's decision to clear some of the park for cattle raising meant that their numbers declined from 450 in 1960 to 260 in 1973. Meanwhile there was a continued threat from surrounding farmers whose small plots of land were hardly sufficient to draw a livelihood.

Thus the Mountain Gorilla Project (MGP) was formed in the late 1970s in order to conserve the gorillas' habitat through education programmes and improved park security, activities that were to be funded through an ecologically sensitive tourism intiative. A model of high-value, low-volume tourism has been promoted, with fees set at almost $200 per day, which essentially equates to a one-hour visit with the primates. In 1989, only 24 visitors, with a limit of 6 visitors per group of gorillas, were allowed each day and there were no problems filling the available spaces. $1 million was raised that year, a sum five times greater than the running costs of the park.

Tourist dollars have certainly contributed to conservation of the mountain gorilla in Rwanda. By 1989, the number of gorillas had risen to 320, a fact largely attributable to the high numbers of tourism-funded guards protecting the gorillas from poachers. In addition, tourist revenue has filtered into the national and local economy, leading to less opposition from local farmers to the existence of a protected area in their backyard.

In Uganda, however, the government forcibly alienated over 1,300 peasants from the land they had been illegally farming within a mountain gorilla reserve in order to make it into a national park. While eventually these people received monetary compensation, only two of them found employment in the new park and the remainder were very bitter about their loss of livelihood. In such circumstances where local people are disadvantaged by the existence of a protected area, it is likely that their reaction, such as poaching animals and extracting other materials from the reserve, could undermine the conservation effort in the long term.

Sources: Based on Panos (1995); Mowforth and Munt (1998).

would be willing to make a donation to improve conservation practices in the park (Hvenegaard and Dearden 1998).

This section now reviews the situation of people living in and around protected areas in various regions of the globe in order to ascertain whether or not they are receiving the economic and other benefits from the protected areas which will lead them to value conservation efforts.

In many Third World countries there are significant populations living *within* protected areas, sometimes legally, often not. We should not assume that conservation and human habitation are in opposition with each other, as in the past many indigenous peoples had effective conservation practices because they simply could not afford to degrade the ecosystems upon which their livelihoods depended (Dasmann 1988). A good example of a protected area which has not displaced local residents and which is successfully promoting local conservation and development is the Annapurna Conservation Area Project (ACAP). The ACAP was established in 1986 in the most popular trekking region of Nepal. There is an enormous strain on the environment here due both to the needs of 8,000 local residents and approximately 40,000 trekkers who visit the area annually. Thus, for example, areas of unstable mountainside have been defor-ested in the past in order to provide lodges with cooking fuel. When the ACAP was initiated, however, means of controlling resource use were discussed and a number of innovative projects supported, including recycling, fuel-saving devices and solar heating. In addition, trekking fees have helped to fund other activities of the ACAP, such as training locals how to service the needs of trekkers and holding workshops for them on how to improve their health and hygiene practices. In order to ensure a diversity of livelihood strategies, training has also been provided in carpet weaving and residents have been encouraged to continue with farming activities and manufacture of handicrafts (Panos 1995). Thus the success of the ACAP is firmly rooted in its philosophy of making the needs of local residents central to the project's aims (Stevenson 1997).

Wearing and Larsen (1996) point to some non-economic benefits of tourism in association with protected areas, suggesting that it can enhance a community's appreciation of their natural resources, because they are gaining economically from these resources, and their sense of pride, because foreigners are travel-ling vast distances to experience their natural wonders. Another non-economic benefit can come from participation in conservation organisations, such as the ACAP, which help to ensure adequate protection of the natural environment on which tourism is based (Pobocik and Butalla 1998). Such organisations can be an important means of capacity-building, as well as instilling confidence in members, as noted in a study of community-based wildlife management in southern Africa: 'Participants indicated that one of the key achievements was the establishment of power sharing processes, which promoted the capacity of communities to share in decision making and also promoted a feeling of self-worth within communities' (Mander and Steytler 1997: 5).

While clearly economic benefits and capacity-building resulting from con-servation projects can improve attitudes of local residents towards conserva-tion, they may also value conservation benefits of the protected area, such as erosion control and elimination of flooding. This can be seen in Figure 6.3, which specifies the extent to which tourism and conservation benefits affected support of local people for the Cockscomb Basin Wildlife Sanctuary in Belize. While tourism benefits are particularly significant, there is evidence that local people in some areas valued conservation benefits as well.

However, if communities do not gain direct benefits from tourism in associ-ation with protected areas, they may be likely to undermine conservation efforts. In Doi Inthanon National Park in Thailand, there are 4,000 people resident within the park who are involved in the harvesting of wood and wild animals, and cultivation of crops (including use of pesticides and artificial

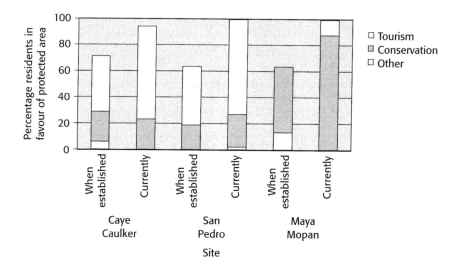

Figure 6.3 Support of nearby residents for the Cockscomb Basin Wildlife Sanctuary, Belize. (*Source*: Based on Lindberg *et al.* 1996: 558)

fertilisers), raising significant resource management issues for parks staff. There is nothing to motivate these residents to practise conservation because all accommodation within the park is owned by park authorities, and it is difficult for local people to find work as guides for birdwatching tours as most do not have a solid knowledge of birding skills or the English language (Hvenegaard and Dearden 1998).

Even when conservation efforts are actually initiated by local communities, perhaps the ultimate form of 'community conservation', it cannot be assumed that the benefits in terms of tourist dollars will outweigh the costs at the community level or that all community members will support conservation imperatives (see the Sunungukai case study, opposite). Thus in the Santa Elena ecotourism project in Costa Rica, where the community itself decided to establish a rainforest reserve on their land as a means of promoting economic diversification, the benefits they gained from this protected area did not always auger well against the costs of having tourists in their community (Table 6.3).

While environmental NGOs can play an important role in supporting both conservation imperatives and the needs of local communities residing near protected areas, it is of concern that some such NGOs are entirely preoccupied with biodiversity conservation. In the past such NGOs have often provoked negative responses from local communities as they are seen as prioritising the rights of animals or other species over the rights of people. Regarding the establishment of a biosphere reserve in South Africa, for example, Brinkcate notes: 'The communities of Cornfields and Thembalihle were most aggravated at the idea that land which they felt was vital to their survival would be used for wild animals' (1997: 72). In the Pacific, similarly, conservationists are sometimes referred to as 'the new

Table 6.3 Main advantages and disadvantages of the Santa Elena
Rainforest Reserve

Advantages	Disadvantages

• Employment
• Money for the community
• Nature conservation
• Building friendships
• Sharing knowledge
  between cultures
	• Increase in the cost of living
	• Change in community values and culture
	• Use of drugs
	• Lack of peace
	• Uneven distribution of tourist dollars, with a lot
	  of money leaking outside of the community

Source: Based on Wearing and Larsen (1996).

missionaries' because they are so concerned with pushing their own agendas.
The interests of environmental NGOs are heavily influenced by environmental
politics, and this influences the extent to which community opinion is sought
and community concerns are integrated into protected area management plans
(Belsky 1999; Purdie 1996; Scheyvens and Purdie, 2000).

Clearly protected areas can help to achieve conservation aims, but the above
comments suggest that efforts must be made to ensure that they concurrently
contribute to local development, with an understanding that development has
not only economic, but also social, cultural and political dimensions.

Case study: Sunungukai ecotourism venture, Zimbabwe

A picturesque site on the banks of the Mazoe River in Zimbabwe is home to the
Sunungukai camp, a small ecotourism development managed by the local community and consisting of community-built chalets and a campsite. It was initiated
by the community but is affiliated to CAMPFIRE, the natural resources management programme discussed in Chapter 5, although Sunungukai does not involve
safari hunting. The camp is on communal land which adjoins a protected area,
the Mupfurudzi Safari Area, offering visitors the option of taking guided walks
into the park to see cave paintings or to view animals. Other activities which can
be arranged include fishing, birdwatching, swimming, walks to view hippos and
crocodiles along the river, and cultural tours of the adjoining village.

The constitution of Sunungukai lists three objectives:

1. to establish a viable campsite to promote ecotourism and conservation of
   natural resources in the Nyagande area;
2. to create employment and generate income to raise the standard of living and
   welfare of the community;
3. to operate the project under the principles of CAMPFIRE.

Sunungukai is a genuinely community-managed venture with committee members who have gained skills in areas such as natural resource management and
leadership. As Morrison and Robinson note, 'Community management and

Table 6.4   Occupancy rates at Sunungukai camp, June 1997–May 1998

Date	Visitor numbers	Occupancy (%)
1997		
June	13	2.7
July	19	4.0
August	13	2.7
September	22	4.6
October	10	2.1
November	13	2.7
December	8	1.7
1998		
January	21	4.4
February	6	1.3
March	21	4.4
April	6	1.3
May	10	2.1

Source: Based on Sunungukai Visitors' Book, June 1998.

control, if financially viable, offers not only pecuniary benefits but also gives the community skills and confidence useful for future development' (1995: 6). Thus as an example of community empowerment, Sunungukai shows much promise.

However, as an example of improvement of local livelihoods, Sunungukai's record is disappointing. Some have suggested that it is economically non-viable (Murphree and Nyika 1997). Certainly occupancy rates for Sunungukai, based on a possible occupancy of 480 for a month (16 chalet beds × 30 nights) have been very low (Table 6.4). This is despite the fact that Sunungukai has received positive feedback from visitors, good commentaries in the Rough Guide and Lonely Planet guidebooks and an award of Highly Commended in the British Airways Tourism for Tomorrow competition in 1993.

One of the major impediments to Sunungukai's economic success is the camp's isolated location and lack of technology. While Sunungukai is located only two hours by car from the capital, Harare, the last 4 kilometres of this is a rough dirt road, and signs indicating the camp's location are inadequate. In addition, many of the tourists the camp attracts are backpackers who take public transport, which makes the journey considerably longer and more difficult. There are no telephones or two-way radios in the immediate area and thus it is difficult to book a chalet or campsite in advance. In such a context, a marketing strategy is absolutely vital but none existed in 1998. Marketing efforts were limited to tourist brochures and even they were in limited supply, with none being available from CAMPFIRE's head office in Harare when this author visited in June 1998.

It took four years for Sunungukai to realise sufficient profit to be able to distribute a modest dividend of Z$120 to members. Members were heartened that they had at last received some direct economic benefit from the venture, although they felt the dividend was very small. Nevertheless they were all very proud of the campsite and chalets they had built and some residents said they felt honoured that tourists would come out of their way to visit them and learn about their way of life. Their enthusiasm has been expressed in the warmth with which they greet visitors (Deaville 1997): '. . . this is the reflection of a healthy community and it attracts or at least impresses tourists' (Friesen 1997: 4).

However, because of the poor occupancy and associated low returns after several years of operation, the overall interest of members has waned. In addition, there have been increasing signs of disregard for conservation in recent years. For example, poaching occasionally occurs in the adjacent protected area and some people have been observed fishing with nets in the Mazoe River, where only line fishing is permitted. Concerns have been expressed that if the project does not meet its aim of facilitating economic and social development in the community, the incentive for people to conserve the natural environment for tourists will diminish (Deaville 1997).

Source: Author's fieldwork, June 1998.

Conclusion

This chapter has shown that biodiversity conservation and tourism can be mutually supportive activities. However, this is only the case if protected area managers and support agencies such as environmental NGOs ensure that local people gain tangible benefits from tourism and related economic activities and thus come to value conservation imperatives. With a change in approach from 'fortress conservation' to 'community conservation', this is certainly possible. Thus staff of the Natal Parks Board are seen by communities residing adjacent to their protected areas more as friends now, whereas 10 years ago they were regarded as the enemy.

In summary, Table 6.5 lists key aspects of ecotourism in protected areas. Note in particular the importance of community involvement not just in terms of gaining economic benefits, but playing an active role in management of protected areas and monitoring of ecotourism activities as well. Thus while the example of the ACAP shows that local people who are resident within protected areas can contribute to the conservation of these areas, it is important that careful planning and monitoring of activities together with local communities take place: (a) to ensure that ventures are economically viable, and (b) to avoid problems, such as those which have arisen within Doi Inthanon National Park because local people have missed out on the benefits of protected areas and associated tourism activities.

Tourism in association with protected areas can result in social, environmental and economic benefits for local people if managed in an appropriate manner. This should embrace the principles of ecotourism outlined above and also discussed in Chapter 5, such as active participation and empowerment of

Table 6.5 Key aspects of ecotourism in protected areas

Location	Protected area such as a national park, state forest or wilderness reserve
Community	Involvement of local community in planning, implementing and managing the protected area, including issues of resource management and economic activities Development of skill base and confidence of local community to ensure active involvement in resource management and economic activities, such as ecotourism Equitable share of economic benefits to local community
Ecotourist	Aims to study and admire natural and cultural aspects of the area
Education	High educational component for tourists, preferably prior information on the history, ecology and cultural background of the area Highly developed interpretation methods, to assist tourists in developing environmental awareness and cultural understanding, where appropriate, and to minimise environmental and social damage
Low impact	Minimal environmental impact Low carrying capacity Minimal negative impacts on local community
Management	High-quality management system which involves local community representatives in decision-making Ongoing monitoring of social and environmental impacts, with assistance from local community members Periodic evaluation of strengths and weaknesses of projects and activities associated with the protected area

Source: Wearing and Larsen (1996: 118).

local people, as well as recognition that people's livelihoods should be enhanced by conservation activities, not undermined.

Questions

1. Explain how the creation of protected areas has often undermined the livelihoods of Third World peoples.

2. How does the 'community conservation' approach differ from 'fortress conservation'?

3. Provide examples of tourism and/or conservation initiatives which effectively meet the dual objectives of conservation and local development.

4. Develop a plan to help overcome some of the barriers standing in the way of the success of the Sunungukai camp in Zimbabwe.

Suggestions for further reading

Ashley, C. and Roe, D. 1998 *Enhancing Community Involvement in Wildlife Tourism: Issues and challenges*, Series No. 11, International Institute for Environment and Development, London.

Wearing, S. and Neil, J. 1999 *Ecotourism: Impacts, potentials and possibilities*, Butterworth Heinemann, Oxford.

Useful websites

IUCN's (World Conservation Union) programme on protected areas:
www.iucn.org/themes/ppa.html

A virtual library on protected areas:
www.wcmc.org.uk/dynamic/pav1/

The Ecotourism Society's conservation page, including information on how NGOs are using ecotourism to support conservation and the well-being of local communities around the world:
www.ecotourism.org/cons.html

Note

1. In 1998 the NPB and the Department of Nature Conservation of KwaZulu Natal merged to form the KwaZulu Natal Nature Conservation Service, and in 2000 they changed their name once more to KZN Conservation. As most of the programmes discussed in this case study occurred before these structural changes and were the responsibility of the NPB, this is the name used throughout the case study.

Justice tourism

Introduction

This chapter examines what many would categorise as a 'new' form of tourism in the Third World: justice tourism. Justice tourism can include cases whereby historically oppressed communities have the opportunity to share with visitors their experiences of past wrongs, thus rewriting the history books in one sense. The term can also be applied to tours of poverty-stricken areas where education and understanding, not horror, are the outcome. In another guise, justice tourism may involve individuals from Western countries paying to come to the Third World to assist with development or conservation work, as they desire to achieve something more meaningful than a pleasure-filled, self-indulgent holiday.

Yet justice tourism could easily be rejected on the basis that it is simply another attractive slogan used to package tourism experiences in a more positive light (Mowforth and Munt 1998). Chapter 5 discussed how the 'eco' label attached to tourism is often simply a marketing tool. Is this the case with 'justice tourism' too or does the label signify real changes in the practice of tourism and in who is controlling tourism enterprises and experiences? This chapter addresses these questions.

What is justice tourism?

While the label 'justice tourism' has not been used extensively to date, authors taking a critical perspective on tourism have commonly discussed justice issues (Britton and Clarke 1987; de Kadt 1979; Mowforth and Munt 1998). Some researchers equate justice tourism with alternative tourism, which has been defined as '. . . a process which promotes *a just form* of travel between members of different communities. It seeks to achieve mutual understanding, solidarity and equality amongst participants' (Holden 1984: 15, emphasis added). Holden's

---

BOX 7.1

Objectives of alternative tourism

- To provide viable options to the exploitative and destructive elements of mass tourism.
- To ensure that the economic benefits of tourism are equitably shared with the people of the host countries.
- To build up mutually enriching relationships between visitors and those visited with due regard to the human dignity and rights of both.
- To ensure that respect for the religious, cultural, social and physical environment is shown.
- To support people's struggles for self-determination in relation to tourism policy.
- To stimulate action-oriented post-travel responses both by the visitors and those visited.

Source: Holden (1984: 15).

---

views are further elucidated in Box 7.1, which lists the building of relationships which recognise the dignity and rights of hosts, and support for people's struggles for self-determination, as objectives of alternative tourism. Apparently just forms of tourism should therefore attempt to redress the imbalance which sees tour operators and tourists from outside of the destination area dictating the form and function of tourism in the destination area.

Other authors draw parallels between responsible travel and justice. For example, Lea states that the three key principles of responsible travel are '. . . to understand the culture that you are visiting; to respect and be sensitive to the people who are hosting your visit; and to tread softly on the environment of your hosts' (1993: 708). Like Holden, Lea's comments stress the need for the opportunity to develop more meaningful relationships between tourists and local people than those based on economic transactions alone. McLaren (1998: 132), who is highly critical of conventional tourism in her book *Rethinking Tourism and Ecotravel,* nevertheless sees relationship-building through tourism as a key mechanism for developing a better future:

> Tourism continues to play a tremendous role in spreading the corporate empire. However, it is an industry that is different from many others. One of its primary functions is to develop human relationships. I see that as a chance to rethink and change our future.

According to the author of *The Community Tourism Guide*, the issue of breaking down barriers between tourists and those they are visiting is at the heart of a just form of tourism: 'Responsible tourism . . . simply means treating local people as *people* – not as beggars, nuisances, servants, con men, thieves or exotic photo opportunities' (Mann 2000: 201).

The relationship between tourists and those whom they visit has been explicitly ignored by many commentators in the past (Mowforth and Munt 1998: 70), but some authors have attempted to overcome this problem. For example, Wenham and Wenham (1984), who in the 1980s were operators of a

---

BOX 7.2

What is justice tourism?

From the point of view of the traveller:

- The knowledge that s/he is not an agent of oppression but is attempting to participate in the liberation process.
- That a travel experience will offer genuine possibilities of forming meaningful relationships with people of different cultures.
- That there is opportunity to experience first hand what other people are doing to create new life possibilities for themselves and others.
- That they will receive adequate preparation for their travel.

From the point of view of the people in tourist-receiving communities:

- Travellers will be seen as people who are coming to share and not to dominate their lives.

- Local accommodation and infrastructure will be used. As far as possible the services of foreign-owned or operated companies will be avoided.

- Tourist sites and shows which degrade or debase the culture will be avoided. Opportunity will be given to local people to develop a real presentation of their culture with pride and dignity.

- Travellers will be required to observe standards of decency and will not be tolerated if their presence is offensive to local people.

Source: Wenham and Wenham (1984).

---

tour agency in Australia called 'Just Travel', suggested what justice in travel means to both travellers and those in the communities they visit. As Box 7.2 indicates, travellers can be part of a liberation process and they should have the opportunity to build relationships with local people; for the local community, economic benefits and pride in their own culture should be maximised through engaging with tourism.

In sum, justice tourism ideally means tourism which is both ethical and equitable. It has the following attributes:

- Builds solidarity between visitors and those visited.
- Promotes mutual understanding and relationships based on equality, sharing and respect.
- Supports self-sufficiency and self-determination of local communities.
- Maximises local economic, cultural and social benefits.

The sections to follow explore various forms of justice tourism, considering in each case whether it is likely that justice will be served or if the relationships so established may simply perpetuate the uneven relationships upon which conventional tourism is based.

Justice tourism in practice

Five forms of justice tourism are elaborated upon below: 'hosts' telling their own story of past oppression; improving tourists' understanding of poverty issues; voluntary conservation work by tourists; voluntary development work by tourists; and revolutionary tourism.

'Hosts' telling their own story of past oppression

In many countries indigenous peoples and other groups have been oppressed on the basis of their ethnicity, religion or beliefs. At its worst, such oppression has included enslavement, civil war initiated by the state, or a legal system – such as apartheid in South Africa – that denies the oppressed group the same rights as other citizens. In the last few decades, legal changes, independence and democratic elections have removed a number of oppressive regimes from power, and the countries which they ruled over have in some cases become popular tourism destinations.

One way in which formerly oppressed peoples are engaging with the tourism sector is to offer heritage tours. Such tours can promote visitors' understanding of human rights and justice issues while simultaneously giving local people the opportunity to speak out and tell their own story of past wrongs. Such heritage tourism does not romanticise, simplify or glorify the past: it simply tells the story of what an oppressed population went through from their own perspective, and reflects on the implications this has had for their lives today. In the Caribbean, for example, there are plans to put together an educational tour package focusing on the sites of the transatlantic slave trade, enabling visitors to appreciate the culture and heritage of the area (Boyd 1999). Similarly, Bartis (1998) has proposed that community-controlled 'Black heritage tourism' be established in South Africa. This is tourism which brings visitors to sites of significance to the anti-apartheid movement, such as the house where Steve Biko resided, or the primary school attended by Nelson Mandela. Bartis (1998) argues that community groups running such tours could benefit significantly through the opportunity to tell the story of their struggles to a receptive audience, after years of having their voices repressed by a hostile government. The significance of such tours should not be underestimated in a country for which 'heritage' for so long has meant 'white heritage':

> South Africa's cultural infrastructure, such as monuments and museums, reflects the needs and interests of the white minority, focusing on aspects of colonial heritage rather than offering a more diverse and sensitive portrayal of South African history. By 1991, for instance, it was estimated that little more than 2% of all national monuments had been explicitly dedicated to black culture and history (Goudie *et al.* 1999: 24).

On a positive note, some efforts have been made to redress this obvious bias under the new regime in South Africa. Examples include museums now displaying scenes of townships and working life for black people and providing information on the work of black organisations and trade unions under apartheid, and monuments erected in the memory of people who died during uprisings against apartheid. Tours of the Robben Island Museum, for many years home to South Africa's most famous political prisoner, Nelson Mandela, attract up to 900 visitors a day and a number of former prisoners are employed as guides (Goudie *et al.* 1999).

Other tours are more concerned with an accurate telling of recent history. Rethinking Tourism Project, which for the first time was offering an 'alternative' tour to Temixco, Mexico, in conjunction with a local NGO, the International Center for Cultural and Language Studies, claimed that tourists would:

> Learn about global tourism and free trade's impacts on Indigenous Peoples of the region, as well as alternative development projects implemented by communities to help retain their culture and heritage, empower local people, create micro-enterprises, and curb youth migration (Rethinking Tourism Project, electronic discussion list, 22 February 2000).

While the types of heritage tourism discussed above certainly offer the potential for visitors to gain a deeper understanding of a country's history and for local people to feel liberated by the retelling of history, this has to be done with cognisance of the levels of interest of different groups of visitors, and presented in a sensitive, yet appealing, manner. There are serious challenges, for example, facing those who are trying to balance the market appeal of just forms of tourism with allowing people to tell their own story of oppression:

> . . . there is a constant and precarious balance between the need for market sustainability and the need for political integrity – the two not always being compatible. Does one, for instance, run the risk of alienating tourists in search of a wild and exotic 'African paradise' by providing them with a diet of 'unpalatable' political detail? (Goudie *et al.* 1999: 24).

This is a similar dilemma faced by Maori tour operators in New Zealand, who sometimes feel that in order to avoid boring tourists, the cultural component of their tours is limited to the telling of popular tales (Warren and Taylor 1994: 16).

Improving tourists' understanding of poverty issues

Some authors have noted an almost voyeuristic interest of particular categories of tourists in seeing poverty as part of their travel adventure. Mowforth and Munt, for example, criticise the way in which poverty has effectively been commodified and people living in slum areas have been 'aestheticised', turned into something '. . . worth experiencing and enjoying' (Mowforth and Munt 1998: 78):

... a range of less savoury realities of some parts of the Third World today – inequality, poverty and political instability – are also there to be enjoyed as part of the tourism experience. They are called upon to both titillate and legitimate travel, to help distinguish these experiences from mere mass tourism and packaged tourists (Mowforth and Munt 1998: 74).

Similarly, Richburg (cited in McLaren 1998: 56) calls independent travellers who seek out sites of famine and human tragedy, 'voyeurs of misery'. He was referring particularly to the situation in Somalia in the late 1980s when numerous independent travellers tried to hitch rides on aid convoys so they could get a close up, personal view of the disaster. While some travellers may have been motivated by a desire, however misinformed, to 'lend a hand', others wished to exploit the situation, taking pictures of the dying to sell on their return home. The latter represents the antithesis of justice tourism.

Not all forms of the tourism of poverty are this disturbing, however. In fact, there is evidence to suggest that tour experiences which include interactions with the poor can increase the understanding of tourists, rather than providing a kind of freak show experience. Ultimately, it is the approach of the tour operators and the attitudes of the tourists themselves to poverty which are critical. For example, in Thailand an agency called Life Travel Service was established with the assistance of academics and development workers to build solidarity among people from different parts of the world. It did this by showing visitors evidence of inequalities between Western and Third World countries and encouraging their support for Thai people's efforts to overcome injustice (Pleumarom 1994). Furthermore, Goudie *et al.* (1999) suggest that to exclude places like townships or shanty towns from a tour operator's schedule essentially isolates them further from a country's social and economic life, reinforcing inequalities of the past:

> In the light of the history of South Africa and current socio-economic/spatial inequalities, it is a serious weakness within the tourism industry that its potential as a tool for economic empowerment and social integration has not been fully realised. Black areas . . . have largely been *terra incognito* for the tourism industry and, consequently, black South Africans have been given little opportunity to participate as partners or leaders within this industry sector (Goudie *et al.* 1999: 27–8).

Interestingly, township tours have now become a popular activity, particularly in Johannesburg and Cape Town in South Africa, but what is most critical is whether these tours offer local people opportunities for economic empowerment and social integration. Some tours of Soweto seem to be making steps in this direction (Box 7.3). While some may argue that such tours bring direct economic benefits to only a handful of township residents, in another way, safe and informative tours of townships help to overcome stereotypes of township life and people. They also provide opportunities for visitors to meet residents

---

BOX 7.3

Soweto township tours

In 1998 there were several official operators running tours of the most notorious township in South Africa, Soweto. Certainly the quality of these tours varies, with some run by outsiders and involving tourists spending most of their time peering out of the windows of their luxury coach to catch glimpses of life in Soweto. Others, such as Max's Maximum Tours, are run by township residents and are more informative and interactive. Max is a long-time resident of Soweto and he insists, for example, that all participants disembark from the mini-coach regularly and speak with Soweto residents who gather around. As noted by Else *et al.* (1997), 'Given the townships' recent history, the friendliness that is generally shown to white visitors is almost shocking.' The Max's Maximum Tour taken by this author involved entering one woman's shack which she shared with her grandson, and hearing her story of how she had come to live in Soweto and what dreams she had for the future. Tour participants were invited to leave donations when they left her home. Max rotated his tours around different houses so as to spread the contributions the tourists were making. The tour ended at a *shebeen* (traditional drinking house) on the street where Max lived and here again, tourists literally rubbed shoulders with the locals.

The general impression of other tourists on the mini-coach was that they had learned a great deal and had a better understanding of the diversity and complexity of life in a township. This is unlike the majority of white residents of Johannesburg, who still stereotype Soweto as a crime-infested area which it would be dangerous, and foolhardy, to enter. As noted in the Lonely Planet guidebook,

> Most white South Africans are completely ignorant of life in the townships and very few have ever been inside one. Their picture is of unmitigated hostility, and a nightmare environment of drugs, superstition, tribal warfare, depravity and violent crime (Else *et al.* 1997: 522).

Source: Author's fieldwork, May 1998.

---

and find out a little about their lives, thus they are helping to overcome the legacy of social and economic exclusion which characterises township life.

Voluntary conservation work by tourists

Tourists who wish to make voluntary work part of their vacation are motivated to varying degrees by a desire to do something active and worthwhile for others, or for the environment, during their travels, rather than taking a traditional 'laze around on the beach' vacation. Engaging in such voluntary work can be seen as socially or environmentally responsible travel (Wearing 2001). This section will focus specifically on voluntary conservation work, while the following section details development work opportunities.

Tours which involve conservation work offer a responsible 'holiday with a difference' to increasing numbers of Western travellers, who often pay significant sums of money for the privilege of doing this work. The cost of the tours covers their subsistence expenses, with accommodation standards varying from basic to luxury depending on the particular tour they choose, plus a contribution to the conservation work of the organisation involved. Projects are typically located in enticing areas such as tropical rainforests, lagoons or beaches. A number of these voluntary conservation tours are summarised in Table 7.1.

The organisations listed in Table 7.1 vary from those with a global focus and an extensive range of programmes to those that are initiated at the grassroots level and focus on one particular programme. Earthwatch Institute is an example of the former, sending around 3,500 volunteers to work with 120 research scientists each year on field research projects in over 50 countries. While Earthwatch claims to do much of its work in collaboration with host country conservation and educational organisations, there is no mention of local community involvement. Volunteers appear to be primarily motivated by their interest in conservation of endangered species. For example, a participant in the Earthwatch turtle project in Costa Rica suggested that the most satisfying aspect of her experience was carrying baby turtles to the sea from the hatchery, a fenced part of the beach where eggs were placed for their safety, and realising that 'we can do something to stop the extinction of this miraculous creature' (Spano 2000: C11). Meanwhile the Golondrinas Foundation, established in a particular area of Ecuador with the dual aims of preserving the cloud forest and developing sustainable agroforestry options, represents a grassroots conservation programme which is directly dictated by local interests. And while Earthwatch Institute charges around $3,000 for a 10-day tour of conservation duty, partly because of a higher standard of lodging but also because volunteers contribute to the costs of Earthwatch's scientific expeditions around the globe, volunteers with Golondrinas pay only $240 a month as a contribution to their food and lodging costs.

The Earthwatch style of tour offers an ideal combination of factors to a particular group of tourists – a picturesque holiday destination which, although providing limited opportunities for self-indulgent pursuits, provides them with the opportunity to contribute to global conservation imperatives. Conservation organisations involved in the tourism business are, however, singled out for criticism by Mowforth and Munt, who feel that:

> A global concern for the environment and the call to 'think globally, act locally', while lofty and harmless in practice, have a tendency to become a crusade (to 'think globally, impose locally') that is devoid of notions of social justice and a concern for local people's perceptions (1998: 181).

This raises an interesting issue: to what extent are these conservation initiatives supported by local communities, and are the communities even aware of their existence? Furthermore, do the initiatives offer any opportunities for local control? Such concerns are typically not addressed on the web pages of the large

Table 7.1   Examples of Third World travel involving voluntary conservation work

Company	Location	Activity	Duration	Cost ($US)
Earthwise Journeys	Belize	Bottlenose Dolphin Research. Participate in a project studying free-ranging bottlenose dolphins along the offshore cayes of Belize. Collect and record data above water, observe and photograph dolphins under water. Accommodation: small lodge on a private caye with over-the-water cabanas and open porch. Free time for snorkelling along the barrier reef and birdwatching	8 days	$1,720–$1,895 includes airfares from Miami or LA
Earthwise Journeys	Costa Rica	Volunteers help build bridges, rain shelters, plant trees, and build handicap access into a rainforest study and preservation area. There are opportunities to work with local people on environmental concerns such as organic farming. All work is under the direction of local leadership and hand in hand with community volunteers. Lodging is in guest houses and is dormitory style	15 days	$1,595
Earthwatch Institute	Kenya	Volunteers will live among the Lou people and help preserve the knowledge of their traditional healers. With few trained medical staff, 90% of the population use herbal remedies. Preserving the details of these remedies is vital in a context of rapid socio-economic change when traditional knowledge could easily be lost	18 days	$1,895
Earthwatch Institute	Costa Rica	Monitor nesting sites of the leatherback turtle. Walk the beach from 8 p.m. to 3 a.m. measuring turtles and recording numbers of hatched eggs. Air conditioned, dorm-style accommodation. Free time during the day for canoeing in the nearby estuary, horseback riding and exploring	10 days	$3,000
Golondrinas Foundation	Ecuador	A grass-roots conservation project located in the Andes which incorporates the participation of local farmers. Aims to conserve 25,000 hectares of highland cloudforest and introduce sustainable agroforestry techniques. Volunteers require some experience in horticulture or permaculture, and advanced Spanish. Volunteers should be prepared for a physical and mental challenge: the work is laborious and the accommodation very basic	1–6 months	$240/month towards food and accommodation

Source: Websites of the various organisations as accessed through Mann's (2000) *Community Tourism Guide*. NB Unless specifically mentioned, costs quoted do not include international travel.

conservation organisations supporting the types of voluntary conservation opportunities discussed above, which suggests that under the guise of global environmental well-being, organisations can forge ahead with such programmes whether or not they have local involvement.

Voluntary development work by tourists

Engaging in development work as part of a vacation is another increasingly popular option for tourists motivated by their conscience. Unlike the conservation work discussed above, the locations of the various development projects are not always scenic, but as with conservation work, there is likely to be some free time for leisure pursuits. Volunteers are typically led by locally based service organisation staff or researchers. Table 7.2 lists a number of different organisations offering development work to tourists.

On first examination of Table 7.2, it may appear that travel with a development focus has much to recommend it. While this argument has some credence, it is important to recognise other perspectives as well. Travel involving development work can be understood in several different ways:

- as 'harmless', giving vent to the altruistic tendencies of a small group of tourists;

- as 'educational', providing for a richer cultural exchange and opportunities for cross-cultural understanding that would not be available on conventional trips;

- as 'helpful', offering constructive assistance to Third World peoples through transference of skills;

- as 'harmful': entrenching inequitable relationships which see the West as having the answers to the developmental problems of the Third World, while failing to acknowledge the place of the West in creating/entrenching such problems or the skills, resources and knowledge of Third World peoples.

The latter view is expressed by Hutnyk (1996) in his book titled *The Rumour of Calcutta*. Hutnyk is cynical about the place of international travellers engaging in 'charity tourism' here, whether for religious groups such as the Mother Teresa Trust or for secular organisations such as the Preger Clinic, informally known as 'Dr Jack's'. The latter provides health care to 'street-dwelling destitutes and others of low economic status' (Hutnyk 1996: 44). Some of the volunteers who work at such clinics are qualified nurses or doctors, while others simply have a desire to help others. Most stay in Calcutta for at least a few weeks, with some remaining for over six months. Voluntary work is the primary reason why a number of these volunteers come to Calcutta, while for others it provides a diversion from their backpacking sojourn through Asia:

Table 7.2 Examples of Third World travel involving voluntary development work

Company	Location	Activity	Duration	Cost ($US)
Preger Clinic	Calcutta, India	Secular organisation offering free health care, on the street, to those of low economic status. Some volunteers are trained doctors and nurses, others assist with administration and more mundane work. The clinic employs some Indian staff. Volunteers are mainly independent travellers	Flexible – often several weeks to several months	Volunteers meet all their own travel and living expenses
Earthwise Journeys	Tanzania	Community development. Volunteers help with infrastructure projects such as repairing structures, enlarging schools, painting classrooms. Free time available for exploring Mt Kilimanjaro, Lake Victoria, the Serengeti Plain and visiting the Masai Mara tribes	19 days	$1,985
Earthwise Journeys	Cook Islands	Volunteers help with health care projects, administrative services, computer training and repair, and general maintenance. Stay in comfortable tourist class accommodation with free time for snorkelling, scuba diving, and hiking on the island	3 weeks	$2,095
Cross-Cultural Solutions	Peru, India and Uganda	Small teams of 2–3 volunteers work with local organisations on many tasks which could include the following: teaching English, stimulating small business activities, assisting women's empowerment groups, assisting local doctors, providing occupational therapy. Evenings are free and volunteers will have at least four days off during their stay	3 weeks	$1,950
Ladakh Farm Project	Ladakh, North-west India	Westerners provide voluntary help on farms. This helps to raise the profile of agriculture and farm life in an area characterised by urban drift of young people, in particular, and attitudes which see agricultural work as inferior. Volunteers are expected to discuss with Ladakhi people problems with Western consumer culture, and show them that they appreciate that Westerners have much to learn from the social harmony and environmental sustainability of the Ladakhi traditional lifestyle	n.a.	n.a.
Karakol Intercultural Programme	Kyrgyzstan	Volunteers stay with local families in Karakol, on the silk route, where they teach English for 12 hours a week. Volunteers bring own teaching materials, which are left in the local library on their departure. Aims to establish friendly relationships between hosts and tourists that continue after the initial holiday	Flexible	Airfares only; no charge for board; small salary paid

Source: Based on information from websites listed in Mann's (2000) *Community Tourism Guide*; Hutnyk (1996); Acott *et al.* (1998). NB costs quoted do not include airfares.

> There is little doubt that most travellers who engage in volunteer work in Calcutta stumble into it with not much more than general notions of commitment and charity. Questions of cultural hegemony, international and class privilege, and the extent of relative economic advantage are, at best, understood in a vague, not an analytical, way (Hutnyk 1996: 44).

Thus Hutnyk does not feel that charity tourism is synonymous with justice tourism. Rather, he suggests that those interrupting their travels to engage in charity work on the streets of Calcutta display a '. . . nonchalant ambivalence' towards their work (1996: 59).

It is argued here that while Hutnyk makes some valuable observations, his comments do not apply to all volunteers, nor to all organisations offering voluntary development work to tourists. As with conservation organisations, the nature and approach of these organisations vary considerably. Some organisations offering development work, such as the Preger Clinic, can be seen as largely altruistic in orientation, and have arisen in response to a direct need for assistance in a Third World country. Others are simply travel agencies with a conscience, organisations which seek to both open the eyes of affluent Westerners to global problems but also, perhaps idealistically, make these people part of the solution to these problems. For example, Cross-Cultural Solutions claims that their programmes '. . . give volunteers from all over the world the opportunity to come face to face with global issues and become part of productive solutions' (http://www.crossculturalsolutions.org/projectindia/ccs.html). Other organisations, such as the Karakol Intercultural Programme (KIP) and Ladakh Farm Project, are more focused on building relationships between people from different parts of the globe, so while some transference of skills may occur, their main motivation is to promote cross-cultural understanding. KIP stresses the cultural exchange element of voluntary English teaching on its website:

> It is not a commercial venture. It is basically a friendship programme. People over here are just as fascinated with your part of the world as you are with Central Asia. . . . [KIP feels it is contributing to] a reciprocal type of tourism in that hopefully in the future the means will be found for the young Kyrgyz to visit their new friend (http://www.geocities.com/TheTropics/Cabana/2715/kipintro.html).

There are also notable variations in the size and reach of organisations offering voluntary development work for tourists. Whereas Earthwise Journeys has numerous projects on offer in a diversity of countries, Cross-Cultural Solutions purposely focuses its programmes on three countries because they argue this will help them to maintain sustainable, long-term programmes. Thus when one group of volunteers leaves, another group replaces them (http://www.crossculturalsolutions.org/projectindia/ccs.html). Further information on the philosophy behind their operations is provided in Box 7.4, including an emphasis on working side by side with locals and empowering, not pitying, local people.

BOX 7.4

Philosophy of Cross-Cultural Solutions

Cultural sensitivity

We believe the people of each culture know and understand what is appropriate for their community. Because local people are the experts, we assist them in carrying out the objectives they deem important, rather than impose Western ways.

Service

Service is the core of our programmes. Our volunteers serve by bringing their energy and skills to help fulfil the goals identified by expert local staff. Dedication to service is far more valuable than any one person's individual skills.

Empowerment

Our philosophy focuses on empowerment, not pity or charity. Cross-Cultural Solutions' partners work to empower people with the skills and knowledge they need to become self-sufficient.

Personal enrichment

Our programmes combine service with real world learning. Volunteers routinely leave the programme with a new appreciation for the host country and its people. Many volunteers say that working side by side with the local people was a life-changing experience.

Source: http://www.crossculturalsolutions.org/projectindia/ccs.html

---

In some cases, volunteers are expected to prepare for their experience by reading briefing notes provided by the organisation and to come with a positive attitude, whereas in other cases they are asked to put considerable thought into what they are doing before they embark on their travels. Ladakh Farm Project volunteers, for example, prepare for their placement by reading the book *Ancient Futures: Learning from Ladakh* (1991), which is Helena Norberg-Hodge's account of the value of traditional culture and lifestyles in Ladakh. This is so they can reflect critically on Western consumer culture in their conversations with Ladakhi people (Acott *et al.* 1998). While KIP volunteers do not require such rigorous personal preparation for their travels, they are asked to bring resources in the form of English teaching materials which they donate to the local library on their departure.

Box 7.4 highlights the different approaches of development agencies offering short-term voluntary work, using the example of organisations involved in the clean-up and reconstruction process in Honduras after Hurricane Mitch devastated large parts of Central America in November 1998. The approaches of these agencies had a direct bearing on the experience of volunteers, and thus on whether their work and their presence in Honduras were harmless, educational, helpful or harmful, to use the categories identified above. While options (a), (b) and (c) in Box 7.5 could all result in tangible local benefits, it is only in option (c) that specific attempts are made to build a relationship between local people and the foreign tourists and for the tourists to gain a better understanding of poverty issues. Options (a) and (c) both somewhat perpetuate the myth that Western society provides the answers for development in the Third World. Box 7.5 confirms that forms of voluntary work which allow for relationships to be built between the tourists and local people can be very effective in highlighting justice issues.

Revolutionary tourism

The term 'revolutionary tourism' was first applied to the visitors, often young, adventure-seeking independent travellers, who flocked to areas such as Nicaragua and El Salvador during the 1980s when civil wars were being fought (Ross 1999) (Figure 7.1). Mowforth and Munt are once again critical of travel to sites of war or civil strife, or 'really dicey situations' (1998: 65), stating that this represents nothing more than another adventure for egocentric tourists:

Figure 7.1 Tourist visiting Sandinista revolutionary statue in Nicaragua. (*Source*: Helen Leslie)

BOX 7.5

Voluntary opportunities for tourists in Honduras post-Hurricane Mitch

(a) Cleaning up in luxury

Hotel operators in Trujillo on the Caribbean coast joined with an environmental group and the Honduran Institute of Tourism to design the campaign 'Relax Trujillo', for which participants paid US$280 to stay in nice beach-front hotels and eat in good restaurants over a six-day period. During the day, however, most of their time was spent helping with the clean-up effort including collecting rubbish off beaches, rehabilitating turtle nesting sites and helping to reforest a national park which suffered major tree damage during the hurricane.

(b) Rebuilding independently of local communities

Honduras was also targeted by a large number of work teams organised outside of the country, which came to assist with the reconstruction effort. Often dressed in uniform T-shirts, they came with their own agendas and provided most of their own resources and equipment. There was very little community involvement. This type of approach engenders dependency and fails to establish relationships of mutual trust and understanding.

(c) Rebuilding alongside local communities

Some Western churches, in conjunction with Honduran partners, provided opportunities for volunteers to assist with the reconstruction effort alongside local communities. Typically the volunteers felt that house construction would be their main contribution during their stay; however, this was different from the intentions of the organisations running these schemes, as explained by one programme coordinator, Don Tatlock:

> If all we were interested in was throwing up homes as quickly as possible, we would ask these folks to send us the money they spend on their airline tickets. What's more important than how many cement blocks they can lay in a week or two are the relationships they can build with the poor during those days, what they can learn about why people are poor, and the impact their presence has on the Hondurans. By giving their time and spending their money to come so far to sweat in the sun with the victims of Mitch, they're conveying a sense of love and caring that pays off in increased self-esteem and encouragement among villagers.

The volunteers learned, for example, how hard-working and industrious local people were and that building relationships with them was more important than constructing houses. Local people responded well to this approach, as seen in the following comment from Teófilo López, a Honduran farmer: 'We don't understand a lot of their jokes, but we understand their solidarity and their sacrifice.'

Source: Based on Jeffrey (1999: 4).

Travel to 'dangerous' Third World countries, to regions suffering civil war and insurrection has become attractive to the bearers of new tourism who have become increasingly preoccupied with the need to distance themselves from tourists (1998: 79).

Certainly for some visitors to sites of civil strife and revolution, and other high-risk areas of the Third World, the thrill of entering a potential conflict zone, rather than any concern for building solidarity or a commitment to justice issues, is their main motivation for travel: [1]

The threat of expulsion is an added attraction for some 'revolutionary tourists'. The prospect of midnight marches through the jungle to skirt immigration check-points adds an edge of danger, and being tossed out of Mexico in the Zapatista cause can only brighten a traveler's politically correct credentials (Ross 1999: 5).

Whether revolutionary tourism can really be deemed justice tourism depends then on whether the tourists simply want to observe revolution or a conflict zone for an adrenalin rush or whether they have an active commitment to a political cause. Certainly enough evidence of the latter exists to be able to reject claims that all revolutionary tourism is more about self-gratification than about education and justice.

A good example of a hotbed of revolutionary tourism is the Chiapas area of Mexico, where the indigenous people have been in conflict with the state since the Zapatista rebellion of 1994. It is claimed that the 'tourists of conscience' who come here contribute significantly to the local economy, make purchasing decisions based on support for cooperatives which are linked to the Zapatista cause, and they have a commitment to the cause that continues after they return home: 'People go back home, look at their photos, talk about their ex-periences, and participate in the solidarity movement', according to Ernesto Ladesma, who manages a local accommodation outlet (Ross 1999: 5). Some tourists pay US$850 for an eight-day trip to Chiapas with the social justice organisation Global Exchange, which is based in San Francisco (Box 7.6). Global Exchange is a non-profit organisation which offers tours as a means of promoting cross-cultural understanding between people in the West and Third World, and educating Western travellers. They offer similar 'reality tours' to countries such as Cuba and South Africa, aiming to put their clients in contact with local people, including community leaders, families and activists, who can inform them about the history and contemporary situation of their country (www.globalexchange.org/tours/). Others travellers come to Chiapas independ-ently, with some attempting to learn about the revolutionary movement and others providing voluntary labour on projects such as construction of schools. For engaging in voluntary labour, taking photographs of Zapatista murals, giving donations and praying with survivors of the 1997 Acetal massacre, over 300 visitors were expelled from Mexico between 1995 and 1999. As discussed in Box 7.6, Global Exchange argues that this is part of a deliberate strategy by

---

BOX 7.6

Global Exchange's tour to Chiapas, Mexico: *Tierra y Libertad*

The attention of the world was riveted on Chiapas when in January 1994, the day that NAFTA went into effect, an uprising led by indigenous Mexicans brought notice to their precarious living conditions. On this tour we will go beyond the headlines to study the unique history and culture of Chiapas. We will examine the historical and contemporary context in which the Zapatista uprising occurred and hear about the modern struggles for economic justice, democracy, indigenous autonomy and human rights.

Our delegation will be based in the colonial town of San Cristóbal de Las Casas and will travel to surrounding communities to speak with indigenous and campesino organizational leaders, activists, educators, students and artisans. We will visit with diverse organizations and their local representatives, including religious and community leaders and human rights groups, and learn of their different visions for peace, justice and sustainable development of their communities. There will be opportunities to dialogue with indigenous campesinos, who have been working for the right to own the land upon which they live and work, and govern their communities according to indigenous traditions and customs.

Prospective tour participants should be aware that on several occasions the Mexican government has sought to expel foreign human rights observers and sometimes participants of educational tours.... Our view is that the expulsion campaign is a systematic attempt to isolate threatened indigenous communities and undermine human rights reporting by keeping international witnesses out of threatened indigenous communities in Chiapas....

While we do not anticipate any major problems during the tour, it is important that all participants be prepared for possibility of being summoned to speak with immigration officials. In all cases, trip participants will receive complete institutional backing from Global Exchange as well as support from allied organizations, including accompaniment by Mexican lawyers.

Cost: $850 from Mexico City
Date: 21–29, July 2000

Source: http://www.globalexchange.org/tours/auto/20000721_TierrayLibertad.html

---

the Mexican government to isolate indigenous communities and keep international visitors, who could potentially be witnesses to unjust government action, away.

The fears of the Mexican government about having oppressive strategies exposed to the world by tourists are legitimate, as tourists have sometimes played important roles as international observers in situations of human rights abuses in other parts of the world. In Tibet, for example, where there has long been a movement for independence from China, journalists were denied access during demonstrations in 1987 and 1988. During this two-year period, therefore, tourists arranged themselves into a loose network to get information on human rights abuses, arrests and torture to the outside world, as well as providing medical assistance to wounded Tibetans. As Schwartz observes,

> The ease with which travelers from different nationalities, a group of strangers, were able to create a clandestine organization and pool their skills . . . is remarkable. But their ready agreement on goals and tactics suggests a common culture of shared perceptions and values (cited in McLaren 1998: 129).

Conclusion

This chapter has examined a number of forms of justice tourism, including black heritage tours which allow hosts to tell their own stories of past oppression to empathetic visitors, and tours of townships which help to increase tourists' understanding of poverty issues. It has also considered the merits of voluntary conservation or social development work by tourists, and visits by tourists to sites where they can express solidarity with local people whose culture and political aspirations are being oppressed by the state.

Undoubtedly new forms of tourism which include poverty tourism, revolutionary tourism and tourism which involves voluntary work, should not automatically be seen as ethically and morally superior to mass, conventional tourism (Mowforth and Munt 1998: 80). There are still plenty of tour operators who are just pleased to be able to exploit the interests of a segment of tourists in poverty, for example, rather than having any commitment to raising tourists' awareness of injustice and building relationships between tourists and local people as part of their tours. However, there is also ample evidence of development agencies, conservation organisations and tour operators which are increasing cross-cultural understanding and raising Westerners' understanding of poverty and justice issues through their work.

From the examples provided in this chapter it is apparent that it is the process by which tourism occurs, not just the product, which signifies whether or not tourism is in fact just. It is not enough that tourism operators, organisations or individuals focus on a *subject*, such as visitation of sites of poverty or civil conflict, because these forms of tourism can be insensitive to local needs and interests. Similarly, there are many seemingly noble conservation projects which have minimal involvement of local communities and may in fact be disadvantageous to them. More important than the subject is the way in which the subject is approached, who controls the subject matter and how much opportunity there is for interaction between tourists and local people. This was evident in the case of American volunteers involved in the clean-up operation after cyclone Mitch struck Honduras, with most volunteers being motivated by charity and only some returning home with a sense that they had gained much more in terms of cross-cultural exchange and an understanding of the lives of the poor than they had given through their labours. Similarly, while some township tours helped to break down stereotypes and show visitors that township dwellers are just people like themselves, struggling for the well-being of their families, other forms of poverty tourism merely attract voyeurs of poverty.

Justice tourism should not be about the rights of Western travellers to explore untamed, dangerous and exotic places and peoples, and nor should it simply be about providing an outlet for the altruistic tendencies of some tourists 'through voluntary work. Rather, justice tourism should be about securing the human rights of those visited, enhancing their well-being and protecting their environments on their terms, and building relationships between tourists and those visited.

Questions

1. List the four key components of justice tourism.

2. Explain the difficulty of achieving historically accurate heritage tours which involve local people telling their own stories of past oppression, while also ensuring market appeal.

3. Provide examples to show the difference between a justice tour of a poverty-stricken area and a voyeuristic tour of the same area.

4. Under what conditions is it most likely that tourists engaging in voluntary development work will gain a deeper understanding of development issues?

5. How can tourism to sites of conflict contribute to people's liberation movements?

Suggestions for further reading

Goudie, S.C., Khan, F. and Kilian, D. 1999 'Transforming tourism: black empowerment, heritage and identity beyond apartheid', *South African Geographical Journal*, 81(1): 22–31.

Lea, J. 1993 'Tourism development ethics in the Third World', *Annals of Tourism Research*, 20: 701–15.

Wearing, S. 2001 *Volunteer Tourism: Seeking Experiences that Make A Difference*, CABI Publishing, Wallingford.

Useful websites

Web pages of Tourism Concern, a British NGO aiming to educate the public and transform the tourism industry by advocating more responsible tourism practices:
    www.tourismconcern.org.uk

Partners in Responsible Tourism – a network of people within the tourism industry committed to promoting responsible tourism:

www.pirt.org/about.html

Information about the ethical tours offered by an Australian organisation, Community Aid Abroad:

www.caa.org.au/travel

Note

1. A discussion on the Tourism Anthropology electronic discussion list in February 2001 suggested that 'dark tourism' is an appropriate term to use when the purpose of a trip or tour is to maximise the 'horror' element of an experience or to glorify conflict (http://www.jiscmail.ac.uk/cgi-bin/wa.exe?A1ind0102&L=tourism anthropology#6).

CHAPTER 8

Gender-sensitive tourism

Introduction

Most tourism development has progressed with scant, if any, regard for the changes it may provoke in gender roles and relations (Wilkinson and Pratiwi 1995).[1] Recently scholars have highlighted this anomaly, showing that tourism has differential impacts on men and women, and women often bear the burden of the greatest negative impacts (Harrison 1992; Kinnaird and Hall 1994; Stonich *et al.* 1995). Still there has been bias in the literature. One could almost be forgiven for assuming that gender issues in tourism are mainly concerned with sex tourism, such has been the focus on this subject in recent years. As Richter (1995: 85) notes, 'Except for sex tours in a few Asian nations, tourism issues of primary salience to women are invisible.' Others suggest that there has been a preoccupation with analysis of employment opportunities in the formal economic sector (Pritchard and Morgan 2000: 132). There are other gender dimensions to tourism processes which should also occupy our concern, as will be explained below.

This chapter starts by reviewing the literature on women and employment in relation to the conventional, mainstream tourism market. It will specify some of the ways in which women have been exploited or otherwise disadvantaged by tourism development in order to demonstrate why gender-sensitive approaches to tourism development are needed. However, this section also reveals ways in which employment in both the formal and informal sectors has been beneficial for many women, offering them opportunities for economic autonomy and greater influence on household decision-making as well. The second part of this chapter then shifts to considering women's involvement in alternative tourism ventures, in order to consider whether such ventures offer greater opportunities for women's empowerment than participation in mainstream ventures. A number of case studies will be used to show that women are not simply victims of inappropriate tourism development, rather, they are responding to tourism in innovative ways and working to secure benefits for themselves and their families from this industry. The case studies also provide ideas on how to achieve gender-sensitive tourism by ensuring that both women's and men's voices are heard when planning for, and managing, tourism development.

Previous studies of women's involvement in tourism have not always been explicitly concerned with ensuring that women benefit more from tourism in the future. This is evident when considering a national symposium on gender and tourism in Indonesia in 1995 which aimed '. . . to increase awareness of the potential of women *to contribute to* the expanding tourism industry and, through that, to Indonesian development priorities' (Wall 1996a: 721, emphasis added). Such an approach considers how involvement of women can benefit tourism development, whereas this chapter is interested in how tourism development can benefit women.

Women and mainstream tourism

It has been noted that for many years tourism researchers were lax in incorporating a gender perspective into their work (Cukier 1996; Pritchard and Morgan 2000). Thus prior to the 1970s, women were virtually ignored as a category of analysis in tourism research. Later, researchers started to 'add in' women and describe differences in the impacts of tourism on men and women, but it is only relatively recently that deeper analysis of issues such as the influence of tourism on gender roles and relations has come about (Swain 1995: 254).[2] Kinnaird and Hall (1996) suggest three reasons why gender-aware analysis of tourism activity is needed, as shown in Box 8.1. Importantly, they note that gender relations in both destination societies and the societies from which travellers derive can influence tourism processes, and they stress that gender relations can be defined and redefined over time in response to tourism activity. This supports the proposition that we should not see women, or minority cultures, or any other group as a static entity who are 'impacted upon' by tourism; rather, they will be influenced by tourism, but they will also respond to tourism in various ways which may alter the nature of tourism development over time.

Postmodern scholars have also identified important gender issues in relation to tourism including the construction and deconstruction of gendered identities in relation to tourism activities. Chapter 3, furthermore, provided case studies of the way in which women and men have been represented as exotic others in tourism promotions and how tourism landscapes have been feminised. There are still other areas of tourism research yet to benefit from careful gender analysis, for example Pritchard and Morgan (2000: 132) make a plea for more tourism research on 'the relationships between masculinist, heterosexual and colonial discourses'.

The discussion on employment of women in tourism below exemplifies how perspectives on gender issues in tourism have changed over time.

BOX 8.1

Why gender-aware analysis of tourism is needed

1. The activities and processes involved in tourism development are constructed out of gendered societies. Consequently, the masculine and feminine identities articulated by both host and guest societies are important components of the types of tourism taking place.

2. Gender relations both inform, and are informed by, the practices of all societies. Therefore, economic, social, cultural, political and environmental aspects of tourism-related activity interact with the gendered nature of individual societies and the way in which gender relations are defined and redefined over time.

3. Discussions of gender and gender relations are concerned with issues of power and control. Gender relations are political relations at the household, community and societal levels. Identifying tourism as an industry based on the economic, political or social power relations between nations or groups of people represents an extension of the politics of gender relations. As such, tourism revolves around social interaction and social articulations of motivations, desires, traditions and perceptions, all of which are gendered.

Source: Kinnaird and Hall (1996: 96, 97, 98–9).

Women's employment in tourism

Three themes pervade research on women's involvement in tourism employment. Firstly, women are shown to occupy predominantly lower-paid and lower-skilled positions, which are often associated with their domestic roles. Secondly, women are expected to fulfil domestic and social responsibilities in their communities as well as engaging in paid employment. Thirdly, many women are happy to have opportunities to work in the tourism sector as this is seen as preferable to the arduous work involved in their traditional roles, for example agriculture. However, a fourth theme which has emerged recently reveals more of the complexities of the situation of women's employment in tourism, suggesting that there is no place for simple assumptions either about the exploitation of women working in the tourism trade, or the opportunities tourism provides for increasing women's status and autonomy. These themes will be covered further in the discussion below.

Literature on women's employment in the tourism industry has overwhelmingly focused on negative aspects of this relationship. Contrary to modernisation theory's assumption that integration of women into the paid workforce is a sign of development, it has been argued that tourism employment typically confines women to the most subservient, poorly paid and low-skilled work (Enloe 1990; Kinnaird et al. 1994; Levy and Lerch 1995). This is particularly an issue for women from minority or migrant ethnic groups (Stonich et al.

1995). Richter (1995: 76) states that women and minorities, '. . . constitute the base of a very steep pyramid, peopled at the bottom with low-paid, part-time and seasonal workers. There are few benefits and little security or mobility associated with such positions.'

Thus while in many cases tourism has opened up more employment opportunities for women than for men, and globally women occupy over half of the positions available in the tourism industry, some suggest that the types of employment available just reinforce the gendered division of labour (Bras and Dahles 1999; Momsen 1994): 'Perhaps it is because the traditional *unpaid* labour of women in society in general is similar to their work in the industry that their condition seems to deserve no comment' (Richter 1995: 76).[3] The cultural positioning of women in different societies certainly affects their options in terms of tourism employment. Thus in the Philippines and in Indonesia women often receive front-line jobs in tourism because they are considered to be more servile and compliant than men and more physically attractive to tourists (Kindon, 2001). Similarly, in the Caribbean, women's alleged caring, mothering nature sees them directed into jobs as chambermaids, landladies or receptionists (Momsen 1994). The way in which the tourism industry relies upon women's subservient, poorly paid labour, based on expectations of women's 'natural' roles and behaviour, is one of the factors which leads Enloe (1990: 41) to comment that 'The very structure of international tourism *needs* patriarchy to survive.'

Women also miss out on higher-status and more lucrative employment opportunities in tourism because social norms restrict the type of economic activities in which women may engage. In both the Himalayan region and in Indonesia, for example, guiding is not an acceptable occupation for women (Cukier *et al.* 1996; Lama 1998; Wilkinson and Pratiwi 1995). In 1992, local people from the fishing village of Pangandaran in Java who took tourists by canoe to a nearby game park could earn up to US$21 per trip, a very good income. However, of the 12 formal guides, none were women and of the 40 informal guides who worked during the peak season, only 5 were women. Many women felt they could not exploit this relatively lucrative economic opportunity because 'Women being involved in guiding is not regarded favorably by villagers, the connotation being that such women are "prostitutes" interested in contacting foreign tourists' (Wilkinson and Pratiwi 1995: 293). Similarly in rural areas of Africa it is common for men to be given preference for jobs when a lodge or other tourism enterprise is established. For example in Mahenye, Zimbabwe, a joint venture agreement between the local Shangaan people and Zimbabwe Sun Ltd, which owns a chain of hotels in the country, saw the development of two tourist lodges on Shangaan land. However, employment at the lodges has been heavily biased in favour of men with only 3 out of 15 positions filled by women at Mahenye Lodge, while at Chilo Lodge 4 out of 38 positions have gone to women (Ndlovu and Mashumba 1998: 187–8). The reasons for this are complex, but derive from both cultural norms and expectations, and employer attitudes. Some of the reasons for employers' reluctance to hire female staff for

---

BOX 8.2

A tour operator's reluctance to employ local women in Zambia

As discussed in Chapter 4, in the Chiawa communal lands of Zambia which border the Zambezi River the Chieftainess granted up to 20 tourism operators, mainly expatriates, the rights to lease land along the river banks and bordering the Lower Zambezi National Park. Her decision was based on the hope that this would bring much wanted investment and jobs to the region. While a small number of jobs were made available to local men, women were completely overlooked. One tour operator from the area cited several reasons why her company did not employ women:

- staff needed to be mobile, as they were often expected to move between the three camps the company owned along the river;
- having women in the camps would encourage infidelity;
- pregnancy/parental leave would be inconvenient;
- the company would have to provide accommodation for families, rather than individuals, as women would not want to leave all of their children to come to work (camps are often quite isolated and there is no public transport service in the Chiawa area); and
- the presence of children and babies could annoy guests.

Source: Author's fieldwork, July 1998.

---

positions in rural southern Africa are suggested by a tour operator working in Zambia, in Box 8.2.

Cultural norms which position women in low-status jobs on the tourism employment hierarchy can also lead to other forms of exploitation. Female employees in service sector roles tend to face particular problems with sexual harassment, for example (Phillimore 1998): 'Women are routinely propositioned and harassed in the context of their waitress, chambermaid and other tourist occupations' (Richter 1995: 78–9).

Another concern not unique to the tourism industry is that in addition to tourism sector employment, most women are still expected to continue to fulfil their domestic and community responsibilities; thus it has been suggested that tourism employment simply adds to the burden of women's already heavy workloads (Goodwin et al. 1998; Levy and Lerch 1995). In the Bay Islands of Honduras, for example, ladino men and women who hail from the mainland are generally given the most menial tourism jobs, but as Stonich et al. (1995: 22) note, 'The position of ladino women is even more serious, given that they hold the jobs with the least status, earn only half that of ladino men, and must confront the double demands of domestic and wage work.'

This raises the issue of whether women prefer informal or formal work in the tourism sector. As a number of authors point out, informal sector jobs for women are often short term and casual (Chant and McIlwaine 1995; Sinclair

1997), the assumption being that this work is therefore less desirable. However, many women prefer informal sector work such as selling sarongs on the beach or operating a food stall as this allows them the flexibility to fit paid work in between their household obligations, and alongside their childcare responsibilities (Wilkinson and Pratiwi 1995). In Bali, 85 per cent of women employed in tourism-related activities are functioning in the informal sector (Cukier 1996). The main problem for many women employed in this sector is that their work is not accounted for in national statistics and not officially recognised as being of importance, thus they receive very little support from the state (Kindon, 2001). They may also face harassment from police or hotel security guards wishing to restrict their unofficial vending activities.

The above discussion points to many problems associated with women's employment in the tourism industry. More recently, however, researchers have developed a deeper understanding of women's position in relation to tourism employment which reveals the complexity of this situation, showing both positive and negative aspects of the relationship. Table 8.1, for example, on

Table 8.1 Positive and negative aspects of tourism employment for women in Puerto Vallarta resort, Mexico

Positive	Negative
• Employment opportunities in a country with traditionally low involvement of women in formal employment • A second tier of informal employment opportunities for women has arisen in terms of domestic work such as childcare and food preparation for women working in the formal sector • At times of labour shortages, women can gain employment in jobs that are normally the domain of men • Economic independence means many women can avoid being tied to a problematic partner • Exposure to foreign gender norms and a relaxation of traditional norms in the resort environment offers greater personal liberty for women • Women have more egalitarian relationships with their partners: '... husbands tend to have greater respect for their wives and treat them accordingly, possibly recognising that their wives can leave them if they want' (Chant 1992: 98)	• The status and remuneration of women's jobs are often inferior to those of jobs held by men, e.g. men carry out domestic occupations as porters or waiters in which they are more likely than chambermaids or laundry workers ('women's work') to get gratuities • Poor opportunities for advancement in many occupations available to women • Older, married women are often looked upon unfavourably by employers who are concerned they will be distracted by pregnancies and family commitments • Many women still expected to work a 'double day', meeting both the demands of formal employment and unpaid domestic duties • Some men have reduced their economic contributions to the household in response to women's financial autonomy

Source: Based on Chant (1992).

women's experiences of tourism employment in the resort of Puerto Vallarta, Mexico, reveals that women value the economic independence, decision-making power and social freedom that have emerged as a result of involvement in tourism.

Important research has emerged to show that employment in the tourism industry has the potential to increase women's autonomy and sense of confidence, and to transform gender relations (Kinnaird et al. 1994; Chant 1992). Chant (1997) argues that the greater economic independence of women who have engaged in tourism in Cebu, the Philippines, has enabled them to enhance their status in the household and establish more egalitarian relationships with men. Meanwhile, Cone's (1995) examination of the lives of two Highland Mayan women involved in selling crafts to tourists revealed that this opened up new economic opportunities to both women, as well as providing them with prospects for establishing genuine friendships with outsiders. These new opportunities signified substantial changes in gender relations for the two women in question who would conventionally only be able to operate outside of their communities in roles as servants in the ladino world.

The situation is often complex, however, as even where women gain autonomy in some areas they may still face obstacles which men do not face and their choice of activities may be constrained by gender norms. Thus while many women in Bali have benefited economically and gained recognition for their skills from engaging in a wide range of small enterprises associated with tourism, these enterprises reinforce the gender division of labour and are largely organised by men (Long and Kindon 1997). Furthermore, Cukier et al. (1996) observed that for jobs in the formal tourism sector in Bali, women often required higher qualifications than men and were sometimes paid less than men in similar positions. Thus economic opportunities for women in tourism will not necessarily overcome, and may even deepen, an inequitable status quo in terms of gender roles, relations and status: 'Tourism, per se, does not bring about a fundamental change in gender and race definitions and the structuring of work. Indeed, it frequently reinforces existing structures and work divisions' (Sinclair 1997: 233).

Inevitably the social change associated with tourism development, but not independent of change generally, results in stress at the household level (Richter 1995). Tensions between men and women may be particularly pronounced when tourism opens up new roles to women, especially roles which allow them to contribute significantly to the income of the household. Apart from delegitimising the role of the male as breadwinner, this may also disturb the balance of power which sees those earning the money deciding on how it is allocated and having a strong influence on other important family decisions as well (Momsen 1994). Thus it is important to recognise that when tourism opens up new opportunities for women to earn money and gain independence, this is likely to unsettle the balance of power within households and communities and may lead to a negative backlash against women, at least in the short term.

Alternative tourism and women

The *nature* of tourism development in destination areas has a marked impact on women's involvement in this sector, such as whether they end up in poorly paid, servile positions or whether they have the opportunity to manage their own ventures. Shah and Gupta (2000: 38) note that 'Women in destinations characterised by smaller hotels and lower levels of investment have proved themselves to be adept at managing small guesthouses and restaurants and running other small enterprises' (Figure 8.1). This suggests that criteria such as being small scale and having minimal involvement of outsiders, characteristics of alternative tourism as discussed in Chapter 1, open up greater opportunities for women's empowerment. The remainder of this chapter thus considers women's involvement in alternative forms of tourism such as ecotourism and village-based tourism, while remembering that, as previously explained, alternative forms of tourism are not necessarily polar opposites to mass tourism and should not be placed on a pedestal where they are immune to critique.

Figure 8.1   Tourist bargaining for a *mantle* (tablecloth) in Panajachel, Guatemala. (*Source*: John Morrell)

To date the impacts of alternative forms of tourism and their potential to enhance the lives of impoverished communities, have rarely been analysed from a gender perspective:

> . . . while some critics of mass, large-scale tourism development have advocated the pursuit of small-scale, 'sustainable', 'alternative', 'responsible' or 'appropriate' tourism which is locally controlled, sensitive to indigenous cultural and environmental characteristics and directly involves and benefits the local population, gender considerations have yet to be placed centrally within such a debate (Kinnaird and Hall 1996: 97).

However, there are useful discussions on related issues, such as the impacts of tourism on village women (Wilkinson and Pratiwi 1995), women's involvement in ethnic tourism (Swain 1993) and mountain-based tourism (Lama 1998). In addition, examples of 'good practice' which show that women are participating equitably in sustainable tourism initiatives, have been compiled in a report for the United Nations' Commission on Sustainable Development (Hemmati 1999). Case studies from these sources and others will be considered below when discussing the potentially empowering or disempowering effects of involvement in alternative tourism for women.

For the purpose of this analysis, the four dimensions of empowerment introduced in Chapter 4 are discussed: economic, social, psychological and political (Scheyvens 1999a). It is easy to be preoccupied with economic benefits from tourism, especially when considering impoverished communities, but development is multidimensional. It is thus also essential to consider issues such as whether a community has control over a tourism initiative (political empowerment), if it provides opportunities for people to develop new skills, gain respect within their communities and thus improves their self-esteem (psychological empowerment), and if it enhances community cohesion (social empowerment). Each of these four dimensions of empowerment is discussed below with relation to women's involvement in alternative tourism initiatives. The same framework could be applied to analysis of the involvement of women, or other groups (such as indigenous people or local communities), in mainstream tourism initiatives as well.

Economic empowerment[4]

Tourism opens up numerous economic opportunities for women, both in formal enterprises and in informal enterprises which require little infrastructure to be established (Figure 8.2). For women to be economically empowered through involvement in a tourism venture, however, they must share equitably in any economic benefits and exert some control over income deriving from tourism. Ensuring women gain economic benefits from tourism is a particularly difficult issue in societies in which men control household finances. There are ways

Figure 8.2   Ndebele women selling jewellery outside their home, South Africa.

around this issue, however, even with an ethnic group such as the Maasai in Tanzania where traditionally women have neither income nor possessions of their own. The Dutch tourism consultancy organisation, Retour, was asked to work with the Maasai to pursue small-scale, low-impact tourism opportunities (van der Cammen 1997). Retour staff eventually convinced the men that they should allow women to be actively involved in tourism, largely for the pragmatic reasons that first, they would otherwise have difficulty gaining funding from development agencies, and secondly, culturally responsible tourists, whom they wished to attract, would not be interested in a society which oppressed women. After working with groups of women to build up their confidence and skills, Retour helped the women to cooperate with youth groups to offer complementary tourism products: campsites, walking safaris and beadwork shops. A major achievement of this venture is that women have been able to retain the income they have earned through selling beadwork:

> Maasai women don't want to radically change their culture. But they do want to create incomes of their own and to put more pressure on men if necessary, to cope with growing needs for income, health-care and education for their children. Empowerment is a process to enable them to achieve these goals . . . (van der Cammen 1997: 163).

While the Maasai women were economically empowered by gaining control over their own income, in other cases economic empowerment has been taken a step further, enabling women to control their own ventures. Women providing services for trekkers in Nepal, for example, were fortunate to be offered training as well as flexible loans for income-generating activities through the Developing Women's Entrepreneurship in Tourism programme (Gurung 1995). Meanwhile in Belize, the Sandy Beach Women's Cooperative, a group of 12 women who decided that they needed to supplement the income their husbands could provide from farming and fishing, established a very successful lodge as part of a self-initiated ecotourism venture. Instead of catering for 'sun and sea' tourists, the Sandy Beach women wanted to attract nature lovers who were interested in the adjacent wetland area, birdwatching, hiking and village tours. Economic success allowed the cooperative to expand from a six-room venture to providing accommodation for 26 guests and seating for over 100 people in an adjacent dining/conference room. In addition to supplementing the family income through lodge management and service provision, women's involvement in the cooperative enabled them to gain valuable skills in business management and marketing, as well as a deepened knowledge of environmental issues. Through their work they have challenged existing gender roles which suggested that women's domain was restricted to the household. They have also gained the respect of the entire village largely because of their approach to tourism, one which promotes understanding of local culture and environmental sustainability and which encourages local involvement, meaning many people have been able to benefit economically from the venture. Multiplier effects, for example, stem from use of local materials and labour in construction of the lodge and local food in cooking, sales of crafts from the lodge and work for local people as cultural performers, demonstrators of traditional food and guides. Thus while women retain their hold over management of the initiative, both men and women have benefited economically from it (Commonwealth Secretariat 1996).

We cannot assume that the availability of an alternative tourism product will equate with greater economic benefits for local women, however. In the Solomon Islands, for example, small-scale ecotourism lodges which have been established by families in the Marovo Lagoon area are seen by outside environmental groups as a favourable alternative to large-scale economic options, such as logging. However, it is largely women's unpaid labour that is used for the cleaning, cooking and laundry for guests staying in these lodges, and in addition the women still have to fulfil most of their domestic tasks as well as extending their food gardens so they can supply enough produce for both their families and their guests (Greenpeace Australia Pacific and Oliver 2001). Furthermore, opportunities for economically beneficial involvement of women in alternative tourism initiatives are somewhat dependent on favourable attitudes of male members of their communities, as demonstrated in the story of a female guide in Box 8.3.

BOX 8.3

A female guide at Sunungukai camp, Zimbabwe

The development of the Sunungukai camp in Zimbabwe was discussed as a case study in Chapter 6. To remind readers, Sunungukai is an ecotourism initiative consisting of community-built and managed chalets and a campsite on the banks of the Mazoe River. While the economic returns from this venture have not been great, those involved have developed a number of business and management skills and the venture, even when it attracts only handfuls of tourists at a time, is a focus for local community pride. In this venture, however, women do not appear to have the same freedom to take advantage of opportunities the ecotourism development offers, as the following example concerning the employment of guides will show.

When my partner and I arrived at the camp we told the manager that we would like to go on a guided walk to the hippo pools the following afternoon. Later in the day I interviewed the manager and asked if they had followed up on a suggestion made in a previous report which recommended employing female guides, on the basis that they might be able to draw attention to various features of the local environment and village life which men ignored. He replied thus: 'Everyone who is capable is encouraged to be a guide. The girls around here are not interested, but it is open to everyone.' The next day, however, the designated guide failed to turn up and in desperation, the manager directed the cook, a woman, to guide us. What ensued was a very interesting, and fun, tour, as we told the manager on our return. He seemed to have difficulty accepting that our substitute tour guide could be taken seriously, however, and insisted, in front of her and us, that she was not a guide and should 'stick to the cooking'.

Subtle and more overt means of controlling women's roles and behaviour can lead to women having little faith in their abilities beyond their domestic duties, and can clearly impede them from following up a range of economic opportunities which ecotourism initiatives could offer.

Source: Author's fieldwork, 1998.

Psychological empowerment

When tourism is developed in a culturally sensitive manner, there seems to be a good chance that it will lead to psychological empowerment. This is an issue particularly pertinent for women as they are often at the centre of efforts to preserve aspects of tradition. Swain (1993: 49), for example, claims that the production of ethnic art by Kuna women in Panama and Sani women in China '. . . serves as a viable way to resist cultural assimilation'. When discussing the Langtang Ecotourism Project in Nepal, Lama (1998) similarly suggests that women are the 'keepers of cultural traditions and knowledge' because many men find employment in towns or with trekking parties and are away from home for long periods of time. Women maintain traditions and therefore build strong communities through supporting religious functions, producing handicrafts, using natural medicines, speaking local dialects, wearing traditional dress and performing traditional songs and dances.

Furthermore the notion that cultural erosion is a necessary consequence of tourism development has been challenged by Fairburn-Dunlop (1994), in her examination of women's involvement in producing craft items for tourists. She explains how Samoan people have been reluctant to embrace conventional, mass tourism because of a fear this will undermine *faaSamoa* (the traditional Samoan way of doing things). In this context, Samoan women here faced a dilemma: whether to produce handicrafts used for household and ceremonial purposes, such as prestige fine mats (made from pandanus leaves) and *tapa* (a cloth made from bark and dyed with distinctive patterns) or to produce goods for tourists. The government tried to encourage the women to sell culturally important items such as large pieces of *tapa* to tourists, but these tourists did not appreciate the cultural significance of *tapa* and were not willing to pay an amount which would cover even the labour costs of the women. Women's committees in the villages thus decided to produce such culturally important items mainly for their own use, and meanwhile they developed new skills in printing *tapa* patterns onto clothing and tie-dyeing sarongs for tourists. Only smaller pieces of *tapa* are sold to tourists, which also ensures the plant materials used in traditional craft manufacture are not depleted unnecessarily. Fairburn-Dunlop (1994: 139) thus postulates that '. . . women have been able to capitalise on the opportunities the [tourism] industry offers because their rights have been safeguarded by customary norms'.

Some development agencies can be credited with assisting local communities to engage in positive ways with the tourism sector, subsequently raising feelings of pride and community self-reliance. Gurung (1995) shows how external development agencies have assisted Nepalese women to develop their self-confidence and become actively engaged in trekking tourism through providing education and training for them. In other cases, development agencies have made clear their expectation that women should be involved in all aspects of their activities, thus giving women the opportunity to develop leadership skills and gain wider recognition within their communities. The Mountain Institute (TMI), for example, which works on community-based mountain tourism in the Himalayan region, expects at least 30 per cent of participants in any of its activities, including committees, study tours and planning workshops, to be women. TMI also seeks to gain men's support for women's involvement in mountain tourism, holding community discussions at which the roles and responsibilities of women in tourism, and the unique skills women bring to tourism, are highlighted (Lama 1998).

Psychological empowerment has also occurred through the work of the Siyabonga Craft Cooperative in KwaZulu Natal, South Africa, which has seen a major growth in the confidence of its members. The women here had sold their crafts alongside the road for several years, when in 1995 the Natal Parks Board agreed to provide land for them to set up a permanent craft outlet. They subsequently raised funds to build a shop on the banks of the St Lucia estuary, where numerous tourists leave their cars before taking a boat ride to see hippos, crocodiles and birds. By 1998 the cooperative had 35 members, including many women who were head of their household. Polygamy is common in Zulu culture and women are often abandoned by their partners, temporarily or permanently, thus economic independence is a matter of survival for many women (Scheyvens 1999b). Involvement in the Siyabonga Craft Cooperative has increased the self-reliance and pride of its members by providing them with a good source of income so they can, for example, afford the fees to send their children to school. It has also given some members the confidence and motivation to go back to school themselves, as they wanted to learn English so they could speak to the tourists who came to their shop, and to learn maths so that they could serve customers, give the correct change and understand the book-keeping system. The grade one classes they attended were held at night at a local primary school. Rather than being ashamed to attend classes at a level lower than that of most of their children, the women were so eager to learn that they complained that the teachers would only hold the two-hour classes on four nights of the week as they wanted Friday nights off (Scheyvens 1999b).

Psychological disempowerment can also occur, however, if tourism work interferes with women's community roles and their spiritual development, leading to reduced social interaction with their wider community and feelings of guilt. In the Solomon Islands, for example, women were often physically isolated from their friends because the guest lodge operated by their family was located on a small island in the Marovo lagoon, away from other villagers. Here women assisting their families to run lodges felt they were forced to neglect God as they did not have the time to spend at church or in prayer groups (Greenpeace Australia Pacific and Oliver 2001). Similarly some women in Bali prefer informal sector work in tourism because this allows them the flexibility to meet their religious commitments (Cukier *et al.* 1996).

Social empowerment

An intangible expression of social empowerment can be seen when tourism results in greater social cohesion in a community. This can be observed in Nepal where women's groups have used tourism as a source of revenue for community projects. For example, Langtang women perform cultural dances for tourists and are using the funds raised to restore their local monastery (Lama 1998). Similarly, funds raised by a women's group in Dhampus were used to build 500 metres of trail, used by both trekkers and villagers, which was widely recognised and appreciated. Rather than simply seeing this as an addition to women's already heavy workloads, Gurung (1995) explains how through such activities women gain greater respect within their communities, and this can indirectly lead to greater freedom for them. For example, because the Dhampus women's group was working on a project to benefit the entire community, men felt compelled to allow their wives to attend meetings, even if this meant the men had to take on domestic roles while the women were absent (Gurung 1995).

However, community benefits from ecotourism may sometimes be biased against women. CAMPFIRE (Communal Areas Management Programme for Indigenous Resources) in Zimbabwe, discussed in Chapter 5, explicitly sets out to empower local communities by allowing them to manage wildlife resources in their area and to determine how they can benefit economically from this wildlife. Advocates of the CAMPFIRE programme claim that social development has been a major benefit to come from the programme, citing specifically the availability of funding for local clubs and for community cultural events such as traditional ceremonies, which enhance community spirit (Dhliwayo 1998: 3). This is true to a large extent; however, differential funding of men's and women's clubs is also evident in some cases and may be a reflection of the larger proportion of men on many CAMPFIRE committees at village level. In the Sunungukai venture, for example, mentioned above, of the small profit realised in 1994 Z\$2,160 was allocated to the all-male football club while only Z\$500 each went to the school and a sewing club (Scheyvens, forthcoming, a).[5]

In communities where culturally and environmentally appropriate forms of tourism are occurring, and where women are involved in running or servicing tourism ventures, this often leads both to greater respect for women and a reconsideration of gender role stereotypes. Examples such as the Sandy Beach Women's Cooperative in Belize show communities that women need not only be restricted to household work, and they may also encourage men's involvement in what are seen as women's domains. Authors writing about countries as disparate as the Solomon Islands and Nepal have noted that where small-scale family enterprises cater for tourists, men have been forced by demand to undertake tasks normally completed by women (Greenpeace Australia Pacific and Oliver 2001). For example, many of the lodges for trekkers in Dhampus are managed by women and they are often more economically successful than the traditional livelihood in the area, agriculture. With the growing popularity of trekking, women have to rely upon the cooperation of their whole families, thus men have been found to be engaging in a much wider spectrum of work than previously, including kitchen work (Gurung 1995). A greater sharing of the workload and appreciation of the value of domestic work have often occurred in these situations.

Political empowerment

In tourism ventures which occur at the community level, there is often a need for a community-based decision-making forum which can convey community interests and act on behalf of the community. This forum may be an existing traditional or government institution, or it may be a specially formed grouping such as a tourism committee. Because of the complex nature of the term 'community', it is very difficult to accurately assess what 'community opinion', let alone consensus, is, even though this is often what is sought. Gender bias in community forums is thus a common problem (Joekes *et al.* 1996). Moore (1996: 29) describes '. . . gendered patterns of exclusion from "public" forums empowered with constructing "community" opinion'. In the Sua Bali (meet Bali, understand Bali) sustainable village tourism initiative in Indonesia, for example, the female owner-manager has not been able to promote as much local participation in her venture as she would like simply because as a woman, she cannot be actively involved in village discussions in the traditional village council, the Banjar. Her lack of voice in the Banjar, a forum dominated by richer males in the village who are very suspicious about her successful tour-ism venture, makes it very difficult for the manager to achieve her aim for a '. . . mutual, careful, coexistence . . . between the village (its culture and the natural surrounding) on the one side and Sua Bali on the other' (Mas 1999: 110).

In other cases, such as ecotourism projects, communities may be asked to designate 'representatives' to sit on park management or other natural resource management boards. However, representation of women in such decision-making structures beyond the village level is notoriously poor both because of societal attitudes about appropriate roles and behaviour for men and women (Lama 1998), and because of what Moore (1996) calls 'sexual policing' of women's movements.

Some communities, however, have genuinely overcome cultural constraints to women's participation in meetings and on decision-making forums. For example, in Palawan village in the Philippines, women have emerged as the organisers and managers of a sustainable tourism project. Ecological degrada-tion of surrounding seas was undermining the local fishing industry, with catches dropping from a household average of 37 kilograms of fish in 1985 to 8.4 in 1989. Meanwhile tourism in the area was growing, based around boat trips to the reefs and islands in Honda Bay for activities such as snorkelling and diving. While this potentially offered the fishing community an alternative live-lihood option, first they had to challenge a cartel of five families which other-wise controlled and monopolised the boat tour business in Honda Bay. Women were active in community meetings held with this cartel, learning to use the legal and political systems to push their cause (Mayo-Anda *et al.* 1999).

Eventually with the support of an NGO (the Environmental Legal Assistance Center) and a local people's organisation, 30 small boat operators created the Honda Bay Boatmen Association (HOBBAI). As suggested in this name, a gender-sensitive approach was not evident in HOBBAI at the outset, even though women were heavily involved in the initiative. The objectives of HOBBAI include operating an ecologically friendly service, alleviating the poverty faced by most local fisherpeople and establishing a fair rota to allow all members of HOBBAI to take turns in gaining an income from tourists, while continuing with fishing activity at other times. Operating a tour boat earns a family twice as much as they would get from fishing for one day.

In one respect, HOBBAI may be seen as reinforcing gender roles as men continue to operate the tour boats while women carry out administration for the cooperative. In another respect, however, women have been highly politicised by their involvement with HOBBAI and are now active in local tourism planning and natural resource management forums. They have lobbied members of the City Tourism Council to gain financial support for HOBBAI and prepared speeches for city council meetings, for example, as well as protecting the marine resource by filing complaints about illegal commercial fishing vessels. With assistance from their NGO partners, a process of participatory monitoring and evaluation is being implemented involving HOBBAI members. This includes collection of data on gender issues such as the distribution of labour and revenue within HOBBAI households.

Similarly, the Makuleke community in South Africa is actively trying to ensure women's voices are heard when important decisions about their future development are made. The Makuleke people in 1998 won a land claim which involves a large amount of land in the Kruger National Park, the key drawcard in South Africa's wildlife tourism industry (Tapela and Omara-Ojungu 1999). The community have agreed that it will continue to be managed as a conservation area but they have the rights to all commercial development associated with the land. Here, community leaders openly espouse their wish for more women to be involved in the planning for future tourism and natural resource management in the land claim area: 'When we call for a meeting we don't want to hear a boys choir only . . . we want everyone to be able to stand up and say, "according to me . . ."' (Lamson Maluleke: Author's fieldwork, June 1998). They realise that an invitation from them for women to speak up will not be sufficient, however, and thus they support work for women's empowerment which is being facilitated by someone from outside their community. 'Our main objective is to raise awareness among women that they can do it – to build their own self-image and confidence and get rid of shyness' (Lamson Maluleke: Author's fieldwork, June 1998). Clearly a close connection exists between psychological and political empowerment.

Conclusions

The key theme running through accounts of women's involvement in tourism in the Third World is that they have been used and often abused by the tourism industry for its own ends, and rarely do they exert any control over tourism forms and processes. Women's labour in tourism has been concentrated in lowly paid, casual and subservient positions where they are vulnerable to exploitation both by guests and their employers. In other cases women have been passed over when more senior positions arise, or cultural constraints have prevented them from pursuing economically lucrative forms of employment, such as guiding. Meanwhile, as Chapter 3 showed, women have been presented as a tourist attraction in their own right, with exotic and/or erotic images of women used alongside pictures of palm-fringed beaches to lure tourists into the ultimate fantasy world.

One key finding to come from analysis of the case studies herein, however, is that women are not simply victims of inappropriate tourism development. Rather, they have benefited greatly from some well-planned initiatives, including many of the alternative initiatives considered in the second part of this chapter, and in other cases they have successfully taken action to ensure that the way that tourism progresses is in their direct interests. Alternative tourism initiatives may offer more positive examples because they are operating at a smaller scale where women have a better opportunity to exert some control over their operations. Examples from both Nepal and Samoa showed how women were helping to ensure the continued pride and dignity of their people by engaging in tourism in ways which protected tradition, rather than feeling their culture was being degraded or 'sold out' to tourism. Establishing their own craft cooperative had significant flow-on effects for the Siyabonga women, boosting their confidence and encouraging several members to expand their education with night classes in literacy and numeracy. Growth in economic independence was another major spin-off from engagement in tourism for women, whether through employment in hotels and restaurants, informal efforts to sell crafts and jewellery, or more elaborate ventures, such as the Sandy Beach Women's Cooperative in Belize. While it is relatively easy to focus on negative aspects of the relationship between gender and mainstream tourism, in particular, it was clear that through mixing with new people and earning an income of their own this also enhanced their sense of autonomy.

Furthermore, significant challenges to norms regarding gender roles and relations often came about through women's involvement in tourism:

> Gender roles are challenged by the foreigners who have different ideas about how either sex can behave. This may influence local people into attempting to emulate the visitors and challenge stereotyped roles, leading for example to more self-confidence and independence amongst women (Macleod 1998: 160).

The success of the Sandy Beach women in managing their venture challenged predominant gender role stereotypes and increased community respect for women. Similarly, when women in Nepal used tourism as a means of raising funds for improving trails or repairing a monastery, such was the community respect for them that the onus was on men to take on non-traditional roles within the household while their wives engaged in this community work. Where women in Nepal managed lodges for trekkers, men also took on work in the non-traditional domain of the kitchen. Meanwhile in Puerto Vallarta, women involved in tourism observed that a more egalitarian relationship with their partners emerged over time. Such examples show that there is potential for involvement in tourism to be an empowering experience for Third World women.

However, both mainstream and alternative tourism initiatives which do not have a specific mandate to be sensitive to the needs and interests of women actively run the risk of disadvantaging and marginalising local women. For example, while women may be allowed to engage in economic activities associated with tourism and have their workloads lightened due to installation of new services, such as water supplies, they are typically poorly represented on so-called 'community' decision-making forums and they do not always have control over the income they earn from tourism. Thus there is a need for gender sensitivity in the planning and management of all tourism ventures. Gender sensitivity does not necessarily mean that a whole stream of women-specific projects or programmes needs to be initiated, however. As Ashley and LaFranchi (1997: 71) point out, '. . . if women have the greatest need for benefits but face more constraints to participation, their problems are only exacerbated if their men feel excluded and hence are opposed to the activities'.

While gender sensitivity and empowerment of women are not likely to be key items on the agenda of most stakeholders supporting tourism development in the Third World, they could be seen as a necessary step for them to achieve broader goals. This is explained with relation to The Mountain Institute's (TMI) recognition that empowering local people helps to secure maintenance of the physical and cultural resources upon which tourism depends:

> . . . [while] empowerment is not the major focus of TMI's work in CBMT [Community-Based Mountain Tourism] in the Himalaya, enhancing women's roles in mountain tourism is recognized as an inseparable factor in developing local capabilities for managing sustainable tourism that supports conservation of the region's rich biodiversity and cultural heritage (Lama 1998: 5–6).

A more gender-sensitive approach to tourism can therefore be seen to be in the interests of all tourism stakeholders. The key issues for stakeholders to consider in any well-planned, gender-sensitive tourism development are:

- Who has access to and control over resources used in the tourism venture?
- What roles are open to women and men in the tourism venture?
- Are both women and men likely to share in both decision-making and the economic benefits stemming from the venture?

While the cultural positioning of women continues to pose constraints to women's beneficial and active involvement in both mass and alternative tourism ventures, such constraints can be successfully challenged. Appropriate strategies will, however, be dependent on the specific nature of gender roles and relations in different societies. Nevertheless many of the examples above show that women are actively working to ensure that tourism benefits themselves, their families and communities, and in the process, they are gaining greater autonomy.

Questions

1. Consider how gender relations in both the destination societies and the societies from which travellers derive can influence how tourism evolves.

2. Provide a list of pros and cons of formal and informal work opportunities for women in the tourism sector.

3. Cite examples of ways in which women can be (a) economically, (b) psychologically, (c) socially and (d) politically, empowered through involvement in tourism.

Suggestions for further reading

Kinnaird, V. and Hall, D. (eds) 1994 *Tourism: A Gender Analysis*, Wiley, New York.
Special issue of *Annals of Tourism Research*, 22(2) 1995: 'Gender and tourism'.
Swain, M. and Momsen, J. (forthcoming) *Gender in Tourism*, Cognizant Communications, New York.

Useful websites

Resolution against sex tourism from the International Federation of Women's Travel Organizations:
www.alphabetaweb.com/sextouri.html

EarthWise Journeys is a tour operator which offers specialist tours for women:
www.teleport.com/~earthwyz/women.html

Notes

1. Gender is defined herein as the social construction of the relationships between men and women and the way in which their identities are framed, whereas sex is a term which only draws attention to biological differences between men and women.

2. To understand how gender analysis has come to play an important role in deepening our understanding of the tourism industry, see Kinnaird and Hall (1994), Sinclair (1997) and special edition of the *Annals of Tourism Research*, 22(2).

3. Phillimore's (1998) research in Herefordshire, England, is one of several examples which reminds us that women in Western countries are also often somewhat

restricted to tourism jobs which constitute an extension of their domestic roles. This is not just an issue for Third World countries.

4. The Tswaing Crater Museum case study in Chapter 12 also provides a good example of the economic empowerment of women through an alternative tourism project.

5. In July 1998, the exchange rate was approximately US$1 = Z$18.

CHAPTER 9

Budget tourism

Introduction

Almost wherever it is viable, Third World governments are actively pursuing tourism growth in their countries. Most focus on the international market and they are particularly interested in attracting higher-spending tourists. No one particularly wants foreign 'hippies' and neither do many place great importance on encouraging local families to see more of their own country. The assumption that catering for higher-spending tourists will bring the greatest benefits to Third World countries is questioned in this chapter, which focuses on ways in which local communities could benefit from involvement in budget tourism. Before we explore this issue, however, it is necessary to examine why the budget sector of the tourist market has been undervalued by many Third World governments.

The bias against budget tourists

For the purposes of this book, budget tourists in the Third World are seen primarily as either the international backpacker market or domestic tourists with limited income. Another category which could be included here are Third World tourists travelling outside of their country but within their immediate region; as noted in Chapter 1, intraregional tourism is a major growth market within both Asia and Africa. Promotion of Third World tourism rarely targets these groups. Of the five tourist 'types' which characterise tourists to southern Africa, for example, efforts to attract tourists are centred on the first two 'types', while the last three 'types' have been virtually ignored by government planners and policy makers (Baskin 1995).

1. organised mass international tourists who travel in charter groups;
2. individual mass international tourists who have travel arrangements made for them;
3. the international low-budget tourist (backpackers);
4. local domestic tourists with reasonable disposable incomes;
5. local domestic tourists with limited disposable incomes.

Domestic tourists are given limited attention in official promotional activities despite the fact that domestic tourism constitutes four-fifths of world tourism flows (Boniface and Cooper 1994: 56). In Peru, for example, domestic tourists outnumber international tourists by almost 7 : 1 (O'Hare and Barrett 1999). Even in internationally acclaimed tourist enclaves, there is often a large proportion of domestic tourists. For example in Goa, India, foreign tourists only make up around 10 per cent of visitors (Wilson 1997: 59). There is particularly scant consideration of this sector in the Third World where foreign exchange earnings occupy the thoughts of policy makers, and the international market is seen as more glamorous than domestic tourism (Richter 1989).

Yet the potential for growth in domestic tourism is enormous, especially within the Third World: 'An exalted middle class with reasonable affluence and disposable income and a strong desire for travel has emerged in all countries, particularly developing nations' (World Tourism Organization 1995: 2). This 'reasonable affluence' may not equate to a great deal of money when translated into US dollars, however it enables growing numbers of Third World tourists to travel within their own countries and regions. Their prime motivations for travel include leisure, religious pilgrimage and family gatherings. In China, the world's most populous country, the growth in domestic tourism has been of enormous significance, with total numbers increasing from 280 million in 1990 to 640 million in 1996, associated with an increase in expenditure from 17 billion RMB yuan to 163.8 billion RMB yuan in this same short period (Wen 1997: 566). Similarly in the rapidly industrialising countries of Asia the number of domestic tourists is growing at unprecedented rates (Figure 9.1).

Box 9.1 lists the objectives of the Kenyan Domestic Tourism Council (DTC), which seems to have identified a number of benefits associated with the domestic tourism sector. Despite such recognition, in practice the government still devotes most of its resources to promoting international tourism and what work the DTC does tends to focus on supporting big hotels rather than budget accommodation outlets (Sindiga 1996).

The international backpacker market has quite a different profile from Third World domestic tourists with a limited income, but they tend to share in common a greater budget-consciousness than other categories of tourists. Backpackers have an independent, flexible style of travel and are thus likely to travel alone or in small groups. They are often keen to share the local lifestyle (Loker 1993: 33), with 'meeting the people' cited as a key motivation for travel (Riley 1988: 325). Recreational activities of backpackers are likely to focus around nature (e.g. trekking), culture (e.g. village stays) or adventure (e.g. river

Figure 9.1   Malaysian schoolgirls visit historic Melaka.

BOX 9.1

Objectives of the Kenyan Domestic Tourism Council

- To promote national unity and integration.
- To enable local people to benefit from government investment in tourism infrastructure including national parks and reserves.
- To expand investment induced by domestic tourism.
- To transfer resources from richer to poorer areas and communities.
- To conserve foreign exchange by encouraging Kenyans to travel within their own country.
- To compensate for seasonal variations in overseas tourism thereby sustaining tourism demand and employment in the sector.

Source: Sinclair (1990) cited in Sindiga (1996: 21).

rafting or riding camels) (Loker-Murphy and Pearce 1995). This is associated with the tendency for backpackers to travel more widely than other tourists, seeking unusual or out of the way locations and/or experiences (Haigh 1995): 'The less travelled route and more difficult way of getting there has a high degree of mystique and status conferral' (Riley 1988: 321). The tight budget many backpackers impose on themselves is largely related to the longer duration of their travels (Gibbons and Selvarajah 1994).

Perhaps because of its association with the 'hippy' and 'drifter' tourism of the 1960s and 1970s, the backpacker segment of the tourism market has not always been welcomed by Third World governments (Cohen 1973; Hampton 1998). In South-east Asia, the interest paid by most government planners to the backpacker sector is either negligible or negative: '. . . the backpacker sector is at best tacitly ignored, or at worst actively discouraged in official tourism planning' (Hampton 1998: 640). And in Bhutan, independent travellers have been banned completely as they are seen as posing a threat to the country's GNH (Gross National Happiness), with only approved tour parties allowed (Wood and House 1991). Meanwhile in Goa, the Director of Tourism stated that: 'Luxury tourism was the way forward. Hippies and backpackers do not bring in enough money' (cited in Wilson 1997: 68).

Certainly there are some good reasons why Third World governments may have reservations about attracting backpacker tourists. For example, because they seek 'out of the way' desinations, Spreitzhofer (1998: 982) argues that the influence of backpackers on Third World societies '. . . proves often to be more lasting and shaping than organized, spatially selective package tourism'. The more lasting influence backpackers may have is particularly a problem when they seek out new destinations but they fail to understand, or simply choose not to respect, cultural norms regarding what is appropriate behaviour in these new locales (Bradt 1995; Noronha 1999). Scanty or excessively casual dress, even in places of worship, drug and alcohol abuse and casual sexual encounters can all cause insult to local residents (Mandalia 1999; Aziz 1999). Such inappropriate behaviour seems to be a problem particularly in backpacker ghettos or enclaves, places where large numbers of backpackers congregate such as Kathmandu, Bangkok and Goa. Backpackers have also been criticised for being excessively concerned with bargain hunting. Thus in order that their funds will last for the duration of their travels bartering may turn into a game in which they ultimately exploit artisans and traders desperate for a sale (Bradt 1995; Goodwin *et al.* 1998; Riley 1988). While such concerns about social behaviour are clearly legitimate, it is also true that backpackers have become scapegoats who are blamed for many of the social ills associated with tourism, regardless of the support they provide for the local economy (Crick 1994, cited in Macleod 1998).

For the reasons cited above both international backpacker tourism and domestic tourism remain low on most Third World governments' lists of priorities for tourism promotion. Some, such as Botswana, are actively discouraging budget tourism as seen in the following policy statement:

Foreign tourists who spend much of their time but little of their money in Botswana are of little net benefit to the country. Indeed, they are almost certainly a net loss because they crowd the available public facilities such as roads and camp sites and cause environmental damage. . . . It is important to shift the mix of tourists away from those who are casual campers towards those who occupy permanent accommodation. Encouraging the latter while discouraging the former through targeted marketing and the imposition of higher fees for the use of public facilities, are obviously among the objectives to be pursued (cited in Little 1991: 4).

While denigrating budget tourists, this policy aims simultaneously to 'provide local communities with direct and indirect benefits from tourism activities' (cited in Little 1991: 6), without specifically considering whether it is realistic for impoverished rural communities to cater for higher-end tourists. Local communities do not usually have the skills, experience or resources to provide services for the top end of the tourism market themselves, thus in worst-case scenarios, such communities miss out completely on the benefits of tourism ventures in their own backyards. The section to follow considers ways in which it might be more worthwhile for these communities to target budget tourists.

The benefits of budget tourism

Communities which provide goods and services for budget tourists can secure a number of benefits. Table 9.1 considers such benefits, first considering economic and then non-economic criteria of development. It is clear that both domestic tourists (DOM) and backpackers (BP) can support development in Third World communities.

Economic development

A key reason behind the negative attitude to backpackers, in particular, has been the perception that their focus on living on a budget means they bring little revenue to the destinations they visit. This perception has been seriously challenged, however, by research in New Zealand and Australia which exposed that, largely due to the longer duration of their stay, international backpackers actually spent more money than any other category of tourist (Haigh 1995; Gibbons and Selvarajah 1994). In Australia, for example, a 1992 survey revealed that the average expenditure per backpacker was $3,267 compared to an average for all visitors of only $1,730 (Haigh 1995: 1). Furthermore, backpackers spread their spending over a wider geographic area, bringing benefits to remote and otherwise economically depressed regions where other tourists rarely ventured, unless it was to dash past in their luxury coach (Baskin 1995; Gibbons and Selvarajah 1994; Loker-Murphy and Pearce 1995; Macleod 1998). Tourism

Table 9.1   Ways in which budget tourists can support community development

Economic development criteria	Non-economic development criteria
Spend more money than other tourists because of longer duration of visit. [BP]	Enterprises are small and thus ownership and control can be retained locally. [BP/DOM]
Adventuresome nature and longer duration of visit means money spent is spread over a wider geographical area, including remote, economically depressed regions. [BP]	Local people gain self-fulfilment through running own tourism enterprises rather than filling menial positions in enterprises run by outside operators. [BP/DOM]
An emphasis on travel to visit friends and relatives or for personal social occasions and religious rituals brings economic benefits to areas not frequented by other tourists. [DOM]	Because they operate their own businesses, local people can form organisations which promote local tourism, giving the community power in upholding their interests and negotiating with outside bodies. [BP/DOM]
Do not demand luxury, therefore will spend more on locally produced goods (e.g. food) and services (e.g. transport, homestay accommodation). [BP/DOM]	Raises appreciation of different cultural, linguistic and religious groups and of common interests of the people of a country, thus it can help foster national integration. [DOM]
Economic benefits can be spread widely within communities, as even individuals with little capital or training can provide desired services or products. Formal qualifications are not needed to run small enterprises; skills can be learned on the job. [BP/DOM]	The interest of backpackers in meeting and learning from local people can lead to more equitable social interaction between backpackers and local people than between guests in 5-star resorts and local people. [BP]
Basic infrastructure is required therefore ensuring low overhead costs and minimising the need for imported goods (e.g. can use bamboo and thatch to create a beach stall). [BP/DOM]	Local servicing of the tourism market challenges foreign domination of tourism enterprises. [BP/DOM]
Significant multiplier effects from drawing on local skills and resources. [BP/DOM]	Government support for domestic tourism indicates rejection of colonial mentality whereby the interests of foreigners were prioritised. [DOM]
Not as fickle as international tourists, e.g. tourism demand less likely to be diminished by threats of political instability or international air transport problems. [DOM]	Budget tourists use fewer resources (e.g. cold showers and fans rather than hot baths and air conditioning) and therefore are kinder to the environment. [BP/DOM]
Less subject to seasonality than international tourists. [DOM]	

BP = backpackers; DOM = domestic tourists.
Sources: Based on information from Hampton (1998), Wilson (1997), WTO (1995) and Richter (1989).

monies are also spread more widely by domestic tourists, especially when the purpose of their travel is visiting friends and family (Richter 1989). Thus in Peru the spatial concentration of tourists which was seen as entrenching existing inequalities was mainly a problem associated with international tourism, not domestic tourism (O'Hare and Barrett 1999).

Both Richter (1989: 105) and Sindiga (1996) argue that the economic contribution of domestic tourism should not be underrated because it requires little foreign exchange to develop, and it is not as vulnerable to fluctuations in numbers caused by seasonality or problems arising from travel booking systems, airline schedules, changing international tastes, perceived security threats or world economic recession. In fact, tourism campaigns can be planned to boost domestic travel in the low season for international tourists. Interestingly, a few countries including Thailand, Indonesia and Malaysia, are paying increasing attention to promoting domestic tourism in the wake of the Asian economic crisis. This crisis saw some significant decreases in international arrivals across the region. Here a *Thai Tio Thai* (Thais Travel Thailand) campaign has been launched. The Indian government has also supported domestic tourism by introducing a subsidised holiday scheme for its employees which has boosted tourism to some areas enormously: '[The] Leave Travel Concession has done wonders for domestic tourism in India. A whole infrastructure, consisting of moderately priced accommodation, catering services and tourist packages have thrived around this scheme' (Shah and Gupta 2000: 41).

Both backpackers and domestic tourists can contribute significantly to local economic development because they purchase more locally produced goods and services than other categories of tourists (Hampton 1998; Goodwin *et al.* 1998; Wilson 1997). Local production of tourism products is typically labour intensive, thus providing good employment opportunities (Macleod 1998). Pobocik and Butalla (1998) compare the economic contributions of independent and group trekkers, the latter being on prepaid organised trips, in the Annapurna Conservation Area Project (ACAP) in Nepal. They found that while group trekkers spent US$31 a day in Nepal compared to only US$6.50 a day for independent trekkers, independent trekkers were found to contribute much more to the local economy within the ACAP. This was because group trekkers usually camped and trekking companies brought in most provisions for their clients, whereas independent trekkers stayed in local lodges, ate local food and drink and purchased local souvenirs:

> . . . group trekkers contribute little to local economies, which is a fundamental factor in the successful trekking agency management paradigm of supplying all needs and reaping all profits. This practice is in direct conflict with the accepted ecotourism paradigm of maximising local economic benefits (Pobocik and Butalla 1998: 163).

Similarly, restricting independent travel to areas such as the Upper Mustang region in Nepal, a policy which intends to protect indigenous people, has been shown to be detrimental to local entrepreneurs and businesses (Ashley *et al.* 2000).

Visitors to the Komodo National Park in Indonesia, attracted by the unique 'Komodo dragon' reptile, also support this trend (Goodwin *et al.* 1998: 41). Tourists in the highest-spending category visit Komodo from cruise ships

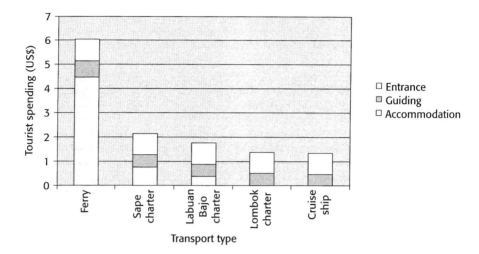

Figure 9.2 Visitor spending in Komodo National Park, Indonesia. (*Source*: Based on Goodwin *et al.* 1998: 41)

which provide all of their food and accommodation, thus they spend very little on Komodo, and the same applies to tourists who use charter boats for their visit. Budget tourists, however, use the government ferry, which necessitates a stay of at least one night on Komodo's main island and consequently they spend two to three times as much money within the park as do the other tourists (Figure 9.2).

Backpackers are likely to support certain economic enterprises developed by local communities which other tourists, because of their less flexible travel schedules, cannot. For example, in 1998 a drum-making workshop, to be held over several days in a rural area, was advertised in the backpacker hostels of Harare, Zimbabwe. It is likely that skilled artisans in other trades, such as potters, carvers and weavers, could offer similar workshops which would be attractive to many backpackers. Food and basic accommodation can be included in the price of such enterprises. In New Zealand, many backpackers in Northland choose to attend a day-long workshop in which they learn from Maori artisans the skill of bone carving. At the end of the day they can take home their own bone pendant, while other tourists purchase these from souvenir shops.

Both backpackers and domestic tourists on a budget do not demand luxury, thus local people do not require sophisticated infrastructure to cater for this market (Polit 1991). As the WTO has noted, catering for domestic tourists '. . . requires only simple installations and infrastructure' (1995: 1–2). The lack of importance of infrastructure is witnessed by 'beach shacks' selling food and drink to backpackers in Goa (Wilson 1997), backpackers utilising road-side services (Figure 9.3), and families letting out rooms in their homes to backpackers in Bali (Wall and Long 1996) or to domestic tourists in Beidaihe, China (Xu 1998). Backpackers have shown interest in staying in very basic

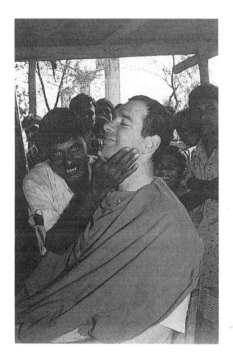

Figure 9.3 Backpacker enjoys a shave from a roadside barber, Bangladesh.
(*Source*: Henry Scheyvens)

accommodation, such as could be provided by a family in a township in South
Africa (see Chapter 7), because of the adventuresome nature of this experience.

When local resources and skills are used to provide facilities for tourists,
there can be important multiplier effects (Cater 1996: 6). On Gili Trawangan
in eastern Indonesia, for example, backpacker bungalows are built of local
bamboo and concrete blocks manufactured in the village, they are furnished
with bamboo tables and chairs made in neighbouring Lombok and curtains
made of the traditional *ikat* fabric (Hampton 1998: 649). Such ventures can be
economically viable even with small numbers of visitors because of low over-
head costs and minimal leakages (Wall and Long 1996).

The spread of economic benefits within communities may also be greater
when catering for tourists on a budget, as more community members, including those who are less well-off, can participate (O'Hare and Barrett 1999). This
is partly because catering for the budget tourist market will not usually require
community members to have any formal qualifications, rather, they can develop
skills on the job. For example, a study in Namibia found that informal sector
activities associated with tourism, including the sale of fuelwood and vegetables
to campers, offered a valuable means of enhancing the livelihoods of the poorest
groups in society. Individuals did not need capital, a broad range of skills or a
good command of a foreign language to participate successfully in the tourism

sector in this way (Ashley and Roe 1998: 21). It has similarly been found that women, often excluded from formal economic activities, are more likely to operate informal tourism enterprises by selling handicrafts, operating food stalls or working as beach vendors (Wilson 1997; Goodwin *et al.* 1998). Domestic tourists and international backpackers are more likely than other groups of tourists to support the informal sector (Shah and Gupta 2000).[1]

The case study to follow highlights the ways in which domestic tourism can promote local economic development, using the example of the largest seaside resort in China.

Case study: Domestic tourism in a Chinese seaside resort

Beidaihe (population = 55,000) is the largest seaside resort in China, attracting approximately 6 million visitors in 1990 (Xu 1998: 46), yet it is virtually unknown to foreigners. Historically, enjoyment of this resort was only available to the privileged of society, but with political change there has been increasing interest from large numbers of Chinese people in domestic travel.

Local people have gained numerous economic benefits from the growth of tourism in the area. Firstly, around 80 per cent of the expenditure of tourists visiting Beidaihe is used for local tourism services including accommodation, food and retail shopping. The remaining 20 per cent is paid for regional transportation. This high rate of local expenditure means high employment in the area, with 40 per cent of locals finding work in tourism-related enterprises (Xu 1998: 47). The amazing growth in service sector enterprises since the initiation of wide-scale domestic tourism is shown in Figure 9.4.[2]

Notably, a wide range of people have benefited from participation in tourism here because of what Xu calls the 'comparatively low entry costs of supplying goods and services to the domestic tourism market' (1998: 47). For example, in

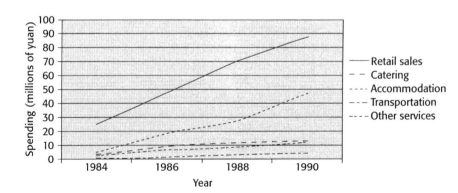

Figure 9.4 Growth of service sectors in the Chinese seaside resort of Beidaihe (in millions of yuan). (*Source*: Based on Xu 1998: 48, derived from *Statistical Yearbook of Beidaihe, 1984–1992*)

1987 there were 680 private guest houses, an increase from only 13 four years earlier. Around half of the primary sector labourers, who generally received low wages, moved into tourism, and others who remained in the primary sector have enhanced their incomes through tourism. Farmers, for example, started selling produce to tourist restaurants. Migrant labourers have also found seasonal work in Beidaihe for several months and while this is not as desirable as permanent work, the wages are much higher than those available in the agricultural sector so the work is welcomed.

The economic benefits of tourism in Beidaihe were clearly reflected in per capita household income figures, which increased from yuan 230 in 1980 to yuan 1,330 in 1991. This compared favourably with the national average, in 1991, of yuan 708. Such facts lead Xu (1998: 44) to the conclusion that, '. . . for most tourist areas in China, the promotion of domestic tourism, compared to international tourism, is a more practical way of achieving local economic development'.

Other aspects of development

It is important not to confine discussions of the relationship between budget tourism and local development to economic criteria. Some significant social, political and environmental benefits which can ensue for communities which cater for budget tourists are discussed below.

Communities providing services to the budget end of the tourism market are more likely to retain control over their enterprises. If they aimed at servicing higher-paying tourists, communities would often need to either become indebted to a lending institution in order to provide high-quality facilities or to bring in other parties. For example, they may end up leasing their land to a private safari operator rather than managing their own enterprise. They would also require sophisticated skills and management experience to cater adequately for the demands of top-end tourists. Controlling one's own enterprise is a positive step in the direction of self-determination for people otherwise dependent on the tourism industry for menial jobs or handouts and is more likely to lead to self-fulfilment. There is a notable difference, for example, '. . . between being a cleaner in a large international hotel compared with being the owner of a small *losmen* [homestay] cooking and serving at tables in their own place' (Hampton 1998: 650).

Hampton argues that encouraging local people to cater to the needs of backpackers also poses a challenge to foreign domination of tourism enterprises within Third World countries:

> Given the political will to constrain the larger players, backpacker tourism could increase local participation in real development, part of a more sustainable long-term strategy which attempts to balance local economic development needs against powerful interests wishing to build large international tourism resorts (Hampton 1998: 655).

An example from Goa, India, highlights this point. Wilson (1997: 69) is concerned that a growing emphasis on luxury tourism development in Goa, which has traditionally catered primarily for the domestic and backpacker markets, may undermine local development:

> . . . this focus on up-market tourism is out of keeping with the present structure of the tourism industry in Goa, which is mainly low-budget and served by a multitude of small hotels, guest-houses, rented rooms, and a host of ancillary services. . . . The danger here is that control over up-market tourism could pass out of indigenous hands into foreign ownership and that these multinationals might be . . . less sensitive to . . . social, cultural, and environmental issues.

When communities control their own tourism enterprises, they are more likely to be interested in participating in local business or tourism organisations through which wider development goals and the well-being of their people can be promoted. In Bali, Wall and Long (1996) explain how a strong tourism organisation was initiated in one neighbourhood where homestays were common. Its aims were to promote tourism in the area, to protect the local environment and to address any issues which concerned the community, including the in-migration of outside entrepreneurs. Forming organisations can therefore help communities gain greater control over tourism development in their vicinity and give them political strength to deal with outsiders, including the private sector and government officials (Ashley and Garland 1994).

While the hedonistic, self-centred attitudes of the beach party style of backpacker may work against developing cross-cultural understanding (Aziz 1999), in general backpackers tend to engage in more social relationships with local people than other categories of tourists:

> Whilst it is no doubt easy to romanticise the extent to which various types of budget travellers mix with locals, they do, in fact, enjoy a fairly positive image with some Sri Lankans precisely because they are easy-going, relaxed and often have the time to talk to local people. By contrast, there are many negative characterizations of those more affluent tourists who travel from hotel to hotel in air-conditioned luxury never stopping to speak to anyone (Crick 1994, cited in Macleod 1998: 162–3).

To support Crick's statement, it is suggested that independent trekkers in Nepal, including many self-designated backpackers, treat their employees (e.g. guides, porters, accommodation providers) 'on more equal terms' than those on group treks organised by outside agencies (Shah and Gupta 2000).

Travel by domestic tourists can expand their knowledge and understanding of their own country, with a subsequent increase in national pride. Richter (1989) further claims that domestic travel can raise people's appreciation of different cultural, linguistic and religious groups and of common interests of the people of a country, thus helping to foster national integration.

Brown (1998a) suggests that countries searching for an alternative, less exploitative form of tourism development than that dominated by the interests of multinational capital, should encourage domestic tourism as this results in greater community ownership of tourism enterprises. Thus if governments give their active support to domestic tourism, this can be seen as representing a rejection of the '. . . colonial mentality, that ascribes more importance to the wishes and tastes of outsiders than to the desires of their own people' (Richter 1989: 105). Presumably governments which support domestic tourism from an ethical standpoint will find ways of making their cultural and natural heritage accessible to their own people. In countries such as Zimbabwe, for example, there is a tiered system of payments for entry into national parks, with cheaper fees charged to domestic tourists. A similar system is applied to hotel accommodation in Fiji and Kenya. An interesting way of overcoming the lack of disposable income which impedes many domestic tourists from enjoying tourism sites has been identified in the case of the Tswaing eco-museum near Pretoria, South Africa. In order to ensure that entrance to the site is open to all people from surrounding areas, including township dwellers and school pupils, the entrance fee can either be paid in cash or by bringing 20 empty drink cans (Kobus Basson, Tswaing Crater Museum Project Manager: Author's fieldwork, June 1998). Conservation organisations could also be interested in subsidising entry of local people into parks in order to foster support for sustainable development principles. It has been noted that in Costa Rica, for example, most poor people show little interest in parks and tourism because they do not have the means to visit parks and other tourism ventures (Thrupp 1990, cited in Stonich et al. 1995). An innovative way of encouraging Kenyans to visit parks is discussed in Box 9.2.

Finally, budget tourists support sustainable utilisation of resources through staying in places which have cheap prices because they do not provide resource-intensive, expensive services. Thus homestay accommodation in much of the Third World includes comforts such as ceiling fans and buckets of water or cold showers, while down the road hot baths and air conditioning are standard requirements of tourists at the luxury resort. Furthermore, the willingness of backpackers to pay good money to engage in activities centred on natural attractions, including game viewing in Africa, trekking in Nepal, or diving and surfing in the Caribbean or Pacific, can also help communities see that there is a value to conserving natural resources in their area. It may even encourage them to form or participate in conservation organisations, cooperating with neighbouring communities to ensure adequate protection of the natural environment on which tourism is based. In Nepal, for example, villages in the popular trekking area of the Annapurna Sanctuary joined the Annapurna Conservation Area Project (Pobocik and Butalla 1998).

From the discussion above it is clear that local communities can gain a number of important economic, social, political and environmental benefits from engaging with budget tourists. Significantly, individuals did not need large amounts of capital to initiate a successful venture. This point is further highlighted in the

BOX 9.2

Kenyans visit their parks for the first time

All his life Samson Ouma has wanted to see a leopard, a cheetah and an elephant. Ouma was born in Kenya, renowned throughout the world for its exotic wildlife. Yet like most Kenyans, he has never seen any, except on television or in newspaper photos.

A million tourists poured into Kenya in 1998, spending as much as US$570 a day to snare the country's magnificent wildlife with their cameras. Mr Ouma earns US$95 a month as a gardener at the British high commissioner's residence. A national park flocking with lion, cheetah and leopard lies a few kilometres from the residence, but Mr Ouma has never been there. He can't afford it. . . . What angers him most is the hijacking of his heritage. 'For tourists, the animals are more important than Kenyans. They think the wildlife belongs to the world', he says.

On a recent sunny afternoon, Mr Ouma waits to board a bus in downtown Nairobi. In a burst of holiday spirit, the Kenya Museum Society is sponsoring an afternoon excursion to Nairobi National Park for the household staffs of its members. Mary James, the high commissioner's wife, is sending Mr Ouma, her cook, her laundry man and five other workmen to the park. . . .

The bus finally sputters into motion. . . . Ninety minutes later, it rolls into the 113 square kilometre park. . . . Suddenly, there's a shout and a stampede to one side of the bus. There, 45 metres away, is a leopard, lazily straddling the branch on an acacia tree, its front paws tucked under its chest. The bus erupts in clapping and shrieks of glee. . . . For the first time, a smile creases Mr Ouma's face. The leopard has enthralled him, melting away his bitterness. 'I'm finally getting something back that belongs to me', he says.

Source: Nelson (2000: 8).

following case study which also recognises that any village-based tourism venture is likely to need support from a range of stakeholders if it is to be successful.

Case study: Noah's eco-cultural tours

Chimanimani is a mountainous and extremely scenic area in the Eastern Highlands of Zimbabwe. The town of Chimanimani is very small, serving as a government administrative centre and service town, in addition to providing hotel accommodation (mainly frequented by domestic tourists) and lodge accommodation (mainly frequented by the many backpackers visiting the area). Noah Majuta is a 24-year-old man who decided to set up a tour guiding service when he realised there was little chance of gaining other employment in the Chimanimani area. He was from a poor family and recently moved to a village by the name of 'Old Location' near to Chimanimani, where he hoped to support his wife and child (Figure 9.5).

Noah started to guide hiking parties into the Chimanimani mountains. He later followed this up with cultural tours after a British volunteer working for the

Figure 9.5   The site of Noah's eco-cultural tours in Chimanimani, Zimbabwe.

Chimanimani District Council conducted a survey of visitors to the area, with respondents stating they would like the chance to see a village and learn about Shona culture and way of life (Helen Steward, Voluntary Service Overseas: Author's fieldwork, June 1998). The Shona are the largest ethnic group in Zimbabwe.

Noah's most popular tour involves walking with visitors from Chimanimani town to Old Location, a distance of approximately 2 kilometres. On the way he points out the traditional uses of various plants and trees, showing where fuel-wood is collected and which trees are used for making toothbrushes or ropes, for example, as well as drawing attention to different species of birds and other wildlife. Visitors are then taken to Noah's home in the village and introduced to his wife and baby daughter. His wife demonstrates how food is traditionally prepared and cooked, as well as drawing on lasting images most tourists have of rural southern Africa: how to strap a baby onto a woman's back and how to carry a bucket of water on one's head. The latter turns into a participatory demonstration with visitors encouraged to try to develop this skill. While his wife finishes her preparations of the meal, Noah provides explanations of such subjects as how their houses are constructed and where they get their water from; this helps visitors, who usually stay in places where they can turn on a tap and there is a seemingly endless flow of water, appreciate that water is a very precious commodity in most parts of Africa. Visitors also have the opportunity to walk around the garden and taste local plants such as sugar cane. Lastly, lunch is served and the visitors and family sit down together to eat. Throughout the tour, information about Shona traditions, such as how to clap to demonstrate thanks or approval, and the significance of totems and marriage traditions in Shona culture, are discussed.

After a signing session of the visitor book, the tour concludes with a walk back to Chimanimani. Some comments from the book include:

> All through our journey in Africa we were looking for tours where we could learn about traditions and traditional ways of life. We were lucky to come here and find your tour.

> What a Zimbabwean experience. Thank you for showing us your lovely village and welcoming us into your home.

Clearly many visitors appreciate broadening their visit to Africa by experiencing not just the nature and wildlife, but local living conditions and cultural norms as well.

Despite Noah's simple living conditions and the lack of modern facilities, he has managed to establish a successful small business. Because he has no car, walking is the means of transportation used. Although he has no telephone, tour bookings can be made with either the information office of the Chimanimani Tourist Association or a nearby hotel, with whom Noah checks in daily.

While for the first few months the cultural tours were run independently of the wider village, Noah soon recognised that not everyone in the village understood why he was bringing foreign people there and this had generated some suspicion and jealousy. He saw the need to secure the approval and support of the entire village for his enterprise, and he felt a good way of doing this would be to contribute a percentage of his revenue to a central fund. Initial talks with the elected village committee revealed that they were very enthusiastic about developing tourism in the village. They were particularly happy that he was willing to pay money into a fund which could be used to support villagers during times of need, for example when arranging funeral ceremonies or if someone required urgent medical attention. A sum of Z$20 per visitor was agreed upon for day visits. In 1998, Noah received Z$100 per person for the village tour, which included lunch. In the future, Noah hopes to expand his enterprise to offer economic opportunities for other villagers. His plans include overnight stays and visits to artisans and specialists in the village.

Noah has developed a successful small tourist enterprise over which he has maintained control, a significant achievement for a villager in an area where the tourist industry is dominated by whites and outsiders. He has even joined the Chimanimani Tourist Association, and is the only village dweller who is a member. There was no major infrastructural investment needed to run Noah's tours because transport was by foot and local communication services were used, and his start-up costs were low because the tours were based on the freely available resources of nature and resources in his own home.

Source: Author's fieldwork, June 1998.

Conclusion

In the past, commentators have distinguished two major limitations for local communities in engaging with the tourism sector: the unequal distribution of benefits and the fact that control often remains with outsiders (Ashley and Roe 1998). This chapter has suggested that if communities serviced the lower end of the tourist market, including backpackers and domestic tourists, they could gain significant benefits and have some control over tourism in their area. Tourism ventures catering for budget tourists are often largely dependent on local cultural and natural resources, and locally managed, thus allowing communities to 'participate with equity in the [tourism] process' (Lillywhite and Lillywhite 1991: 89g).

The tendency of Third World governments to ignore budget travellers in their promotional strategies could be to the detriment of local economic and social development. It can also entrench existing regional inequalities (O'Hare and Barrett 1999). Backpackers bring in considerable amounts of foreign exchange which is dispersed far more widely than most proceeds from tourism. Domestic tourists may not have a lot of disposable income, but, like backpackers, a large proportion of their money is used on locally produced products and services, therefore supporting artisans and service sector workers and avoiding import leakages. There are also significant non-economic benefits which can come to communities from engaging with budget tourism. As this chapter has shown, aiming 'low' can lead to empowerment of local communities by building upon the skills of the local population, promoting self-reliance, developing the community's confidence in dealing with outsiders and enhancing people's pride in their own culture.

This chapter and Chapters 2 and 3, however, also raised concerns about the behaviour and attitudes of backpackers, which can be harmful or offensive from the perspective of local peoples. This may particularly be the case in backpacker ghettos or enclaves.[3] Tourism involves both 'hosts' and 'guests' and responsibilities by both parties (Pearce 1995). Backpackers should not assume that by choosing what they see to be an 'alternative' method of travel, the ethics of their travel experience will be beyond scrutiny. As Noronha (1999: 5) concludes,

> If backpackers would like to distance themselves from the unjust face of global tourism, there's a long trek ahead. . . . Backpackers need to be more critical, more honest – and less selfishly enthusiastic – about how they currently benefit from a patently unfair global system.

Thus there may be a need for better education of the backpacker segment in order to allay some of the concerns Third World peoples have about their social behaviour. Guidebook publishers (especially Lonely Planet and Rough Guides) and travel agencies could play a role here, providing backpackers with

---

BOX 9.3

How to be a responsible budget traveller

1. *Learn about your host country* so you are able to observe local dress codes and customs. Respect other people's culture and values.

2. *Don't be judgemental.* Criticising or condemning local traditions, cultures and religions will leave you at odds with people who feel strongly about them. Remember that what dictates life in the country you are visiting is rarely identical to your own environment.

3. *Getting to know local people* will expose you to goings-on in town, demystify certain misconceptions and facilitate healthy exchange of ideas for mutual benefit.

4. *Buy local.* Buying Coke or Pepsi gives money to multinationals. Buying fresh fruit juice gives money direct to local people. Consider donating to a local community project.

5. When you are shopping, remember that your 'bargain' means low wages for the maker. *Pay a fair price.*

6. *Ask permission* before taking photographs, even if your subjects are little children.

7. When booking a local tour enquire who is running it and *who benefits*. Make sure tour guides have permission to visit communities, and that they are working closely with local people and paying a fair price.

8. Appreciate the richness of seeing and participating in a different way of life. *Don't search for a home away from home.*

9. Remember that some communities don't want visitors. If in doubt, don't go.

Source: Tourism Concern (2000).

---

thoroughly researched information on appropriate behaviour and cultural norms in their chosen destinations. Non-governmental organisations can also play a role, as shown by Tourism Concern which recently published a brochure for backpackers with a checklist on how to be a responsible budget traveller (Box 9.3).

Despite such concerns, it is clear that local communities can gain significant benefits from engaging with tourists on a budget. The success of Noah's enterprise in the case study above demonstrates that it is possible for relatively poor Third World people to tap into, and benefit from, the tourism industry. While Noah's success derives largely from his own initiative, it is important not to underestimate the support he received as well. In particular, a British volunteer helped him with market research, and membership of the Chimanimani Tourist Association assisted with networking and marketing. It is unrealistic to expect community members to have at their disposal the wide range of resources, skills and information which may be needed to initiate and control a successful small business, even one directed at budget travellers. For this reason, Chapters 10–12 provide examples of ways in which government bodies, the private sector and NGOs can provide appropriate support for communities involved in tourism.

Questions

1. Do the local economic benefits of encouraging domestic tourism outweigh the macroeconomic benefits, such as foreign exchange earnings, which a country can achieve through promoting international tourism?

2. How can domestic tourism contribute to a greater spread of benefits within a country than international tourism?

3. Imagine that you are a tourism consultant who has been asked to brief the government of Zimbabwe on the benefits of backpacker tourism. Specifically, you should make five points on the ways in which local communities can benefit from this sector and three points on strategies the government could put in place to support communities which wish to encourage backpacker tourism.

4. Some writers have suggested that backpacking is no longer an independent endeavour but rather just a variant on institutionalised, mass tourism whereby backpackers follow a well-trodden route through various countries and continents. Reflect on possible pros and cons of such an institutionalised form of backpacking from the perspective of local communities.

Suggestions for further reading

Hampton, M. 1998 'Backpacker tourism and economic development', *Annals of Tourism Research*, 25(3): 639–60.
Ghimire, K. (ed.) 2001 *The Native Tourist: Mass Tourism Within Developing Countries*, Earthscan, London.
Sutcliffe, W. 1999 *Are You Experienced?* Penguin, London.

Useful websites

Lonely Planet's thorn tree site offers some enlightening and interesting perspectives on backpacker travel:
thorntree.lonelyplanet.com/thorn/repliesflat.pl?Cat=&Topic=243499&view=expanded&sb=7

The site of the charity Surf Aid which aims to ensure that the surf industry and surfers themselves put something back into the impoverished destinations, such as the Mentawai islands off the coast of Sumatra in Indonesia, where they go to surf:
www.surf-aid.org

Tourism Concern's site reporting on their Young Travellers' Conference held in April 2001:
www.tourismconcern.org.uk/frame.htm

Notes

1. It must also be noted, however, that in some cases it is extremely difficult for poorer people servicing the budget tourist market to make a profit simply because they are in competition with many others. O'Hare and Barrett (1999) identify this as a significant problem in the case of hostel operators in Peru, for example, who generally have low occupancy rates of 10–20 per cent.

2. As Lew (2001: 110–11) notes, while interested in pursuing economic development through tourism, the Chinese government did not allow domestic tourism in the early 1980s as they felt this would put too much pressure on the country's accommodation and transport services.

3. Note that Elsrud (2001: 608) distinguishes between experienced backpackers and newcomers. The latter have come to be known as 'sun, sea and sex backpackers', and it is this group that may be more likely to behave in a culturally inappropriate manner.

Promoting development through tourism

CHAPTER 10

Roles for governments

Introduction

Governments have incredibly important roles, and responsibilities, when it comes to tourism development in the Third World, particularly if they are concerned about issues of sustainability (Brohman 1996a; Clancy 1999; Harrison 2001): 'sustainable development can only be achieved when tourism is managed in a controlled and integrated manner and is soundly based in careful and effective legislative restriction' (France 1997c: 213). Thus it is up to governments to set the ground rules, or regulations, within which tourism takes place. And it is governments that have the power to establish policies which can determine whether a country follows a path of tourism development dictated primarily by overseas interests and capital, or one which seeks to achieve economic gains for local people and the state while preserving the integrity of social, cultural and environmental features of their country. However, moulding tourism to suit their own interests is a major challenge for any government:

> Policy makers can only proceed from what already exists . . . and that is a powerful and still growing, highly integrated, international tourism industry. How to coax that behemoth into less (self-) destructive behaviour is the main task ahead (de Kadt 1990: 33).

Too often a lack of control by governments over the volume and nature of tourism development has led to a country's dependence on foreign products, foreign investment and foreign skills (Baskin 1995; Britton and Clarke 1987). This is particularly of concern in the context of Third World destinations and small countries in general whose development can therefore be strongly influenced by overseas investors (Britton 1982; Brohman 1996a). There is already a global economic concentration of wealth in tourism, witnessed by the domination of the package tourism industry by a small number of key players with advanced forward and backward linkages which enable them to control aspects of the industry. For example, company mergers taking place in Britain are likely to result in just four tour companies controlling up to 90 per cent of outbound charter capacity. These companies do not just own tour operators in Britain and abroad, they also own hotels, self-catering accommodation, airlines, cruise ships and retail chains (O'Connor 2000). The managing director of Sunvil Holidays, Neil Josephides, states that such dominance is not in the interests of destination countries such as his home, Cyprus:

> Thomson combined with Preussag will control 20 to 30 per cent of tourism to Cyprus. Tourism represents over 20 per cent of the country's Gross Domestic Product, so the operators don't just control the hoteliers, they control the country. It's very depressing (cited in O'Connor, 2000: 5).

A number of issues concerning government roles and responsibilities in tourism development are considered in this chapter. First, the challenges facing governments wishing to pursue a self-determined form of tourism development are explored. This is followed by a section on the nature of tourism development which questions what types of tourism may be most beneficial for Third World countries. The chapter then moves on to explain the roles the state can play in planning for and regulating tourism development. Finally, strategies for governments to support community involvement in tourism are explained using case studies from Costa Rica and Namibia. Ideas will be presented both concerning appropriate ways of overcoming barriers to equitable tourism development, such as restrictive building codes, as well as means of actively encouraging and providing incentives for desirable forms of tourism development.

Outside influences on Third World tourism development

Potentially the state can play an important role in controlling overseas investment in tourism and the activities of private developers. However, advocating a strong role for the state in tourism planning, regulation and management seems anomalous when the current market-driven, neoliberal economic climate dictates a minimalist role for government actors (Hoogvelt 1997; Brohman 1995). Furthermore, many Third World governments find that their economic policies are at the mercy of supranational organisations. This is particularly the case with those that have come under direct pressure from the International Monetary Fund (IMF) to adopt policies which encourage high levels of foreign investment as a means of earning foreign exchange to pay back mounting debts. Thus,

> Governments which in public espouse the fine-sounding language of the sustainable and ethical high ground of local community tourism development may be subject to external pressures . . . which dictate a policy of economic liberalisation and foreign exchange maximisation (Mowforth and Munt 1998: 257).

While policy makers in the Third World are often lured by the supposed economic benefits tourism can bring in terms of gross revenue, this takes no account of such important factors as the repatriation of profits. Furthermore, even if they do manage to hold on to a generous proportion of the profits from tourism, opening up their borders fully to foreign investors may lead to diminishing self-sufficiency and self-determination. Brown thus asserts that it is essential for government planners to 'look and act beyond simplistic gross figures' (1998a: 214). Globalisation places countries with weaker economic systems in a very vulnerable position in relation to other, more powerful countries (Burns 1999b).

Interestingly, international conservation organisations can also be seen as placing considerable pressure on Third World governments. While they prioritise the environment, which may make them seem a great deal better than other supranational organisations with purely economic motives, they often do this at the expense of local community interests and livelihoods[1] (Brown 1998b; Mowforth and Munt 1998).

While these external forces mean it can be very difficult for Third World governments to implement tourism policies which serve community and national interests, they are not completely impotent. As Parnwell (1998: 213) argues, 'The local, national and global are . . . drawn together in complex interrelationships rather than the global simply swamping and ultimately superseding the national and sub-national.'

The nature of tourism development

Many people assume that in Third World contexts, tourism growth is necessarily beneficial because it will contribute to economic development. As we saw in Chapter 2, however, the relationship between tourism and development is complex and often only tenuous positive links exist. Yet still we find authors such as Raguraman (1998: 534), who complains that tourism in India has shown a 'dismal performance' because their share of world tourist arrivals and world tourism receipts declined between 1981 and 1995. For this same period, however, tourist arrivals and tourism receipts in India both actually showed a steady increase. Any further increase in tourism in India may have been at the expense of social and environmental well-being, especially if issues such as the distribution of tourists were not considered. This is an issue which seems to have been clearly understood by, interestingly, the tourism department in the state of Himachal Pradesh, India. Rather than just planning for accelerated tourism development, they supported the dispersal of tourism to ensure both that there was not undue pressure at one site and that the benefits tourism brought were spread more widely than existing popular sites (Shah and Gupta 2000).

Just as a large influx of tourists may not always spell development, certain types of tourism may not be desirable for Third World countries or communities, thus we need to consider how governments can influence the *nature* of tourism development. Essentially they can choose to take a 'hands-off' approach and just let tourism develop according to national and international demand and the marketing strategies of travel agencies and tour operators, or they can try to attract particular types of tourists which they feel will bring the most benefit, and least harm, to their country. Five governments which have made concerted efforts to control the nature of tourism development, rather than allowing tourism entrepreneurs and investors to dictate the form and function of tourism in their countries, have their strategies outlined in Table 10.1. While the Maldives seeks to control tourism by spatial means, developing separate tourism enclaves on otherwise uninhabited islands as a means of protecting traditional lifestyles and religion elsewhere in their country, Samoa has promoted small-scale, ecotourism initiatives, and The Gambia banned all-inclusive holidays. Both Bhutan and the Seychelles have restricted the number of tourists, Bhutan by limiting visas and the Seychelles by putting a cap on the number of hotel beds available. In addition, Bhutan has declared some religious sites off limits to tourists in order to preserve their spiritual integrity.

However, some governments which are purportedly attempting to promote alternative forms of tourism have contradictory policies in place (Pearce 1992). For example, while the Kenyan government's development plan for the 1994–96 period sought to shift the focus of tourism from mass tourists to upmarket ecotourists, this contradicted other broad goals emphasised in this plan, including maximising tax revenues and foreign exchange earnings (Sindiga 1999: 118). Neither can a government expect to be able to both gain maximum revenue from tourism while encouraging involvement of local entrepreneurs (Shah and Gupta 2000). Compromises will often need to be made.

There are many examples of governments which have tried to control the nature or volume of tourism by focusing exclusively on higher-end tourists. In the early 1980s, the government Tourist Office in Papua New Guinea offered no support at all to guesthouse owner-operators, choosing instead to refer visitors to large-scale, Western-style hotels (Ranck 1987: 165). The case of governments prioritising large-scale tourism development is also clearly played out in Indonesia, where luxury tourism has been promoted as a strategy for modernisation. The national policy supports resort development and hotels with star ratings, providing every encouragement to foreign investors, but small-scale tourism initiatives are officially meant to be supported by the ill-equipped and less powerful local and provincial governments (Dahles and Bras 1999a). This is despite the fact that small-scale, local companies are often 'more successful in generating income, employment, and government revenue than larger, internationally-owned establishments' (Brohman 1996a: 56), thus suggesting that governments wishing to maximise the revenue they gain from tourism should focus at least some of their attention at this lower level.

Table 10.1   Examples of Third World governments with restrictions on tourism development

Country	Tourism strategy
Bhutan	No tourism prior to 1974, when strictly controlled tourism was introduced. Development plans are focused around preserving the country's GNH (Gross National Happiness), thus annual tourist arrivals were restricted to 2,000 up until 1985. Arrivals have gradually increased, hovering around the 5,000 mark annually in the late 1990s. Tourism is further controlled by requiring tourists to pre-book through one of the registered tour operators in Bhutan, or their counterparts abroad. A minimum spending requirement (which was US$200/day in the late 1990s) has provided a further deterrent to independent and budget travellers. All tourists must stay in government-approved accommodation. The impacts of tourism are carefully monitored by government officials and religious leaders so that concerns over social or environmental degradation can be quickly addressed. This led to the closure of some temples and monasteries to tourists in 1988 after religious leaders complained that the spiritual integrity of these sites was being undermined by tourism
The Gambia	In October 1999 the government banned all-inclusive holidays (where the cost covers all transport, accommodation, meals and activities for tourists) because tourists were spending most of their time and money in their resort, and local businesses could not benefit economically from tourism. [NB This ban was short-lived – see Box 10.1 for an explanation]
Maldives	Receives over 300,000 tourists annually, more than its population, but impacts are minimised by policies which have led the World Tourism Organization to cite the Maldives as a model of sustainable tourism development. Tourists are restricted to a number of designated resort islands, that is, previously uninhabited islands established solely as tourist havens. They are not free to visit other islands inhabited by locals at their leisure, although day excursions to some of these islands are provided. To avert negative environmental impacts, resort developers are only allowed to build on 20 per cent of an island's area, buildings cannot exceed the height of the surrounding vegetation, and all services, including water and sewage treatment, must be provided by the developers. Water cannot be taken from other islands
Seychelles	The government has enacted a number of innovative sustainable development policies, including some relating to the tourism sector. The number of beds for rent has been limited to 4,500 (there are 76,000 residents), based on an estimation of how many tourists the country's ecosystem could cope with. When demand increases, the supply will remain the same so prices simply increase. Buildings can be no higher than a palm tree and water use in hotels in monitored. A proposal that tourists take their waste home with them has not yet been put into place
Samoa	Tourism planning supports small-scale, locally controlled, nature-based tourism development as opposed to the larger-scale resort development common in neighbouring Fiji

Sources: Based on information from Inskeep (1997), Lyon (1997), Paskal (2000), Tourism Concern (1999b), Weaver (1998b) and Wood and House (1991).

BOX 10.1

The Gambia's ill-fated ban on all-inclusives

All-inclusive resorts provide accommodation, most meals, transport and leisure activities for tourists, all for one price. They have been very popular in The Gambia for some time, but have been derided by many local people because they do not encourage tourists to go out-side of their resorts to purchase goods and services. Indeed, as the fees for these resorts are mostly paid to travel agents in Britain and other European countries it appears that leakages from all-inclusive resorts can be particularly high.

Due to pressure from organisations such as Gambia Tourism Concern, the Gambian government decided to ban all-inclusives from October 1999. This ban had a short life, however. It was lifted in December 2000 because of concern about the loss of tourists to other countries, especially some in the Caribbean offering all-inclusive resorts. Now the Gambian government is actually encouraging new foreign investors to build all-inclusive resorts, with tax concessions as an added incentive (*In Focus* 2000, 38: lift out Campaigns Update).

This is an example of the increasing power of a small number of travel companies with a high degree of vertical integration, which allows them to shift thousands of clients from one destination to another when the conditions in a particular country no longer suit them (Akama 1999).

In practice, most Third World governments invest a great deal more of their limited resources in securing benefits of tourism at the national level, including encouraging foreign investment and attracting international tourists, than they do in supporting the active involvement of local communities in this sector: '. . . if anything, the "benefit to residents" is a poor partner of the need to protect "long term investments" . . .' (Mowforth and Munt 1998: 284). In focusing their attention on attracting large-scale investors Third World governments have effectively subsidised investment in tourism by outsiders (Shah and Gupta 2000):

> in many Sub-Saharan African countries, public funds have served to speed up the accumulation of capital by the MNCs, while investment codes have mainly facilitated tax evasion and export of capital by the middle class and national bureaucracies (Brown 1998a: 240).

If they wish to support local development and ensure communities have a role in managing tourism rather than simply providing labour in tourism enterprises owned and controlled by outsiders, governments may need to look at encouraging other forms of tourism. Too often, as discussed in Chapter 9, tourism planners see backpackers or domestic tourists on a budget as liabilities, rather than recognising that these segments of the market present local people with numerous income-generating opportunities (Hampton 1998; Wilson 1997). Poorer members of communities, in particular, typically do not have the skills, experience or resources required to cater for luxury tourists and they can only gain access to the industry through the informal sector. Yet tourism planners tend to ignore the informal sector or to see its existence as problematic, rather than seeking ways to actively support this sector (Timothy and Wall 1997; Dahles 1999).

A related concern is the tendency for Third World governments to move tourism 'up scale' in areas which have become popular with budget tourists. This can result in the loss of important economic advantages for local people as well as loss of control over tourism enterprises. This is certainly a concern in Pangandaran, a fishing village in Java which has developed into a beach resort. The government's promotion of upmarket tourism here has led to major landownership changes such as development of a five-star hotel on what was previously communal village land. As noted by Wilkinson and Pratiwi (1995: 295), it is lower-class people who are most likely to be disadvantaged by the government's upgrading of tourism in Pangandaran: 'They face the possibility of being displaced from their homes and losing employment in their informal sector jobs as the tourism product moves up-scale and creates demands for higher standards of facilities and services.'

Clearly governments need to carefully consider the nature of the tourism they wish to pursue before formulating their plans and policies. Simple assumptions, such as asserting that attracting luxury tourists will maximise a country's benefits from tourism, are not always based on fact and typically ignore the needs and concerns of many poorer people who could gain economically from servicing tourists. This may be regarded as acceptable in countries such as the Maldives or Bhutan where the government wishes to minimise the overall number of tourists in order to protect the indigenous population, but could be hotly contested in other countries such as Indonesia and India where lower-income people are heavily involved in servicing tourists through the informal sector.

Planning for and regulating tourism development

When faced with immediate developmental challenges such as poverty and indebtedness, it is not surprising that Third World countries do not always accord tourism planning a high priority (Douglas 1998; Raguraman 1998). It is generally not a lack of planning per se but a lack of effective planning, and implementation of plans, that is the main impediment to appropriate tourism development in Third World countries.

Table 10.2 documents the evolution of public sector approaches to planning for tourism. In addition to growing recognition of the need to involve communities in tourism planning, there is now a stronger focus on taking an integrated approach to planning which stresses that environmental and social impacts of

Table 10.2 Public sector approaches to planning for tourism

Era	Tourism planning stage
1950s	Virtually no public sector tourism planning
1960s	Candyfloss image of tourism at official levels, reluctance to consider tourism as equal to other economic sectors; government priority focused on investment incentives and operation; little or no critical analysis of sector; minimal attention given to practicalities of implementation; spread of the blueprint approach to master planning
1970s	Tourism planning approaching its apex; focus on luxury resort tourism; ideology of 'planners know best'; continuing lack of political will in shaping tourism development to the destination's own needs and aspirations; recognition in mainstream planning of community involvement; corporations follow international strategies
1980s	Acknowledgement of economic, sociocultural and environmental impacts of tourism, giving rise to recognition of the need for comprehensive and coordinated goal-setting framework; recognition in North America of need for community involvement
1990s	Recognition that if not fully planned, tourism fails to deliver the economic benefits expected by Third World nations; total destination management seen as the way forward with sociologists, anthropologists, environmental scientists and human resources specialists joining physical planners

Source: After Burns (1999b: 331–2).

tourism are equally as important as economic ones. While there have been significant improvements in tourism planning, the phases depicted in Table 10.2 are not discrete categories and we can still find evidence of some problematic approaches to tourism planning. For example, Britton (1987a) observed that tourism development in the South Pacific was largely influenced by international interests rather than local needs and concerns, a planning approach characteristic of the 1970s, but this is still the case in countries using tourism as a means of paying back foreign debts. Also Akama (1999) identified that the Kenyan government pursued a policy of large-scale tourism development including high-rise hotels and luxury beach resorts through to the early 1990s, so not all governments caught on to the trend for developing more socially and environmentally sensitive tourism policies which emerged in the 1980s. Furthermore, as authors writing about countries as diverse as Eritrea (Burns 1999b) and Vanuatu (Douglas 1998) have noted, tourism planning in the Third World often relies on foreign consultants who have an inadequate understanding of the social and political context in which they are working and fail to consult widely with local communities.

There is now wide support among tourism researchers for a strong role for local communities in tourism planning (Ashley 2000; McMinn and Cater 1998; Trousdale 1999; Woodley 1993). However, turning this rhetoric into reality appears to be very difficult in practice (Joppe 1996), at least partly because government interests and priorities often diverge greatly from those of local communities (Mowforth and Munt 1998). As noted by Wall (1996b: 41), 'Planning is a political process that empowers some and disadvantages others, often strengthening the position of the powerful and further undermining the position of the weak.'[2]

For tourism planning in the Third World to be effective and responsive to community interests, there needs to be a coordinated system of planning. Too often government ministries or departments dealing with issues with a strong relation to tourism, such as natural resources and conservation, are fragmented (Brown 1998a; de Kadt 1990). Similarly, there is inadequate coordination of planning from national to regional and local levels. Often national planning is overly top-down while at the local level, officials lack capacity and resources to effectively implement tourism plans and regulate development. Yet it is at the local level that public sector planners can be more responsive to local needs and interests: 'Local authorities, through the production of integrated plans and development control powers, are best placed to assess the characteristics of the local environment and the priorities, needs and attitudes of local people to tourism' (Hunter 1995: 92).

National governments have responsibility for acting on matters which are vital to the success of tourism but over which communities have no control, such as airline schedules, investment policies and data collection. For example, because in most cases Third World countries constitute long-haul destinations for international visitors, governments need to negotiate with airlines to ensure that adequate transport services are provided to allow a good flow of tourists (Sinclair et al. 1992; Woodley 1993). When Air Nauru and Polynesian Airlines withdrew their air services to the tiny Pacific island of Niue during the 1980s, this seriously undermined Niue's tourism industry (Ryan et al. 1998). Meanwhile, government investment policies determine whether basic infrastructure will be developed to a stage regarded as adequate or attractive by potential tourism developers, and whether these developers receive any incentives such as tax breaks (Oppermann and Chon 1997).[3] Also, in order to plan adequately for tourism development and carry out effective marketing, governments need to collect statistics and other information on visitor arrivals, popular destinations and expenditure patterns (Lea 1988). Information-gathering for resource inventories and ongoing monitoring of the social, environmental and economic impacts of tourism are critical as well and can help governments, for example, to establish clear regulations regarding water and soil quality and waste production, and to define carrying capacity levels for different resources to avoid overexploitation.

Good tourism plans and policies need to be complemented by effective legislation, and enforcement of this legislation, to ensure that private sector developers do not impinge on the well-being of local communities and environments. Parnwell (1998: 228) cites Hall (1994) in stating that 'the impact of tourism depends crucially upon the ownership of regulatory power'. It is critical, therefore, that governments play a strong regulatory role rather than allowing elites or international interests to usurp or bypass state control. Efforts to regulate tourism development can include use of planning controls, placing conditions on investment, implementing legislation concerning land tenure and access (for example, whether to allow investors to purchase or only to lease land), and allocation of licences or concessions to tourism operators (Ashley 2000; de Kadt 1990). In the past tourism in many Third World countries has been notoriously poorly regulated, leading, in Kenya's case, to 'an unplanned and haphazard mushrooming of tourism and hospitality facilities' (Akama 1999: 19).

While many Third World countries now have effective regulatory frameworks which should be particularly successful in controlling environmental impacts, they do not always monitor for such effects or enforce these regulations (Wall 1996b). When this happens, there can be environmental degradation to the extent that tourism drops off considerably. This is exactly what happened when the acclaimed Long Beach on Boracay Island was polluted by sewage, leading to a 70 per cent decrease in tourist arrivals in the 1996 (Trousdale 1999).

Government regulations are often fiercely resisted by industry players, however, who claim that the best option is for them to self-regulate their activities. Examples of self-regulation will be provided in Chapter 11. Not all industry players are supportive of self-regulation in practice, however. For example, UK tour operators claim that host governments are responsible for establishing and implementing regulations which will result in more sustainable forms of tourism development (Forsyth 1995). In an ideal situation government regulation, including establishment of clear ground rules, should be complemented by an industry which is willing to self-regulate (Trousdale 1998).

In addition to good governance at the national level, including effective planning, policy making, legislation and regulation, there is a need for strong and effective governance at the local level. Poor governance, for example the way in which favouritism can lead to a lack of enforcement of regulations, is seriously undermining the quality of tourism and the benefits it could bring to Third World peoples. For example, on the island resort of Boracay in the Philippines, a government official received serious threats when she persisted in reporting to the mayor's office development violations by tourism entrepreneurs. As Trousdale (1999: 859) notes, 'Violent reprisals are clearly understood in the community, helping to limit criticism and obscure governance transparency.' There is no way that community participation in planning can become a reality when the political views of community members are essentially repressed in this way.

Strategies to support community involvement in tourism

Table 10.3 outlines a number of strategies governments can enact to support community involvement in tourism, including ways in which they can plan for and regulate tourism development, market tourism, and facilitate community

Table 10.3   How governments can support community tourism enterprises

	Policies that support community tourism enterprises
Tourism planning and policy	• Clear policy statement in support of community tourism enterprises • Local participation in tourism planning • Community involvement and benefit key criteria in government planning decisions on formal sector tourism • Budget-style tourism, including domestic tourism, is actively encouraged • A planning system for approving new tourism enterprises that (a) requires private sector interests to talk with local communities and (b) is easy for rural people to use
Tourism marketing	• Marketing of community tourism enterprises – not just wildlife, beaches or luxury resorts – by the national tourism marketing body • Emphasis on people and culture in national marketing • Providing market information to community tourism enterprises
Tourism regulations/ standards	• Accommodation grading system which allows for 'simple' accommodation such as campsites and homestays • Health and safety standards that are appropriate for informal tourism enterprises • Simple regulation procedures not requiring access to the capital city, large sums of money or complicated forms
Land-use planning	• Land-use planning that incorporates community views, recognises tourism as a land-use and supports multiple land-uses
Tourism training and licensing	• Capacity-building for rural residents, or for residents of poorer urban areas, organised or sponsored by government • Courses, licences and exams that are accessible to local people, and provide qualifications that are appropriate for local enterprises, e.g. locally run courses to be registered as a guide
Joint ventures between community and private sector	• Supportive policy providing incentives for private companies to negotiate with communities • Regulations/tenure arrangements that give power to communities • Government recognition of community institutions with legal powers to enter contracts
Information, staffing and extension	• Dedicated staff, such as community tourism officers, based in regional areas to advise and support communities initiating tourism enterprises • Information provided to the formal sector on how to work with communities and enhance local benefits
Park pricing and development	• Parks run in ways that stimulate enterprise opportunities for neighbours (e.g. craft markets, local guides) • Complementary rather than competitive enterprise development inside park • Providing park visitors with information on local enterprises • Giving neighbouring communities a tourism concession inside the park • Collecting a levy from each tourist for a development fund for surrounding communities
Credit	• Access to credit for small and medium-sized enterprises

Source: After Ashley and Roe (1998: 30–1).

access to training and credit. Fundamentally, governments that wish to prioritise local interests in tourism can choose to adopt a participatory planning model which encourages local involvement and ensures that local concerns are heard right through to national planning levels (Ashley 2000). They can also make a commitment to directing assistance, first, to enterprises which are not capital-intensive, as it is at this level that the use of local skills and services is maximised, and secondly, to promoting tourism based on local technology, including transport, food production, handicraft and accommodation services (Goodwin *et al.* 1997). These forms of tourism employ many low-income people directly and provide indirect employment to others who provide raw materials, such as vegetables for cooking or hand-woven fabric for curtains. Such strategies which can result in excellent economic outcomes including poverty reduction and a decrease in the number of unemployed people, would provide a challenge to the thinking of many governments which for years have assumed that they can achieve maximum returns from investment in, and encouragement of, the luxury tourism market.

When comparing bids for tourism concessions, governments could do well to learn from South Africa's Strategic Development Initiative which gives priority to investors whose bids included plans for encouraging local development (Koch *et al.* 1998, cited in Ashley *et al.* 2000). In addition, governments could put more effort into dispersing tourism areas both to help avoid problems which arise when tourism grows too quickly in one destination, and to spread the benefits of tourism. In doing this, they do not need to keep opening up 'undiscovered areas', rather they can assist other mainstream destinations to market themselves (Shah and Gupta 2000).

Neopopulist theorists would argue that ideally, communities should dictate the form and function of tourism development and have full control over any tourism ventures in their area. In reality, however, local people often lack the experience and resources needed to establish successful tourism ventures. Thus as Baskin (1995: 111–12) notes, 'In order for . . . small initiatives to thrive, institutional support is required.' This institutional support can come from governments, NGOs or the private sector, and can involve provision of information, networking opportunities and capacity-building through skills training. Several roles that governments can play in supporting community involvement in tourism will be explained in the paragraphs to follow.

Governments can play an important role in providing, or coordinating, appropriate training to upskill local people engaging in tourism enterprises. Training in small business skills, management and marketing is particularly relevant. Such training is particularly relevant, and should be available to both those operating formal and informal enterprises. There are, for example, cases of local government bodies providing specific training to street vendors in cross-cultural communication, foreign languages, and health and safety regulations (Timothy and Wall 1997).

Governments should also ensure that findings from monitoring and research on tourism issues are publicised widely. For example, if local government officers find that tourists are avoiding certain beach locations because they feel harassed by persistent vendors, this information should be made available to the vendors rather than simply sending out their report to regional business associations and asking the police to be more vigilant in controlling vendors. In such cases appropriate action may be for a community meeting with government officers where vendors can propose possible solutions, such as the creation of an ethnic market, which would become a drawcard for tourists and preclude the need for vendors to patrol the beaches for customers.

Benefits can also come to communities from dialogue or collaboration with private sector partners. Governments can act as a catalyst for such relationships by making discussions with communities a prerequisite to gaining planning consent for a tourism venture. They can also require that social issues are researched when environmental impact assessments are carried out (Ashley 2000: 28). Promoting joint venture opportunities between communities and the private sector can be an effective strategy for governments that wish to overcome the problems and economic dependence associated with foreign ownership of tourism assets and control over the industry. Also to protect areas new to tourism from foreign domination, provincial or state governments can put in place protective legislation which makes it impossible or difficult for outsiders to purchase land in the area (Shah and Gupta 2000).

However, 'One of the most significant determinants of control in the tourism industry is ownership and investment. In most peripheral communities financing for tourism development is not available and must come from outside interests' (Woodley 1993: 145). Thus in addition to actively encouraging private sector players to talk with communities, governments can ensure that these communities have sufficient equity to engage in joint ventures from a relatively powerful position by either making loans available to them or by giving them secure tenure over what is often their greatest asset, the land. Ashley (2000) states that in Namibia, devolution of tenure rights is one of the main ways in which the government has supported community involvement in tourism, as this enables communities to influence the direction of tourism development and gives them some market power. Communities may need to be empowered in other ways, however, such as having access to lawyers to ensure they do not bear most of the risks of joint ventures and that they have some political voice, or control, over the ventures rather than just contributing economically (Sinclair et al. 1992).

As discussed in Chapter 6, in the past state-funded conservation initiatives such as the creation of protected areas have often gone ahead for the good of the environment and the good of tourism, but to the direct disadvantage of indigenous peoples. This should not, and need not, be the case. Great efforts are now being made in a number of Third World countries to ensure local benefits from tourism in conjunction with conservation estates so that local people will in turn support conservation. Park authorities that wish to support communities living inside or around protected areas can, for example, help to establish permanent outlets for locally produced crafts within park boundaries or commission them to work as guides or to provide cultural performances for visitors. Furthermore, to ensure surrounding communities have a voice in planning for future development, places for representatives can be established on park management boards. Governments can make such representation a legislative requirement. This allows local people to work for strategies to ensure that conservation and tourism are complementary activities. Of concern, however, is the intention of governments in countries such as South Africa and Zimbabwe to cut funding for the conservation sector, based on the expectation that protected area authorities should become self-funding over time (Scheyvens forthcoming, a). While politically expedient at present, the interest of these authorities in promoting the development of local communities may wane in the future if government cuts go ahead and economic survival becomes their main preoccupation.

Another key role for governments is to provide supportive legislation to enable communities to establish viable enterprises. Restrictive building codes may mean that it would be too expensive for most people to establish accommodation facilities up to government standards even when in reality, a basic traditional house with the addition of bathroom facilities would suffice. In the Solomon Islands, for example, building codes are based upon Western standards, making it very difficult for small-scale tourism ventures to be developed. Using traditional construction methods and materials, local artisans cannot meet the requirements of the building code. It has been estimated that if building regulations were adhered to, a small-scale tourism venture would cost around US$100,000. The villagers in one area went ahead and built their own basic guest house, however, at minimal cost using mostly local materials and labour, which has attracted a steady stream of visitors (Sofield 1993: 737). Similarly, in the past the Namibian government had regulations for the registration of tourism accommodation facilities to ensure minimum standards, which effectively impeded the involvement of communities in this sector. There was no provision for tourists to stay in simple rondavels with access to basic ablutions; rather, the lowest category of accommodation had to provide five bedrooms and modern plumbing (Ashley and Roe 1997). The issue of setting appropriate standards for tourism services also applies to guiding. Official tourist guides may need to pass extensive tests to gain a government endorsement, thus disqualifying illiterate or semi-literate guides who may be excellent at their trade. In some cases, government plans to protect ethnic minorities from the excesses and intrusions of tourism have effectively prevented these people from benefiting from tourism. This has occurred, for example, in Sa Pa in Vietnam and Upper Mustang in Nepal (Shah 2000, cited in Ashley *et al.* 2000).

Governments can provide great support to small-scale and community ventures by the way in which they market tourism to their country. They can, for example, promote a wide range of tourism options rather than just those appealing to mass or luxury tourists. Thus in some countries the government tourism office provides visitors with information on guest house accommodation in villages as well as hotel accommodation. Ideally governments should also try to inform tourists of the advantages of supporting small-scale and community ventures.

In order to demonstrate the implications of good versus poor government support of community involvement in tourism, the following sections examine case studies of government tourism strategies in Costa Rica and Namibia.

Case study of weak government support: Ecotourism in Ostional, Costa Rica

Ostional beach lies within Ostional Wildlife Refuge, which is a nesting ground for Olive Ridley sea turtles. Relatively low, but steadily increasing, numbers of tourists interested in wildlife protection visit this site, which therefore seems an ideal location for an alternative tourism initiative with strong community involvement. However, although the 400 local people have a high level of community organisation, they have played little role in tourism development and therefore reaped few of the benefits of tourism in the area.

Campbell (1999) asserts that this lack of community participation and management in tourism is due to two factors. First, the community has received no support from the government. Instead the government's only interest in tourism in the area has been to collect taxes from accommodation providers and extract entrance fees from visitors entering the turtle refuge area. While the University of Costa Rica has a research laboratory within the refuge, their only concern has been in minimising the impacts of tourism on the nesting patterns of the turtles. Secondly, the community lacks information and experience relating to tourism development. Thus even though many local residents feel that tourism is positive for local development, they have great difficulty in identifying economic opportunities tourism could provide them with. In fact, 82 per cent of respondents identified two or fewer opportunities. Furthermore, they did not have a realistic idea of constraints to their participation in tourism initiatives, as only 11 per cent felt that monetary issues might stand in their way and 5 per cent recognised that there were legal impediments, such as restrictions on land use within the reserve (Campbell 1999).

Thus while theoretically ecotourism in Ostional offers great potential for community involvement through provision of food, accommodation and guiding services, it is likely that tourism initiatives will be dominated by individual entrepreneurs, both Costa Ricans and foreigners, in the future, with very little community control. Rather than adopting a regulatory approach to tourism in the area, a proactive approach from government could see regional tourism officers assisting communities such as that at Ostional in accessing the information required on both impediments to their involvement in tourism and providing ideas for appropriate, beneficial community involvement in tourism.

Case study of strong government support: Namibia

During the 1990s the Namibian government, with the support of NGOs and donors, implemented strategies which actively support community involvement in tourism. Some of these strategies are outlined in Table 10.4. Particularly important in creating an enabling environment for community tourism initiatives are the policy and legal changes which encourage communities to establish

Table 10.4   Government support for community involvement in tourism in Namibia

Strategy	Details
Legal rights	In 1996 a legal amendment stated that while wildlife remains the property of the state, communities can form defined management units ('conservancies') which means they are legal guardians of the land and receive conditional use rights over wildlife. Thus they can develop their own tourism enterprises involving consumptive (e.g. hunting) or non-consumptive (e.g. photographic safaris) use of this wildlife
Policy support	There is explicit support for community involvement in tourism in the 1994 White Paper on tourism. Thus when private operators have sought government approval for their enterprises, tourism planners have asked them to seek local approval even when residents actually do not have legal rights over resources. In 1998 the tourism policy was reviewed and comments called for on a new draft tourism policy which places increasing emphasis on community involvement. This is evidenced by the following objectives of the policy, to • 'facilitate better access to factors of production for previously disadvantaged groups, and for women; • improve the enabling environment for the small scale and informal sector; • protect the bio-diversity of Namibia; • embark on economic utilisation of Namibia's natural resources, to the extent possible for a sustainable use of these resources, for the creation of employment and income at both national and community levels' http://www.tourism.com.na/nampol.html
Networking, advocacy and training	In 1995 the government established NACOBTA, the Namibian Community-Based Tourism Association. NACOBTA provides advocacy, training, funding and business advice to help set up effective community tourism projects, and has plans to improve publicity of the projects by initiating a marketing and booking service

Sources: Based on information from Ashley (2000), Kavita (2000), Namibian government (www.tourism.com.na/nampol.html)

conservancies. Conservancies allow communities to earn revenue from tourism in association with their communal lands in the same ways as landowners on commercial land can gain from tourism. In order to encourage communities to capitalise on these new rights the government, through the 1998 draft tourism policy, plans to support training which is targeted at community involvement in tourism and to reinforce the rights of those developing tourism enterprises in association with conservancies (http://www.tourism.com.na/nampol.html).

Such changes have had a major impact, as communities have started to become active in establishing campsites, joint venture tourism projects (such as Damaraland camp discussed in Chapter 11), and offering guiding services, sales of curios and fuelwood. These enterprises have enabled many communities to improve their livelihoods by supplementing the income they gain from agriculture, which is typically minimal because apartheid policies pushed many local people onto marginal land (Kavita 2000).

The government has also impeded community involvement in tourism in some circumstances, however. For example, the wildlife rights of conservancies are conditional, which means communities cannot always influence commercial tourism development (Ashley 2000). Past governments must also claim some responsibility for failing to invest in building the skill base of people in rural areas where the disempowering legacy of an apartheid system remains. Few communities have access to credit or capital, or experience in operating a business. Others are impeded by a lack of infrastructural development in rural areas: 'Without adequate roads, signage, safe water and public toilets, many rural communities with a rich natural and cultural heritage are unable to capitalise on their assets and attract tourists in significant numbers' (Kavita 2000: 9).

Conclusion

Traditional approaches to tourism planning have been top-down and have failed to adequately consider social and environmental issues. As noted by A'Bear et al. (1993), we cannot rely on bottom-up development alone to empower local people, improve their lives and result in better natural resource management. States must face up to their responsibilities in this regard, rather than assuming that the private sector will act in an ethical fashion or that the voluntary sector will ensure local level participation. In practice, however, many governments have been concerned largely with macroeconomic issues, and their legacy is often seen in the form of tourism policies which offer incentives for foreign investors but fail to encourage local participation in the tourism sector. While such policies can help governments to meet their foreign debt obligations, repatriation of profits means that the benefits are often not as great as anticipated and meanwhile the tourism sector becomes dominated by outside interests, rather than the country's own concerns and priorities.

The greatest challenge for Third World tourism planners in the new millennium may be to implement clearly formulated policies which have community and national interests, rather than the interests of supranational institutions (such as the IMF), international investors or local elites at their heart. It will be difficult to achieve this, however, unless the structures of good governance are clearly in place, including transparency of decision-making structures, effective and accountable leadership, a strong legislative framework and enforcement of regulations (Trousdale 1999). Only then will it be possible for states to seek to control the way in which globalisation affects their countries. A fundamental problem at present is identified by Parnwell (1998: 214):

> ... rather than the regulation *of* globalisation, whereby the state picks and chooses those aspects of international engagement which may suit the country's particular interests and needs, governments are more typically involved in regulation *for* globalisation, anxiously seeking to secure global competitiveness to ensure that some crumbs fall in their direction.

It is certainly possible for Third World governments to resist the pressures they may face from outside institutions and to follow a more self-determined, sustainable development path. As de Kadt (1990: 27) asserts, '. . . it is only the state which can provide the conditions for movement towards greater sustainability'. Some Third World governments are already forging a clear direction for tourism development within their shores. There is no single formula for the approach Third World governments should adopt if they wish to prioritise local and national interests, however, and this chapter has discussed a number of quite diverse strategies. The Maldives, for example, protects the social well-being of the local population by minimising their contact with tourists, while the Namibian government supports specific strategies to encourage involvement of local communities in tourism. What both show is that governments can determine their own agenda for tourism development, based on their country's resources, needs and interests.

Many excellent examples of strategies governments can implement to support community involvement in tourism have now been discussed, but the key is that resources are devoted to putting community participation into action. Priority should be placed on coordinating training to build the capacity of communities, providing them with access to capital and, where relevant, secure tenure over communally held land. Communities should not be expected to initiate ventures entirely on their own, however, as in some cases they may prefer to draw on the relevant resources and experience of the government and the private sector through joint venture arrangements. Chapter 11 develops this theme further with a discussion on roles and responsibilities of private sector tourism actors.

Questions

1. Explain the pros and cons of pursuing high-value, luxury tourism both from the perspective of (a) a government Treasury official, and (b) a community leader.

2. Why does the way in which a government manages conservation issues have great significance for the tourism sector in general, and the way in which communities engage with the sector, in particular?

3. List at least three strategies a government can implement if it wishes to support community involvement in tourism.

4. Critically evaluate the worth of 'enclave tourism', such as the development of resort islands in the Maldives separated from local communities. The following quote may help: 'On the one hand they [resorts] serve to concentrate the adverse impacts of tourism to clearly defined and confined areas but, on the other, any positive impacts which might have arisen locally will be likewise confined' (Cater 1995: 196).

5. Go to the first website below and look up three different Third World countries. Consider, in each case, how the government tourism office chooses to promote its country and what this might tell us about the nature of tourism development that is being pursued in each case.

Suggestions for further reading

Brown, D. 1998 'In search of an appropriate form of tourism for Africa: lessons from the past and suggestions for the future', *Tourism Management*, **19**(3): 237–45.

De Kadt, E. 1979 'Politics, planning and control', pp. 18–33 in E. de Kadt (ed.), *Tourism: Passport to development?*, Oxford University Press, Oxford.

Oppermann, M. and Chon, K-S. 1997 *Tourism in Developing Countries*, International Thomson Business Press, London (Chapter 2: Tourism and development).

Trousdale, W. 1999 'Governance in context: Boracay Island, Philippines', *Annals of Tourism Research*, **26**(4): 840–67.

Useful websites

A directory of government tourism offices worldwide. While most individual country sites are devoted to promotional material, some also provide information on tourism policy and planning:

www.towd.com/

The draft tourism policy of the government of Namibia, with a notable focus on community involvement:

www.tourism.com.na/nampol.html

Notes

1. This issue was also raised in the discussion on conservation work by tourists in Chapter 7.

2. For example, it has been suggested in the case of Indonesia that past governments have used tourism 'as a conscious measure . . . to strengthen central control over outlying areas' (Cater 1995: 192).

3. Note, however, that investment in infrastructure for tourism can place a heavy burden on limited government resources. For example, while public funds are used to establish water supply systems which can fill hotel swimming pools and irrigate golf courses, local families may have one water pump to share in their village.

Roles for the tourism industry

Introduction

The tourism industry is rarely identified as an appropriate agent for facilitating the development and empowerment of local communities, largely due to its self-serving profit motive. However, it would be lax to focus a discussion of what can be done to facilitate the development of communities involved with tourism just on the need for governments and non-governmental organisations (NGOs) to take action. While the preceding chapter has shown that governments have a pivotal role to play in setting and enforcing regulations to protect local communities, while also providing mechanisms to support involvement in tourism by communities, and the following chapter will focus on support from NGOs, in the final instance we are still faced with the need for change within the industry itself. Rather than thinking of the industry as a monolithic entity serving no other purpose than to promote economic growth regardless of the cost, this chapter explores ways in which segments of the industry can, and are, changing their practices. Associated benefits for Third World communities will also be highlighted.

A point already made several times in this book is that for tourism to bring maximum benefits and minimal harm to local communities in the future, it will not be sufficient to support their involvement in alternative tourism initiatives. Since the late 1980s there has been an escalation in the number of alternative tour operators on the market, but the changes they are implementing will mean little overall if the mainstream tourism industry fails to reassess its operations: 'Despite moves by the smaller "alternative tour operators", tourism is still a mass event and the operations of large, transnational companies (TNCs) have come to dominate and control most areas of tourism development' (Sobania 1999: 81). It has been suggested for example that tourism in Europe, the world's most visited destination region, will in the future be dominated by only six tourism companies (*Der Spiegel* 1998 cited in Sobania 1999: 81). What is needed, therefore, is transformation of the modus operandi of the mainstream tourism industry, including large companies operating in a multitude of different countries and with a high degree of vertical integration. While in the past tourism NGOs have tended to focus on supporting local action groups opposed to tourism development, there is now a greater focus on working *with* the industry for change. For example, the British NGO, Tourism Concern, has redefined its mission statement to make influencing the industry central to all of the organisation's work, thus it reads: 'To promote change in the tourism industry towards just, sustainable and participatory tourism development' (Lara Marsh, Tourism Concern, pers. comm. June 2000). Radical change may be hard to achieve in light of the attitudes of many industry players, however:

> The chaos brought about by industrial scale tourism is shrugged off by the travel industry which blames it on consumers or governments. Excuses offered by the travel industry such as 'it's what the consumer wants' or 'these local governments don't have proper planning regulations' . . . don't stand up when seen in the light of other businesses (Burns 1999a: 5).

Yet change is evident within the mainstream tourism industry, and this has often been driven by outside forces such as tourism watchdog and environmental pressure groups in the 1970s and 1980s, and more recently by state institutions and holidaymakers themselves. The latter are increasingly showing the industry through their spending decisions that they have a social and/or environmental conscience. Thus while recognising constraints to meaningful change in tourism industry operations, this chapter also highlights examples of good practice to show what can be achieved and what roles the private sector can play in developing a more equitable and responsible tourism industry. As noted by Husbands and Harrison (1996: 1):

> Responsible tourism is *not* a tourism product or brand. It represents a way of *doing* tourism planning, policy, and development to ensure that benefits are optimally distributed among impacted populations, governments, tourists, and investors.

Tourism operators are at the face of interaction with local communities, thus much of this chapter will be dedicated to what they can do to promote community development and empowerment through their work. However, interesting examples are also provided of the roles that guidebook writers, airlines, travel agents, food and accommodation providers and tourism associations can play. All such industry stakeholders fit into Cheong and Miller's (2000) category of 'tourism brokers'. These authors suggest that we pay particular attention to the power of brokers as 'they compel the tourist to function in a certain way', and they 'are prominent in the control of tourism development and tourist conduct' (Cheong and Miller 2000: 381, 386).

Efforts by tour operators to promote community development

As highlighted in the introduction, tourism industry players are not generally seen as advocates of community development. This point is illustrated in Table 11.1, which suggests that all tourism stakeholders except the industry have some interest in community development. Unless the attitude of industry is reversed, the trend which sees 90 per cent of the money spent on tourism and travel around the world going to companies from industrialised countries will continue, while local communities continue to bear the brunt of negative impacts from tourism (http://www.teleport.com/~earthwyz/tourism.htm).

Despite some cynicism about the likelihood of the tourism industry showing a concern for local communities, an examination of tour operators indicates that some are involved in innovative schemes to bring tangible benefits to their 'host' communities. Figure 11.1 shows that British tour operators have sometimes voluntarily adopted environmentally and socially responsible practices, such as giving donations to schools and charities in the destination area and supporting indigenous tourism ventures (Forsyth 1995). Alternative tour operators which attract high fee-paying clients seem more likely than mainstream operators to engage in sustainable tourism practices, however, as shown in Lew's (1998b) research on ecotour operators in North America and the Asia-Pacific region (Figure 11.2). For example, over 75 per cent of the respondents in Lew's study hired local guides, as opposed to less than 20 per cent of the operators in Forsyth's study. Almost half of the ecotour operators provided a percentage of tour profits to local organisations. Furthermore, a study comparing adventure, fishing, cruise line, golf and ecotourism operators in the United States and Canada showed that ecotourism operators had a 'more heightened sense of ethical conduct' and were more likely to follow a code of ethics (Fennell and Malloy 1999: 938).

Table 11.1   Priorities of different tourism stakeholders

Stakeholder	Community development	Conservation	Industry development
Local residents	**	*	
Development NGOs	**	*	
Conservationists	*	**	
Government officials	**	*	**
Donors	**	**	*
Tourism industry		*	**

Source: After Ashley and Roe (1998: 10).

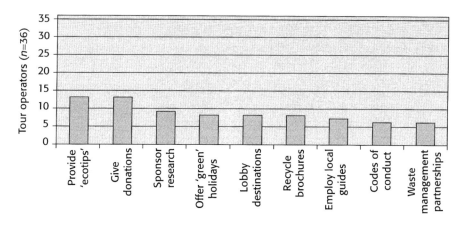

Figure. 11.1   Sustainable tourism practices adopted by British tour operators. (Source: Based on Forsyth 1995: 217)

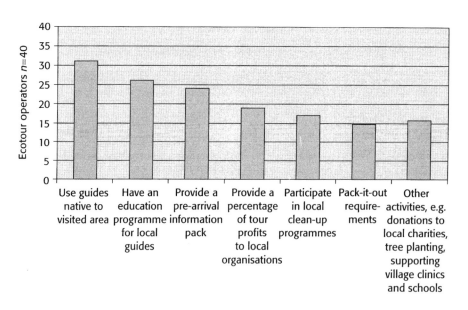

Figure. 11.2   Sustainable tourism practices adopted by ecotour operators in North America and the Asia-Pacific region. (Source: Based on Lew 1998b: 99)

A critical question we could ask of tour operators involved in seemingly altruistic activities, however, is whether they are actually handing any control over tourism to local stakeholders. Mann (2000) provides a three-point scale – from responsible tours, to partnership tours, to community tours – to indicate the degree of community participation different tour operators encourage. In 'responsible tours', a commercial tour operator provides direct benefits to local communities through avenues such as donations to community projects and training local people to be tour guides. For example, tour operator Himalayan Kingdoms has an annual budget for supporting local charities (Mowforth and Munt 1998: 203), and Wildland Adventures aims to maximise the financial gains for local communities from tourism by providing training and employment, particularly for indigenous peoples:

> We give preference to employment of qualified services provided by local communities whenever possible rather than depending exclusively on expatriates or upper-class residents to provide accommodations, guides and staff.... We encourage native peoples, especially of minority ethnic groups with little political power or meaningful economic opportunity, to participate in the operation of our trips as guides, cooks, office staff and managers. We favor local ground operators who are willing to help educate, train and hire indigenous staff (http://www.wildland.com/ecotourism/ecoprinciples.htm).

Despite the benefits they may bring, if 'responsible tours' are controlled entirely by outsiders they are still lower on the scale of community participation than the other two types identified by Mann. At the highest end of the scale, genuine 'community tours' are hard to find, as at this level the community initiates, manages and controls tourism ventures entirely on its own. Many communities simply do not have the important combination of business skills, marketing experience, capital, information on clients or networks to operate at this level. 'Partnership tours' come somewhere in between in the scale of community participation, providing opportunities for a community to cooperate with an outside agency, such as a private tour operator or NGO. This allows the community to have some say in the planning and management of tourism enterprises but they do not have total control. For example, in O'Grady's (1981) checklist for tour operators, he suggests the communities should be involved in advance planning of tours and associated activities (see Box 11.1). 'Partnership tours' can be a particularly appropriate arrangement in situations where communities lack skills and business knowledge vital to the successful functioning of a tourism enterprise (Mann 2000).

Bintang Bolong River Camp in The Gambia provides an example of 'partnership tours'. This camp was established by a French businessman, but with the support of local villagers. The benefits to the villagers have been diverse: sales of materials for construction of bungalows and a restaurant; employment in the resort and associated development of new skills; free electricity; use of some resort transport; and a 10 per cent share of net profits (Wheat 1999a: 7). By examining the Australian company Just Travel, we can see an example of 'partnership tours' which are in practice close to 'community tours' on Mann's spectrum. In this case communities in the Third World initiate and plan the tours, while the role of the tour operator is to attract clients, prepare them for their experience and encourage post-tour reflection:

BOX 11.1

Checklist for responsible tour₁operators

- When the tour is planned, is there full participation by both hosts and guests, or does the group arrive and present a list of their needs and wants?: 'The expectations of both parties must be fully discussed and understood' (O'Grady 1981: 56).
- Are groups kept to manageable numbers (8–15)?
- Does one person understand local customs and speak the local language? Have they fully informed visitors before they begin their travel?
- Does a knowledgeable local person help to guide the group throughout their stay in a country?
- Do they stay long enough in one place to gain an appreciation of the people, culture and environment?
- Are there opportunities for the group to reflect on their experiences and discuss issues with the host during their stay?

Source: O'Grady (1981: 56).

> Pretour preparation is a vital part of any Just Travel experience with several days of learning about the country, the culture, its problems and achievements. Post-tour reflection is also important and participants are encouraged to continue to foster international solidarity with new-found friends (Wenham and Wenham 1984: 09/1).

Any profits from Just Travel are reinvested in alternative tours and ventures in the Third World.

In recent years there has been increasing support for tour operators wishing to transform their practices so they are more in line with responsible tourism. In Australia, for example, the Responsible Tourism Network has been formed by travellers and travel industry personnel concerned about promoting responsible tourism. In addition to efforts to ensure that local communities in the developing world maximise the benefits they can gain from tourism, this organisation provides services for the tourism industry, including assessment of company practice, evaluation of tourism products for wholesalers and resellers, and marketing of appropriate tourism products (www.caa.org.au/travel/rtn/index.html). What is also needed, however, is adequate education of travel agency staff so that they are aware of the range of alternative tourism options and can advise their clients on ways of supporting responsible forms of tourism: 'Undoubtedly "good travel agents" will help promote and influence "good tourism" ' (Wood and House 1991: 64).

As suggested above, 'partnership tours' provide good opportunities for beneficial involvement of local communities in tourism. The following section goes on to elaborate on ways in which equitable partnerships between private sector and community stakeholders can be developed.

Partnerships between industry players and local communities

In order to (a) network with existing tourism services and products, and (b) benefit from the resources and skills of the private sector, it can be beneficial for communities interested in tourism ventures to collaborate with the private sector. This collaboration can be as elaborate as a joint venture luxury lodge, or as simple as an arrangement for a hotel to buy their fruit and vegetable supplies from local villagers. However, it is uncommon for communities to enter into such agreements on a level playing field precisely because of the skills, business experience and resources they may lack. Thus Cater (1995: 201) is concerned that indigenous operators 'cannot hope to compete with the extensive image, power and resources of multinational companies'. Given that 'the fate of tourism projects is sometimes a test of political power and mobilization by different segments of society or different interest groups' (Husbands and Harrison 1996: 12), if private sector actors have more power, then they will be likely to negotiate an agreement which prioritises their interests. Sinclair *et al.* (1992: 60) also warn that a stake in ownership of a tourism venture by local people does not necessarily equate with control over the venture's operations. Thus without adequate support, communities can end up receiving only token economic benefits (e.g. employment in menial positions) from joint tourism developments rather than broader benefits, such as equity in the venture or training for skill development. Community partners will thus typically need strong support in both negotiating and managing such partnerships over the long term. Such support can come from lawyers, NGOs (see Chapter 12), or business advisers.

Examples of partnership opportunities are provided below, starting with the Phinda case study which shows that surrounding communities have gained considerable economic and infrastructural benefits from the development of a luxury lodge but they do not exert a great deal of control over the venture.

Case study: Conservation Corporation Africa at Phinda, South Africa

Conservation Corporation Africa (CCA) is the largest private company in South Africa involved in wildlife tourism. The 17,000 hectare Phinda wildlife reserve in KwaZulu-Natal province is the only one of their developments in which CCA actually owns the land. Four luxury lodge complexes (a rock, mountain, forest and vlei lodge) have been developed at Phinda and tourists have the choice of a range of activities including game viewing, canoeing, fishing and birdwatching.

According to CCA's promotional material, 'Phinda is acclaimed as South Africa's most responsible wildlife tourism project, with its goals of wilderness restoration and community participation' (CCA 1997: 17). With almost 30,000 economically disadvantaged people living around the reserve, community participation is seen as vital to ensure support for Phinda's conservation efforts (Carlisle 1997). CCA does not run joint ventures with local communities; rather, they have established a development fund to benefit these communities (the Rural Investment Fund, or RIF). There are very practical reasons behind this initiative, as seen in the aims of the RIF:

1. to ensure that ecotourism is endorsed by local communities;
2. to promote rural economic development;
3. to advance conservation frontiers (CCA 1997: 23).

CCA guests, who are taken on tours of local communities at their own request, provide most of the funding for the RIF. This money has been used to build 20 schoolrooms and a clinic, to purchase a computer and generator for one school, and to provide training for members of development committees and community leaders. CCA's contribution to the RIF is their management and administration of the fund, which they estimate costs them R500,000 per year. It has been suggested that the RIF provides an excellent example of how 'a private company can act as a catalyst in mobilising funding for community projects' (Wells 1996: 44).

Phinda has also directly contributed to economic livelihoods of the local people in several ways. First, employment has been provided. The land that CCA bought to establish the Phinda reserve was formerly used for raising cattle, game and pineapple. Ecotourism at Phinda, however, is more labour intensive than any of these former uses, employing 350 people in 1998,[1] compared to 64 people employed by the previous landowners. It is estimated that with very low employment rates in this area, the average wage earner supports 10 family members (Les Carlisle, CCA: Author's fieldwork, May 1998). All employees who have worked at Phinda for over six months are involved in training programmes, some of which cover basic skills such as literacy and numeracy. Secondly, Phinda has supported local entrepreneurs, helping one to establish a brick-making business which originally sold bricks for the first lodge at Phinda, and allowing another to set up a charcoal-making business in the reserve using wood which needed to be cleared. The charcoal business employs seven people. Thirdly, Phinda allows sustainable harvesting of certain plants from the reserve, including medicinal plants, wood and thatch (Cherry 1993).

When asked why CCA is apparently so keen to develop positive relationships with surrounding communities, Les Carlisle, Manager of the Phinda reserve, commented: 'Our understanding is that if the local economy does not continue to develop, we don't have a future. We have to get that local community to develop' (Author's fieldwork, May 1998). He also acknowledged that it was beneficial for Phinda that the surrounding communities are now partially dependent on the reserve for their future: 'If they poach, it's not us they're stealing from but themselves.' Outside commentators recognise that for companies such as CCA, interest in local community development is based on pragmatism rather than a philosophical commitment to equity and justice:

> The private reserves, where investors are primarily concerned with wildlife as a business, probably become involved in CWM [community wildlife management] because it makes for good publicity, limits land claims and may limit

the negative activities of unsupportive communities adjacent to their property (Mander and Steytler 1997: 7).

While surrounding communities have gained some direct economic benefits from the establishment of the Phinda reserve, this is not a joint venture and as such they have very little effective control over the way in which the reserve is managed and tourism is promoted in the area.

Source: Author's fieldwork, May 1998.

In many cases local communities could benefit from selling services or products to tourists, including food, crafts or guiding services, but they lack market access. Through developing economic linkages with tourism outlets and agents such as souvenir shops and hotels, such access can be assured. This can offer important economic opportunities for poorer members of communities, in particular, who do not have the capital to establish their own enterprises or the skills to find formal sector employment (Ashley and Roe 1998). Too often such linkages have been shunned by members of the tourism industry, however, because of perceptions of unreliable supplies or low-quality products. Some industry players have been more accommodating, and have found that supporting local producers and service providers can be mutually beneficial. This can be seen in the 'Adopt a Farmer' scheme in St Lucia, a popular island destination in the Caribbean (Box 11.2). In this simple example, there are clear benefits for hotels, restaurants and local farmers, who through a partnership are also saving significant amounts of foreign exchange which would otherwise be spent on importing food and beverages for tourists. As well they are meeting a demand from tourists who hope to find foreign cuisine to accompany their foreign holiday experience, rather than an imported selection of the same food they could eat at home: '. . . when I was in The Gambia, every single item that I ate at my hotel was imported: the eggs, the jam, the wheat for the bread, the milk, tea, coffee, cheese, fruit and vegetables' (Wheat 1999b: 3).

Rather than establishing a tourism venture in isolation from other tourism products and services in the area, it can be very useful for communities wishing to attract tourists to work together with existing enterprises. For example, villagers on the banks of a river who wish to provide accommodation for tourists could offer their services to a canoe safari operator in the area, or they could negotiate a deal with an overland truck company to provide their clients with meals and with campsites equipped with basic toilet and washing facilities. Such overland trucks are a popular means of travel in Africa, yet they typically purchase most of their provisions from big cities and therefore can enjoy rural areas while spending very little money there (Ashley and Roe 1998). Another means of tapping into the existing tourism market would be for villages offering homestay accommodation to be included on routes of backpacker bus services. The Baz Bus in South Africa, for example, travels along routes popular

BOX 11.2

'Adopt a Farmer' scheme in St Lucia

Higher-class hotels often import a majority of the food they serve their guests. This is the case even in countries with a strong agricultural base in contexts where local people could benefit greatly by the opportunity to sell their surplus fruit and vegetables to hotels and restaurants. Relationships between local farmers and food outlets have not developed well in the past, however, due to a number of factors including complaints that peaks in the demand for agricultural produce may not match peaks in supply, quality of produce may be inferior and there is insufficient variety of produce on offer from local farmers.

In response to such concerns, an 'Adopt a Farmer' scheme was initiated by the St Lucia Hotel and Tourism Association in an attempt to assist farmers to diversify their crops to meet the needs of the hospitality industry. One or more farmers would thus be 'adopted' by a hotel on the scheme and would then work closely with both chefs and food and beverage managers to meet the needs of the hotels and ensure quality produce.

The benefits to local hotels of being able to serve fresh, local produce are obvious, and farmers have also gained from learning about how to respond to market demand, developing skills in producing a wider variety of crops, gaining regular income from sales of produce, and earning premium prices for their produce when high quality is maintained. The government of St Lucia also benefits from fewer import leakages.

Source: Based on Tourism Concern (1999a).

with backpackers, offering a flexible drop-off and hop-on service at a number of specified backpacker accommodation providers. There were no village stay options on their schedule in 1998 (Author's fieldwork, May 1998).

Joint ventures which see community resources being used for tourism in exchange for profit-sharing, jobs and other material benefits have also become increasingly popular. Such ventures ideally allow communities to gain skills and confidence in dealing with outsiders but without having ultimate responsibility for the effective running of the business, while simultaneously earning some revenue. In practice joint ventures vary considerably, however, in terms of the degree of control accorded to local communities. Two very good examples of joint ventures which are leading to community ownership over time are provided in Box 11.3.

Non-economic partnerships can also provide important benefits for local communities. For example, local business or tourism associations can run mentoring schemes which link successful tourism entrepreneurs or managers with fledgling community enterprises, helping them to get established or to find strategies to tackle constraints to business success.

While partnerships with the private sector have the potential to bring economic benefits to some people living in 'host' communities, many more of these people are affected on a daily basis by the behaviour of tourists who come to their area. It is vital, therefore, that tourists are well informed about ways in which their actions while on holiday can benefit, rather than harm, local communities.

BOX 11.3

Examples of joint tourism ventures between communities and private companies

Damaraland Campsite, Namibia

A successful joint venture which aims ultimately to give the local community full control and ownership has been developed in the rocky desert landscape of the Torra Conservancy, Namibia. Here a South African business, Wilderness Safaris, established an upmarket accommodation site named Damaraland Campsite in 1996. Ten per cent of the average US$200 occupancy rate per night is paid to the Torra Conservancy. More significantly, Wilderness Safaris have signed a contract which states that they will hand over ownership of Damaraland Campsite to the community in 2006. Meanwhile 13 members of the local community are employed at the camp and can develop appropriate skills and knowledge regarding the management of this successful tourism enterprise (Koro 1999b).

Rainforest Expeditions, Peru

In Peru, a private operator, Rainforest Expeditions, developed a partnership with the village of Infierno which splits the profits of an ecotourism initiative, with 40 per cent going to the company and 60 per cent to the community. After a 20-year period the ownership of the venture will pass into community hands (Stonza 1999).

Giving good advice to tourists

If tourists are to behave in an appropriate and respectful manner when visiting groups of people from vastly different cultures, it is vital that they are well prepared for their visits (Pearce 1995). Without information regarding issues such as ways they can respond to beggars or how one should dress on the street, tourists can find themselves in awkward situations and they may also inadvertently curb local development opportunities:

> We want to interact with local people and enjoy a new environment when we visit a developing country, but all too often we don't have the guidance we need to get the most from our holiday without undermining local customs and culture. And it isn't just tourists who are losing out. People in these destinations often depend on visitors to support the local economy. Without the added confidence good information provides, many holiday makers won't venture beyond the confines of their hotel, depriving local markets, restaurants and other businesses of essential income (Voluntary Service Overseas 1999: 1).

The onus is now increasingly being placed on tour operators and guidebook writers to provide their clients with information on how to behave in a manner which is sensitive to local social, economic and environmental conditions

(Wood and House 1991). The roles that these two groups can play in providing travellers with appropriate information are discussed separately below.

Tour guides or tour operators can play a critical role in mediating relationships between tourists and local people in the destination area. Where they prepare their visitors well with background information on the culture of the people and provide advice on appropriate behaviour, it is more likely that a mutually beneficial cultural exchange will take place. Some operators have made considerable efforts to provide good information to their visitors, such as the German operators who show videos on charter flights to Third World countries about appropriate behaviour for visitors (Wood and House 1991). Such initiatives are the exception rather than the rule, however. A Voluntary Service Overseas (VSO) study of advice given to clients by British tour operators showed that the majority provided inadequate or poor information (Box 11.4). According to VSO (1999), operators could easily make improvements to the advice they give by, for example, adding extra paragraphs on the local economy,

---

BOX 11.4

Survey of advice given by British tour operators

In 1998 Voluntary Service Overseas (VSO) commissioned a survey of 50 small, medium and large tour operators in Britain who sent travellers to Kenya, Tanzania, The Gambia, India and Thailand, to see what types of advice they offered their clients. Advice criteria were developed based on the four following categories:

1. *Respecting local people* (e.g. asking before taking photographs; respecting private property).
2. *Respecting local customs* (e.g. dressing so as not to cause offence; behaviour in holy places).
3. *Interacting with the local economy* (e.g. opportunities to buy local products and use local services; responding to poverty).
4. *Respecting the local environment* (e.g. conserving local resources; not touching coral or picking flowers).

The survey found that while a number of companies were good at providing advice on one of the above categories, particularly environmental issues, they neglected other issues such as social and cultural sensitivity and support for the local economy. It also found that smaller operators were more likely than medium or large-sized operators to provide 'very good' or 'good' advice, but that there were also a number of small operators that offered little or no advice to clients. Meanwhile the large operators, who are responsible for the vast majority of outgoing tourists from the UK, were mainly ranked as offering 'minimum', 'inadequate' or 'poor' advice. Two large operators, however, BA Holidays and Kuoni, came close to the top of the rankings (Figure 11.3). Thus we cannot assume that small, alternative companies will offer better advice to travellers than large companies, and we should not write off the potential of large companies to provide good advice which is in the interests of their clients and of communities in the countries they visit.

BOX 11.4 (CONTINUED)

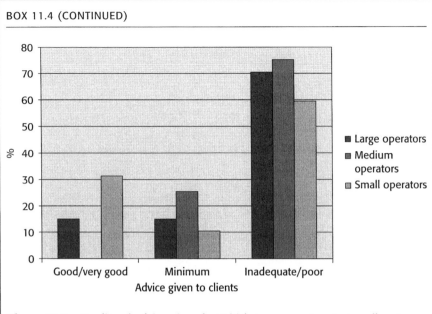

Figure 11.3   Quality of advice given by British tour operators to travellers to selected Third World destinations. (Source: Based on VSO 1999)

Source: Based on Voluntary Service Overseas (1999).

culture and environment to the 'facts about the destination' section of their brochures, and displaying country-specific advice in a clear manner, rather than relegating it to the small print.

Not surprisingly, self-proclaimed alternative tour operators based in Third World countries are leading the way in terms of providing extensive advice to visitors. Ramesh Jangid runs 'Alternative Travels' in his native state of Rajasthan, India, with tours which focus on staying with families in rural areas, using local transport and taking time to discover an area rather than rushing from place to place. Detailed information on preparation for the journey and points about Indian life are provided to clients before their departure. As Jangid (1997: 4) notes,

> We are, I know, expecting a lot from the participants: a good knowledge of India, respect for local customs and laws, and responsible participation in the day-to-day programmes. . . . We expect our European co-ordinators to do far more than just find clients and send them to us. The ones who are sensitive to alternative tourism devote a lot of time to 'orientation programmes'. These study circles and lectures before departure giving general and practical information about our country enable the participants to adapt their behaviour to the new surroundings and make them open-minded to new discoveries.

It is increasingly recognised that guidebook writers also have an enormous responsibility in terms of providing travellers with information which is both accurate and which helps them to act in an appropriate manner when visiting foreign destinations. Guidebooks have revolutionised the world of travel, especially travel to the lesser-known world. While in the 1960s, for example, backpackers numbering in their hundreds made their way across Asia each year, the publication in 1974 of Lonely Planet's first guidebook, *South-East Asia on a Shoestring* (which has come to be known as the 'yellow bible'), contributed to the demystifying of travel in Asia to such an extent that now hundreds of thousands of backpackers flock to this part of the world each year. The fact that travellers will often argue with locals that something is not right because it does not say that in their 'bible' (Sanchez-Gonzalez 1999/2000: 16), is testimony to the power that guidebook publishers have.

Guidebooks are mostly written by outsiders, and without the input of local writers it is unlikely that they will clearly represent the nuances of local culture. Aziz (1999/2000: 4) is concerned, for example, that some guidebooks limit information about the local culture to warnings, '. . . depicting local traditions as nuisances that need to be worked around. Explanation is brief and traveller-focused instead of explaining underlying cultural reasoning.' Backpackers are one sector of the tourism market which tends to rely very heavily on guidebooks for information because this suits their flexible travel schedules. As noted in Chapter 9, because they do not demand luxury standards backpackers can bring considerable opportunities for local communities to be involved in, and benefit from, tourism. There were also some concerns raised about backpacker behaviour, however, which suggest that guidebook publishers need to be very careful about the sort of information they are providing to travellers. In making strange and remote locations seem readily accessible they are opening up new areas and the people who live there to masses of potentially insensitive travellers. Criticisms have also been made about guidebooks popular with backpackers which overemphasise a 'best bargain' mentality (Anderson 1999/2000). This can lead travellers to believe they have to bargain hard to avoid being 'ripped off' by every vendor, hotel owner or tuk tuk driver they come across, when in fact they may be exploiting artisans and traders so desperate for a sale that they accept unreasonably low prices for their products (Bradt 1995).

Some guidebook publishers have certainly made strides, however, to increase the breadth and depth of the information they provide their readers, particularly with regard to cultural and environmental issues (Anderson 1999/2000). Lonely Planet, for example, has an ecology section it its India guidebook, but their environmental sensitivity has not exempted Lonely Planet from being chastised by NGOs for ethical reasons, as will be seen in the following section. Rough Guides' Indian book discusses dam projects and deforestation, and it also includes detailed information on local culture, history and politics. The writer of this book acknowledges, however, that this information may be ignored by many travellers:

... we know that many readers look little further than the listings sections, and at best only skim read our painstakingly researched sketches of contemporary Tamil politics, pigeon fancying in Agra, or sandalwood smugglers in the Nilgiris. That said, I still like to think some of our good intentions rub off and that our approach and insights inspire rather than stifle intelligent interest in the countries we write about (Abram 1999/2000: 5).

Meanwhile, Tourism Concern commissioned a special guidebook, *The Community Tourism Guide* (Mann 2000), devoted to community tourism sites around the Third and Fourth worlds.[2] As well as providing geographical listings of 'exciting holidays for responsible travellers', this guide provides an extensive introduction to issues and principles regarding community tourism, indicating a clear commitment to ethically sound tourism.

The following section moves on to consider how much attention the tourism industry in general has paid to ethical issues concerning travel in the Third World.

Support for ethical issues

To date issues of ethics have generally only been given prominence in tourism industry dialogue when discussions focus specifically on environmental ethics. As the industry's commitment to environmental issues is covered in the following section, this section will consider social ethics. While the World Tourism Organization (WTO) has tried to lead the way by releasing a Global Code of Ethics for Tourism in 1999, thus suggesting principles by which the actions of all stakeholders in tourism should be guided, in practice the code focuses mainly on the rights of tourists and the industry, rather than the communities affected by tourism (Wheat 1999c). Thus while Article 5 stresses the right for host communities to benefit from tourism, in Article 6 the obligations of stakeholders in tourism development are seen in a relatively simplistic light which emphasises protection of clients rather than protection of the people in the places that are visited by their clients.[3] Such inconsistences do not suggest that the WTO is truly committed to ensuring a fair deal for communities involved in tourism.

A forum on Fair Trade in Tourism held in Britain in 1999 and attended by a wide range of tourism stakeholders, identified some impediments to the effective implementation of ethically sound practices in the tourism industry. Even when tourism industry players *want* to be involved in ethically sound initiatives, the practicalities of running a successful business may sometimes stand in the way of the good intentions of both small and large tour operators, for example:

> Small operators who are committed [to ethical tourism], are faced with isolation and a constant struggle to stay in the business with competitive prices and an adequate consumer base without compromising their principles. Large firms are constantly engaged in trying to undercut each other and in initiating mergers in order to remain competitive (http://www.gn.apc.org/tourismconcern).

Furthermore, fragmentation within the industry can hamper support for fair trade:

> Faced with the enormous complexity of suppliers and sometimes complicated political and social conditions in destination communities, it can be difficult to be 'pure' and 'politically correct' throughout the whole of a company's operations (http://www.gn.apc.org/tourismconcern).

Yet some promising initiatives are emerging. Chapter 7 provided examples of tour operators for whom ethics was an integral part of their tours, for example those providing opportunities for clients to build solidarity with oppressed peoples. Malloy and Fennell (1998) also note that many tourism industry players are voluntarily adopting codes of ethics; however, most of the statements in these codes favour environmental and social issues while ignoring economic impacts and benefits. Furthermore, the Fair Trade in Tourism project itself is planning to establish fair trade policy guidelines and measures of fair trade in tourism, with the aim of promoting development and self-reliance in Third World communities. As Evans and Cleverdon (2000) point out, industry-level initiatives (such as establishing consumer awareness of fair trade in tourism ventures) in Western countries which relate to the tourism product will have to be complemented by local economic development strategies within Third World countries if fair trade in tourism is to become a reality (Box 11.5).

A number of organisations within the tourism industry have chosen to take a stand on specific ethical issues. In 1997, for example, the International Federation of Women's Travel Organizations (IFWTO) adopted a resolution against sex tourism. Through this members of the IFWTO resolved '. . . never to promote or assist in the promotion of travel, tours or programs designed for sexual exploitation and to encourage local, regional and national measures to prevent and eradicate "sex tourism"' (www.world-tourism.org/sextouri/ifwto-a.htm).

Similarly, private sector tourism interests have increasingly been involved in campaigns to deter travellers from entering countries where human rights abuses abound, despite the implications this may have for their profit margins. An interesting situation developed, for example, when East Timorese people voted overwhelmingly for independence from Indonesia during a referendum in August 1999, sparking a violent backlash from Indonesian troops and their supporters in the territory. A number of human rights groups advocated boycotting tourism to Indonesia and they were supported by large travel agencies such as Flight Centre, operating in New Zealand and Australia, which refused to service clients wishing to travel to Indonesian destinations such as Bali

BOX 11.5

Dual approach to a fair trade relationship for the tourism industry

1. North (consumers and operators)

Consumer product

- targeted initially at the more aware, 'alternative' tourist
- niche market as for fairly traded coffee, crafts, etc.
- requires fair trade 'branding' through certification/guarantees and monitoring
- must be adopted by associations such as the Association of Independent Tour Operators (UK) and retail chains
- must be promoted in the media, e.g. guidebooks, print and broadcast.

2. South (host-producers and local operators)

Local economic development

- fair trade relationship with tour operators and other fair trade organisations (e.g. crafts, cultural, aid)
- preferential relationship with regional/national host government and institutions (financing, credit, planning, employment, training, promotion)
- requires use of small-medium enterprise business networks
- requires joint promotion and marketing, training, technology sharing and transfer (e.g. IT, marketing).

Source: After Evans and Cleverdon (2000: 144).

during this time. Similarly, the East Timor conflict provided the catalyst for the British Guild of Travel Writers to take their first ever ethical stance on travel to a particular destination: they issued a press release urging tour operators and tourists to boycott Indonesia until there was peace in East Timor. The guild's vice-chairman, Peter Lilley, provided the following explanation for their action:

> It is quite unacceptable that foreign holidaymakers should continue to visit Bali and Lombok after the appalling catalogue of atrocities in East Timor – carried out with the tacit approval of the Indonesian authorities. . . . Individual tourists and tour operators offering holiday packages to Bali and Lombok have got to examine their consciences. It is all too easy to stand by and convince oneself that the matter does not concern you or that there is nothing you can do (cited in Wheat 1999d: 5).

While the British Guild of Travel Writers are openly supportive of travel boycotts for ethical reasons, this is not the case with one of the major guidebook publishers, Lonely Planet. NGOs have been urging tourists to stay away from Burma[4] because of the direct links between the development of tourism and human rights abuses in this country (Parnwell 1998). Specifically, millions of

Burmese have been forced to provide labour on the military regime's projects, including tourism development, which they hope will attract private investment. In addition, income generated through tourism supports the military government. The Burma Campaign UK and Tourism Concern have gone so far as to call for a boycott of Lonely Planet publications, because they published a new edition of their guide to Burma in January 2000.[5] Their actions were in direct contradiction to the wishes of the country's pro-democracy leader, Aung San Suu Kyi, as quoted below:

> Guide book writers should listen to their consciences and be honest about their motivations. Profit is clearly their agenda. It's not good enough to suggest that by visiting Burma tourists will understand more. If tourists really want to find out what's happening in Burma – it's better if they stay at home and read some of the many human rights reports there are (http://www.tourismconcern.org.uk/frame.htm).

The greatest power to influence the industry undoubtedly comes from its clients. This is particularly obvious with respect to 'green' consumers demanding environmentally sustainable products, but also occurs with social issues. For example, Leheny (1995) noted that the reluctance of Japanese women to travel to 'sex tourism' destinations has forced the Thai government to look for ways to 'clean up' its tourism industry. Women travellers generally are being increasingly recognised as an important segment of the tourism market. In fact, they make up over 50 per cent of tourists in some specialist segments such as ecotourism (Obua and Harding 1996; Pearce and Wilson 1995). This power of numbers could give women travellers greater opportunities to influence the nature of tourism products and the future of tourism development. Indeed Enloe (1990) suggests that feminist action from the consumers of tourism could lead to positive change within the industry.

Efforts to achieve environmental sustainability

The corporate world in general has latched on to the popularity of 'green' discourse (Milne 1998), thus it comes as no surprise to find tourism businesses supporting a wide range of environmental initiatives, from donations to conservation organisations to efforts at self-regulation. Undoubtedly some tourism businesses have come up with excellent schemes to support environmental sustainability but the real question remains, is the mainstream industry supporting just the greening of its *image*, or the greening of its *practices*? Some suggest that environmental measures are adopted by tourism companies purely for reasons of self-interest, and this theory is supported by a survey conducted by state tourism and environmental institutions in Germany. The survey found that tourism businesses would support environmental measures under certain conditions, specifically:

- if they reduced costs, e.g. through water or energy savings;
- if they improved the image of the business, lending them a competitive edge;
- if they resulted in fewer complaints from clients;
- if they improved the attractiveness of a destination when otherwise pollution, traffic noise and so forth was detrimental to business;
- if they helped to preserve in the long term the natural resource base upon which tourism is dependent (cited in Sobania 1999: 88).

Clearly economic advantages – in terms of cost savings, increased business and improved image, with customers often willing to pay premium prices for a green product – are the greatest motivation for tourism businesses with an interest in supporting environmental protection measures. The tourism industry is acutely aware that it is facing increasing media scrutiny at the same time that the public is demanding to see evidence of corporate responsibility. However, it would be overly cynical to reject all environmental initiatives by tourism businesses on the basis of industry self-interest:

> To dismiss these expressed environmental concerns as merely marketing ploys is to understate . . . the importance of these concerns expressed both within certain social groups and by the companies themselves; many small companies have an undeniably genuine commitment to environmental issues (Mowforth and Munt 1998: 62).

Several very large companies associated with the tourism industry are now implementing environmentally friendly practices. In Germany, for example, nearly every large tour operator employs an environmental manager. The major German tour operator, Studiosus Reisen, also lists available aeroplanes with their respective energy consumption in their catalogues (Sobania 1999). British Airways (BA) provides another example of a large corporation with a good reputation for environmental awareness. BA's efforts to achieve environmental sustainability include:

- the establishment of an Environment Branch which ensures other branches are adopting appropriate practices by meeting regularly with their directors;
- offering environmental awards (specifically, the 'Tourism for Tomorrow Awards', one of which was awarded to Sunungukai camp, discussed in Chapter 6);
- reviewing the location of its main airports and their impacts on the local environment;
- using external consultants to undertake research; and
- initiating a Green Light programme through which employees are encouraged to provide suggestions for ways of minimising the environmental impacts of BA.

These efforts are laudable and many other tourism companies could learn from them, but to keep BA's environmental efforts in perspective, in relation to general company operations the £425,000 BA spent on its Environment Branch in 1995 constituted under 0.06 per cent of the company's operating profit for 1995/6 (Mowforth and Munt 1998: 219). Furthermore, it is important to recognise that larger tourism companies have greater resources than smaller ones (Milne 1998), and while this puts them in a better position to invest funds in environmental initiatives, this also makes it more likely that they can manipulate environmental tools and use 'greenspeak' to influence public opinion to serve their own ends (Sobania 1999).

With this cautionary note in mind, the following section moves on to consider specific efforts by the industry to regulate its own environmental practices, and explores why the industry is so supportive of self-regulation.

Self-regulation of industry activities

With continuing rapid growth in tourism internationally, regulation of this market will be absolutely critical in the future both for the well-being of the planet as a whole, and to ensure the protection of the resources and interests of local communities in destination areas. The tourism industry generally proffers strong support for self-regulation rather than government regulation (Milne 1998).[6] Garrod and Fyall (1998: 201) comment on the enthusiasm with which members of the industry have embraced tools for the management of tourism: '. . . although the academic debate regarding sustainable tourism is really still in its infancy, the tourism industry itself has already begun to react energetically to the sustainability imperative'. However, industry support for self-regulation does not necessarily equate with a strong motivation towards pursuing sustainable tourism more generally. As mentioned in Chapter 10, a survey of British tour operators revealed that the majority felt that host governments had most, or total, responsibility for promoting sustainable tourism:

> Not one commercial operator interviewed saw ultimate responsibility for action [for implementing sustainable tourism] as lying with themselves. This . . . casts great doubt on the effectiveneess of current self-regulatory measures, and suggests that many of these may indeed be superficial or seeking to achieve good public relations rather than long-term change (Forsyth 1995: 226).

Thus when considering environmental tools tourism companies are now using, including environmental auditing, codes of conduct and certification schemes, we need to consider whether '. . . they promote genuine change in practices or cosmetic change which serves as good publicity but which makes little effective difference' (Mowforth and Munt 1998: 235). Environmental auditing is a process which tests or verifies aspects of environmental management (McManus 2000), but the focus is on means of making a company's operations more efficient, with efficiency being narrowly perceived as a means of cost reduction. Codes of conduct, or practice, generally refer to 'A set of guidelines laying down standards, to which members of a profession or association are expected to adhere in the exercise of their activities' (Medlik 1993: 32). However, there are no universal standards which guide the construction of codes of conduct in the tourism industry (Lew 1998b), leaving it open to individual operators to devise a list which suits their interests, may not be based on consultation with affected communities, and may require little effective change in the way in which they operate (Forsyth 1995). Meanwhile they can still cite adherence to such a code in their promotional material (Mowforth and Munt 1998). An additional problem with codes of conduct is that they often cannot be enforced because they do not include measurable criteria. For example, if conservation of resources and reduction of pollution are advocated, *how much* conservation and pollution reduction is sufficient (Garrod and Fyall 1998: 202)? It is also worth noting that both codes of practice and environmental auditing generally lack verification by an independent body: 'The industry will gain credibility for its internal changes only if it subjects them to external criteria and assessment' (Mowforth and Munt 1998: 221). Without both measurable criteria and independent verification, there is a danger that 'Rather than to solve the sustainability problem . . . simple guidelines and codes of good practice may serve only to trivialise it' (Garrod and Fyall, 1998: 202).

Another increasingly popular tool used by the industry is certification schemes. Certification schemes typically involve setting standards by which a particular economic activity can be monitored, and putting in place a system to verify that appropriate means are being used to reach these standards. Supporters of certification schemes argue that they are more verifiable and rigorous than other means of self-regulation, such as codes of conduct, and in practice, many certification schemes do involve strong input from an independent body. The industry's most prominent certification scheme, Green Globe 21, however, recently received heavy criticism in an independent report commissioned by the WWF, entitled *Tourism Certification: An analayis of Green Globe 21 and other certification programmes* (WWF 2000). One concern was a lack of clarity in use of its logo, as Green Globe logos are awarded as soon as a company commits to undertake the certification programme. The logo for achieving certification is only slightly different from the original logo. Another problem raised was that to achieve certification, companies are required to have a management system in place for reducing environmental impacts, but they are not required to meet standard, measurable criteria on environmental performance. The importance of a well-recognised, credible certification scheme for the tourism industry was strongly supported, however, and a number of suggestions made concerning how this could be achieved:

1. There are over 100 certification schemes used within the tourism industry at present. An umbrella accreditation body is needed to establish universal standards and allow comparisons among the different schemes.
2. Logos must only be awarded to companies which achieve stated performance criteria, not simply for establishing environmental management processes or signing up with a certification scheme.
3. Certification should cover social and economic aspects of sustainability, not just environmental sustainability (WWF 2000).

A sector-specific certification scheme for the hotel industry has been adopted in Costa Rica. Here the national tourism institute (ICT) has evaluated hotels with its sustainable tourism certification programme. It has been suggested that the scheme's greatest success has been to change the attitudes of tourism business people: 'They have more of a holistic vision now. . . . They are not thinking just about their business, but also about the environment in which it is immersed' (Rosaura Monge, ICT natural resources division, cited in Greentour Email Discussion List posting, 13 June 2000).

Conclusion

The tourism industry, particularly as it operates in the Third World, has received a lot of bad publicity often based on the activities of large-scale corporations, profit-hungry developers and tour operators with few scruples. It would not be fair to use this information to characterise an entire industry, however, and as this chapter has shown, private tourism stakeholders are responding positively to pressure from various domains to display greater social and environmental responsibility. These changes should not be taken for granted in an industry characterised by extreme competition and where the short-term need to make profits could easily stand in the way of long-term strategies to improve business practice, from an ethical standpoint (Forsyth 1995).

It is not difficult to find examples of good practice, such as Just Travel and Rainforest Expeditions, given the size and breadth of the industry. However, as Mowforth and Munt (1998: 209) comment: '. . . such initiatives are laudable and are worthwhile in themselves; they are to be encouraged. But their ability to solve most, if not all, of the problems caused by the tourism industry is imaginary.' What is more important than a few good examples of tourism ventures is that there is a general change in the operations of tourism industry players so that it is not profits alone which dictate how all decisions are made. Examples herein include evidence of ethical responsibility in the British Guild of Travel Writers' travel boycotts, and those supporting the Fair Trade in Tourism initiative. Widespread evidence of corporate responsibility in the tourism industry is needed, however. Cannon (cited in Burns 1999a: 4–5) suggests there are five elements to corporate responsibility:

1. 'the social, economic and moral responsibilities of firms and managers;
2. compliance with legal and voluntary requirements for business and professional practice;
3. the corporation and the environment;
4. the challenges posed by the needs of the economically and socially disadvantaged;
5. management of the corporate responsibility activities of business.'

While this chapter has shown that the tourism industry is quite strong on complying with requirements for business and professional practice (point 2), and that companies, even large ones such as British Airways, are increasingly implementing environmentally sound practices (point 3), there is less evidence of the industry rising to the challenges of economically and socially disadvantaged peoples, particularly in destination areas (point 4). Thus while tourism industry players have made considerable efforts to act in a more environmentally sensitive manner (Holder 1996), they have often failed to take on board some of the broader principles of sustainable development, especially justice and equity (Milne 1998). It is important that increasingly popular regulatory measures such as codes of conduct cover social and economic issues as they relate to local communities, not just environmental criteria. Also, while the actions of some operators in providing donations and other assistance to community organisations, health clinics and schools are undoubtedly appreciated by the communities concerned, this could just be seen as a means of 'keeping the locals happy' so that they will continue to cooperate and be welcoming to tourists. There is little overall evidence of communities occupying tourism destination areas in the Third World having the power to influence the industry to minimise the harm and maximise the benefits they gain from tourism. While some operators and service providers (such as lodge owners) are engaging in profit-sharing initiatives with local communities, it is relatively rare to find communities actively managing tourism enterprises, on their own or in partnership with private sector interests. This is perhaps where the biggest changes still need to come about.

Thus there is a need for vigilance on the part of government agencies responsible for regulating tourism (Chapter 10) and NGOs (Chapter 12), to ensure that the industry is promoting responsible tourism, not just promoting increasing tourism dressed up in environmental clothes to deceive a public eager to consume green products. To the industry, government regulation is seen as an unnecessary interference and hindrance to their operations, and something which inherently opposes the dominant free market doctrine (Mowforth and Munt 1998). If regulations requiring independent verification are put in place, however, to measure the level of compliance with certification schemes, codes of practice and the like, this will certainly benefit consumers and aid them in making responsible choices about their travel options.

Questions

1. When the private sector engages with a local community in 'partnership tours', explain what benefits each party can get from this relationship.

2. If you were to book a hiking trip in the Andes with a self-proclaimed 'responsible tour operator', list five criteria you would expect them to meet.

3. Suggest some measures which large tourism organisations, such as tour operators and airlines, can implement in support of environmentally and socially sustainable tourism.

4. Is there a fundamental tension between the main motivation of the tourism industry, to make profits, and the more recent interest of the industry in supporting environmental sustainability?

Suggestions for further reading

Bhattacharyya, D. 1997 'Mediating India: an analysis of a guidebook', *Annals of Tourism Research*, **24**(2): 371–91.

Fennell, D.A. and Malloy, D.C. 1999 'Measuring the ethical nature of tourism operations', *Annals of Tourism Research*, **26**(4): 928–43.

Font, X. and Buckley, R. 2001 *Tourism Ecolabeling: Certification and Promotion of Sustainable Management*, CABI Publishers, New York.

Krippendorf, J. 1987 *The Holiday Makers*, Heinemann, London (Chapter 16: School for a more human tourism).

Mowforth, M. and Munt, I. 1998 *Tourism and Sustainability: New Tourism in the Third World*, Routledge, London (Chapter 7: The industry: lies, damned lies and sustainability).

Stonza, A. 1999 'Learning both ways: lessons from a corporate and community ecotourism collaboration', *Cultural Survival Quarterly*, **23**(2): 36–9.

Useful websites

For examples of 'best practice', profiling companies whose activities contribute to the long-term development of communities and environments in which the tourism industry operates, see Business Enterprises for Sustainable Travel (BEST):
   www.conference-board.org

For references and links on accreditation, certification and rating systems for sustainable tourism, see:
   www.kiskeya-alternative.org/certif/refer-certif-eng.html

For examples of responsible tourism operators, see:
   www.dreamweavertravel.net/eco.htm
   www.teleport.com/~earthwyz/tourism.htm

Website of the World Travel and Tourism Council (WTTC) whose members are chief executives from all sectors of the travel and tourism industry. They work with governments to promote the industry:
   www.wttc.org/

Briefing paper on corporate social responsibility in the tourism industry:
www.tourismconcern.org.uk/fair%20trade/corporate_social_responsibility.htm

Notes

1. Around 20 employees with specialist skills were brought in from outside the area, while the rest were locals.

2. The Fourth World is a term sometimes used to refer to indigenous communities still living as 'colonies' within either Western or Third World countries.

3. For the full text of the Global Code of Ethics for Tourism, see www.world-tourism.org/pressrel/CODEOFE.htm.

4. Note that the military junta changed Burma's name to Myanmar, but pro-democracy groups still prefer to use the name Burma.

5. Lonely Planet have sent responses to those who have criticised publication of the Burma guide, defending their action on the grounds that withdrawing their guide-book would effectively silence one of the regime's long-standing critics. They also point out that there are ways travellers to Burma can ensure that their money supports local communities rather than the military. For more details of their perspective, see http://www.lonelyplanet.com.

6. Milne (1998) suggests that self-regulation may simply not be workable because many of the resources upon which tourism depends, including national parks, coastal areas and waterways, are common property resources, thus there is little incentive for private business operators to act in an environmentally responsible way when using these resources.

CHAPTER 12

Roles for non-governmental organisations and local action groups

Introduction

This chapter focuses on ways in which non-governmental organisations (NGOs) can support communities that wish to engage with tourism. In an ideal world, communities would devise and initiate sustainable and successful tourism ventures entirely by themselves, but at present the reality is that they often lack the experience, networks and skills to be able to do this, and thus appropriate outside assistance is often required (Mann 2000). Also examined in this chapter are the means by which NGOs and local action groups can work with communities which are seeking to influence the nature of tourism development, or to protect the rights and well-being of people living in areas of extensive tourism development. Parnwell (1998) asserts that the emergence of NGOs and advocacy groups within a number of Third World states has enhanced local power to resist or transform tourism.

NGOs have been identified as civil society actors which are well placed to effectively promote community development (Brohman 1996b; Edwards and Hulme 1995). This is largely because they are not-for-profit organisations, and they do not directly represent the interests of the state. Thus it is suggested that NGOs can provide a neutral means of support for communities, and play advocacy and watchdog roles, for example. The involvement of NGOs in tourism planning and management has not always been valued in practice, however. For example, an assessment of the extent to which stakeholders involved in the planning of a tourism project in Brazil represented the diverse interests of those who would be affected by the project, revealed that there was disturbingly low participation of environmental NGOs and community groups (Medeiros de Araujo and Bramwell 1999).

While NGOs may have a great deal to offer the tourism sector, this does not mean that they should escape critical analysis: 'NGOs can clearly have an important role in building local economies and in advocacy for policies that strengthen local control, [however] not all NGOs are created equal' (Mowforth and Munt 1998: 186). A useful way of discerning whether NGOs take an approach which emphasises dependency of local people, or an approach which facilitates local empowerment, is to draw on David Korten's (1987: 147) classification of three generations of NGOs:

1. welfare/relief;
2. self-reliance through capacity-building;
3. sustainable systems development, including advocacy and involvement in the policy process.

Korten is essentially suggesting that NGOs which are situated primarily in the first generation cannot hope to challenge or change existing inequities in society. And while those in the second generation are promoting capacity-building for self-reliance, they are not yet equipping people with the means for self-determination within their social and political lives. This framework will be used in the conclusion of this chapter to analyse the effectiveness of NGOs which have a self-professed interest in the tourism sector.

The discussion to follow will focus mainly on the positive aspects of NGOs showing that they can be very important players in the tourism field, particularly if they use their resources, networks and technical expertise to facilitate the empowerment of communities which wish to be, or are, involved in tourism. The strategies these NGOs use are broken into two categories:

1. those which actively support involvement of communities in tourism;
2. those focusing on minimising the negative impacts of tourism.

With relation to this second category, the work of local action groups is also explored. For example, there are very strong tourism lobby groups in Goa, India, but not all are formalised into what we might call NGOs. NGOs and local action groups whose main focus is campaigning about the negative impacts of tourism can be found in both the Third World and the West. Western-based NGOs are often well placed to assist with funding and publicity for community tourism initiatives, and to raise the awareness of Western travellers and tour operators about alternative, responsible travel options. Meanwhile, Third World NGOs are better positioned to work directly with communities to build capacity, facilitate collaborative ventures with private sector partners, provide technical support, training and information, and arrange study tours to tourism sites for community members.

Strategies of tourism NGOs which support community involvement in tourism

Among the primary motives of NGOs encouraging communities to be involved in tourism are poverty alleviation, the desire to diversify local economies, and capacity-building among local people (Ashley and Roe 1998: 9). The specific strategies of such NGOs which are examined below and summarised in Table 12.1

Table 12.1   Strategies of NGOs which support community involvement in tourism

Strategy	Activities	Examples
Information and awareness-raising for communities	• Market surveys on tourism potential • Dissemination of information on tourism options for local communities, e.g. small- versus large-scale ventures, collaboration with the private sector • Study tours of tourism sites for community members	• Noah's eco-cultural tours (see Chapter 9) – a British volunteer conducted a market survey to determine ways in which Noah could expand his guiding business • Sunungukai camp, Zimbabwe (see Chapter 5) – Zimbabwe Trust and overseas volunteers arranged a study tour which highlighted ways they could improve their facilities for tourists and avert potential problems
Building capacity and increasing confidence	• Building confidence of community members in dealing with government officers, private sector interests and tourists • Training in marketing, management, customer service • Publishing books on the 'how-to' of community involvement in tourism, such as constructing a cultural village or providing guided tours	• NGOs in Nepal – provide education and training to develop confidence and skills of women involved in trekking tourism • Indonesian Ecotourism Network – produced training material on community participation in ecotourism and a book on 'How to become a good ecotourism guide'
Networking	• Bringing people together to work on tourism issues or projects • Forging partnerships with local communities • Providing a representative body for community tourism initiatives • E-mail discussion groups • Attracting funding for community tourism initiatives • Creating linkages between communities and existing tourism enterprises, e.g. communities could supply lodges with produce	• Tourism Concern (UK) – coordinated formulation of a Himalayan trekking code with resident groups and overseas tour operators • Rethinking Tourism Project (USA) – electronic newsletter which keeps indigenous groups informed about tourism conferences, meetings and policy-making forums • Namibia Community-Based Tourism Association (NACOBTA) – represents community tourism initiatives including campsites, traditional villages and craft centres, accessing training and funding on their behalf

Table 12.1   *(cont'd)*

Strategy	Activities	Examples
Promotion of responsible tourism within the industry	• Promotion of responsible community ventures to the tourism industry • Running not-for-profit tours which have a social justice and/or cultural exchange element • Attempts to transform the way in which interests in the mass tourism industry approach their work • Awards for responsible tourism	• ACTSA – campaign for 'People-First' tourism to southern Africa which encourages the UK tourism industry to support initiatives which benefit local people • Global Exchange (see Chapter 7) – organise tours to Chiapas, Mexico, where visitors learn about the revolutionary struggle and local development initiatives • VSO (UK) – WorldWise Tourism Campaign encourages hotels to source their products locally and tour operators to ensure their tours bring local benefits • Studienkreis für Tourismus und Entwicklung (Germany) – 'ToDo! Awards' reward environmentally and socially responsible tourism
Promotion of responsible tourism among visitors	• Information for tourists on ways to support community involvement in tourism • Guidelines for tourists on how to behave and respect cultural norms in the destination country • Information for tourists on activities/countries to avoid on their travels because they violate human rights	• Tourism Concern (UK) – published *The Community Tourism Guide* • Equations (India) – helps travellers locate environmentally and culturally sensitive tourism projects in India • Tourism Concern (UK) and VSO – produce in-flight videos to inform travellers of appropriate behaviour and cultural norms in their destination country • Gambia Tourism Concern – produced a brochure entitled *Tips for Tourists*
Implementing conservation and development programmes	• Supporting ecotourism initiatives as a means of local communities benefiting from resource conservation initiatives • Building capacity so that local communities can be involved in protected area management (e.g. sit on parks boards) or management of wildlife on communal lands	• Conservation International, Ecotourism Department (Washington, DC) – provides training to support community-based ecotourism programmes • CAMPFIRE and Zimbabwe Trust – training in wildlife management and democratic processes for making decisions about proceeds from safari hunting tourism

Sources: Based on information from Bah (1999/2000); Gurung (1995); Joppe (1996); Mann (2000); Scheyvens (2002); http://indecon.i-2.co.ed

are: information and awareness-raising for local communities; building capacity and raising confidence; networking; promotion of responsible tourism; and implementation of conservation and development programmes.

Information and awareness-raising for communities

An important role NGOs can perform is to provide communities with information about ways in which they can be involved with tourism before they decide whether or not this is a viable or desirable path for them to follow (Joppe 1996). Local people cannot participate equitably in a tourism venture without adequate information and the confidence to ask questions and put forward ideas. For example, inadequate information can make communities vulnerable when considering joint venture agreements with the private sector. There is a need for appropriate mechanisms to foster information dissemination, especially in countries where impoverished rural communities have been disenfranchised from the domains of power for many years. For example,

> . . . one of the greatest requirements in South Africa today, is to enable communities to rediscover themselves and to participate fully in an integrated political, social, cultural and economic milieu along with the opportunities and responsibilities that this offers (A'Bear *et al.* 1993: 1).

In essence, information is essential to overcome the disadvantage that most local communities face when engaging with the tourism sector, that is, 'The local destination remains relatively isolated from the international market, receiving tourists but not understanding or playing any part in controlling the terms on which, and the processes by which, they arrive' (Goodwin *et al.* 1997: 5).

Pearce (1995) and Timothy (1999) thus suggest that education of host communities is vital for socially appropriate, sustainable tourism development. This education can take a number of forms and evolve over a number of stages. Pre-tourism development, for example, could include involving communities in market research. A market survey is very important in establishing whether or not a proposed tourism venture will actually be viable in the form in which it is planned, yet communities often need outside help, which NGOs can provide, to do this (Joppe 1996). They need to consider, for example, whether or not tourists are already attracted to the location. If not, and if the site is somewhat isolated or distant from major transport and communication routes, it may have low potential for attracting tourists. Chapter 9 discussed the case study of Noah's eco-cultural tours in Chimanimani, Zimbabwe. Noah had originally guided tourists on treks through the picturesque Eastern Highlands, but with the help of a market survey conducted by a VSO volunteer working for the local council, Noah could see that there was a real demand for cultural tours in the area as well. On the basis of this information he diversified his small business and has found he is in more demand for the cultural tours than for the mountain tours.

BOX 12.1

The value of study tours

A very useful exercise can be for NGOs to organise for community members to go on a study tour to visit existing community tourism ventures so they can learn about the pros and cons of tourism from others who have pursued this option. This is very important, as many communities initially expect to earn a great deal of money from tourism and this is simply not realistic in many cases. In other situations, they may be able to benefit economically from tourism, but if they do this by leasing their land to a hotel developer, for example, this may be at great cost to their local ecosystem because of inappropriate disposal of wastes from the hotel and it may result in social and cultural breakdown. By talking to people on their own level who have already tried such ventures, it is easier for community members to accurately weigh up the value of pursuing different forms of tourism – such as a large joint venture lodge versus a small self-run bed and breakfast business – and to decide whether tourism is a desirable strategy for their development. Through study tours people can also learn about potential problems they may encounter, and ways of providing adequate facilities for tourists.

It is important, however, that a wide range of interest groups from within communities have the chance to benefit from the information garnered from study tours. For example, when leaders of a community near Sodwana Bay, South Africa, were invited by the Natal Parks Board to attend a study tour to assess ecotourism ventures, they insisted that a video camera should be made available so that they could record what they had seen and show this to the rest of the community on their return. Otherwise, they explained, such trips may be seen largely as 'perks' for select community members rather than educational exercises to help the community make informed plans for the future (Jone Porter, Natal Parks Board: Author's fieldwork, May 1998).

NGOs can also encourage communities to be involved in tourism planning, provide opportunities for them to engage in study tours of other tourism sites (see Box 12.1), and disperse information on the potential and pitfalls of community involvement in tourism. Preferably such information should be translated into local languages and should use visual media, such as videos. Once tourism is established, efforts can be made to ensure that local communities are aware of the patterns of tourism in their area, including most popular sites, busy times and how tourists might behave.

Building capacity and raising confidence

If communities choose to go ahead with a tourism venture, they will generally need ongoing training to (a) build their capacity to run a successful venture, and (b) develop their confidence to deal with tourists, private sector partners or government agencies, from whom they may need permission to establish a tourism enterprise. Too often it is assumed that the presence of wildlife or cultural features in a site of scenic beauty, combined with a community enthusiastic about developing a tourism venture, is sufficient to make the venture successful. There are unfortunately numerous cases of communities generating funding to build structures and employing people to service and manage a small tourism enterprise and then feeling bewildered and disappointed when the tourists do not 'just pour in'. For example, at Sunungukai Camp, in rural Zimbabwe (discussed in Chapter 6), the community won a British Airways 'Tourism for Tomorrow' award for establishing chalets for tourists in a picturesque riverside location; however, these chalets have extremely low occupancy rates. Without proper management and publicity, even seemingly ideal community tourism initiatives can fail.

Both communities themselves and outside sponsors, such as donors, have not always recognised the amount of management and marketing experience which is needed by a community if they are to run a successful tourism venture. Tourism as an enterprise has in many countries been dominated by outside operators – from overseas or large cities – thus without adequate preparation and training, few local people are likely to have a good understanding of how tourism ventures work or what tourists want. In addition, they often have to compete with established tourism ventures run by agencies with excellent customer service skills and business management expertise. While tourists supporting community tourism ventures may not expect all of the comforts of home, the romantic vision of sleeping in basic thatched roof huts can soon come into conflict with Western expectations of service and facilities if it starts to rain and there is a leak above one's head. Similarly, many tourists are not prepared to bathe with a bucket of cold water or use newspaper, water or grass instead of toilet paper.

Some NGOs have initiated excellent initiatives to build capacity. In Nepal, NGOs have assisted women to develop their self-confidence and become actively engaged in trekking tourism through providing education and training for them (Gurung 1995). Meanwhile in Indonesia, INDECON (the Indonesian Ecotourism Network) has supported capacity-building by establishing training material to facilitate community participation in ecotourism in selected areas and by publishing a book *How to Become a Good Ecotourism Guide* (http://indecon.i-2.co.id).

Networking

Because of the relative lack of power of local communities in relation to other players in the tourism sector, networking can provide an important means of sharing information and forging partnerships. This can involve bringing different stakeholders together to work on tourism issues or projects. Tourism Concern (UK), for example, coordinated formulation of a Himalayan trekking code with resident groups and overseas tour operators. Other NGOs have formed regional, national or international forums for sharing ideas and information on tourism. An example of a national-level body is the Namibia

Community-Based Tourism Association (NACOBTA), which represents community tourism initiatives including campsites, traditional villages and craft centres, accessing training and funding on their behalf. Other NGOs rely on electronic forums to publicise their work and build linkages among likeminded people around the globe. Rethinking Tourism Project, for example, distributes its electronic newsletter to over 400 indigenous people's groups and organisations.

Promotion of responsible tourism within the industry

In recent years NGOs have started to make efforts to shape the direction taken by the tourism industry. Some have done this by promoting alternative forms of tourism which are both sustainable and responsible, to ensure that private sector operators and the travel industry in general are aware that these options exist. The forum on Fair Trade in Tourism mentioned in Chapter 11 supported this notion, suggesting that just as NGOs such as Oxfam (UK) had established successful outlets for fair trade commodities such as coffee and crafts, it was possible to promote fair trade in tourism (see Fair Trade Forum Report – http://www.gn.apc.org/tourismconcern/). An example of an NGO promoting the involvement of communities in tourism is ACTSA (Action for Southern Africa). Moving on from its previous anti-apartheid work, ACTSA endeavours to support peace, democracy and development across southern Africa. As such it has identified tourism as one means of achieving local level development. Through the 'People-First' tourism campaign ACTSA actively challenges the UK travel industry to put African people first when planning their holidays. To stem the flow of leakages, for example, they encourage the industry to support hotels which source their products locally and to support tourism ventures which ensure profit retention by local communities (Liz Dodd, Policy Officer for ACTSA, pers. comm., 10 September 1998). The latest stage in their campaign has been the launch of postcards which attempt to draw the attention of travellers to the fact that local people often miss out on the benefits which come from tourists' visits to their lands (Figure 12.1).

Other NGOs are more directly involved in promoting responsible tourism. Chapter 7 discussed several non-profit organisations which were running tours to promote social justice and to provide opportunities for a two-way culture exchange. Examples included Global Exchange, which organised tours to Chiapas in Mexico, and the Ladakh Farm Project in north-west India. Rethinking Tourism Project, a United States-based organisation particularly concerned with the effects of tourism on indigenous peoples, has also initiated a new project whereby they are collecting case studies of tourism initiatives owned and managed by indigenous peoples, in the hope that this will provide '. . . a model and protocols for governments, non-governmental organizations, academics, and others to work in balance and equity for sustainable tourism' (www.txinfinet.com/mader/ecotravel/resources/rtp/rtp.html).

The back of the postcard reads:
Don't cut local people out of your holiday. More and more people like you are choosing to travel to new destinations. Over 10 million people visited southern Africa last year. But for many local people the best tourism brings is a few badly paid jobs. For every £10 you pay for a holiday often only £1 stays in the country you visit. It doesn't have to be like this. Your holidays have an impact – make it a positive one.

Figure 12.1   Postcard distributed as part of ACTSA's 'People-First' tourism campaign. (*Source*: Action for Southern Africa, www.actsa.org; Photo: Henner Frankenfeld/picturenet.africa.com)

Meanwhile, Voluntary Service Overseas (VSO) in Britain have implemented their WorldWise Tourism campaign which urges a wide variety of stakeholders, from individual travellers to large hotel chains, to act in a more economically and socially responsible manner (Box 12.2). NGOs have also developed schemes for awarding tourism initiatives for meeting social or environmental criteria (Box 12.3).

Promotion of responsible tourism among visitors

NGOs can play a very important role in influencing tourists' preferences and practices, both through making them aware of their travel options and providing

BOX 12.2

Voluntary Service Overseas – WorldWise Tourism campaign

Action for individuals

- Sign a WorldWise Tourism campaign postcard that urges the travel industry to provide holidays that benefit local people more.

- Organise a public meeting or similar event in your workplace or community to discuss local and international tourism issues. Be sure to ask local travel agents, tourist board officials and others.

Action for travel agents

- Stock VSO's WorldWise leaflet in your agency.
- Insert the leaflet into ticket wallets or flight confirmation envelopes for tourists travelling to the developing world.

Tour operators

- Give your customers more information about the people and places they will be visiting in your brochures, including advice on how they can visit locally owned facilities and resorts.
- Develop a policy for your business on how the holidays you provide could be of more benefit to people living in the destinations you visit.

Hotels

- Start by buying more goods and services locally and reducing imports. Start an environmental management programme within the hotel.

Source: Extracted from Wheat (1999a).

BOX 12.3

Criteria used for 'socially responsible tourism' awards

The German NGO, Studienkreis für Tourismus und Entwicklung (Institute for Tourism and Development), presents 'ToDo! Awards' annually for socially responsible tourism. Their criteria are stated as:

- raising awareness among local people of the impacts of tourism
- participation of a broad range of local people in tourism
- good working conditions for local employees, including pay, security, hours and training
- reinforcement of local culture
- minimisation of the social and cultural damage caused by tourism
- developing new partnerships between the tourist industry and local people
- helping to develop socially responsible tourism in destination areas
- environmental sustainability

Source: Mann (2000: 199).

information to guide their behaviour in their destination country. For example, some NGOs have recognised that rather than simply criticising the tourism industry, they should support local communities by promoting good tourism practices. As mentioned in Chapter 11, Tourism Concern thus commissioned the *Community Tourism Guide* (Mann 2000), to provide information for tourists seeking environmentally friendly and socially sustainable tourism options. Meanwhile in India, Equations helps to direct travellers towards responsible tourist projects.

Preparation of visitors for their travel experience is regarded by some NGOs as a critical strategy to ensure that cultural exchange is the outcome of visitor encounters with the local population. For example, visitors can be given information on sensitive issues, such as how to behave appropriately in a foreign cultural setting, and their attention can be drawn to unethical tourism practices and some alternatives. Pearce (1995) suggests that if tourists are not empowered with information about the nature of local communities and the environment in the area they are visiting, it is more likely that both tourists and locals will experience culture shock, or cultural arrogance will be displayed by the tourists:

> Culture shock may be experienced by both visitors, who are confused by the signals, symbols and style of the visited culture or by locals who have to confront the rule-breaking behaviours of outsiders. While some rule breaking by visitors is unintentional . . . cultural arrogance is the continued practice of following one's own cultural rules while disregarding the sensitivities and reactions of the local community (Pearce 1995: 144).

One classic example of visitor rule-breaking is naked sunbathing on public beaches. Pearce (1995) claims that in southern Thailand this behaviour has offended locals to the extent that they have begun to commit crimes against the visitors.

While the onus should be on tour operators to provide appropriate pre-trip education to visitors,[1] many are reluctant to do this lest they are seen as imposing restrictions on their clients who just want to take off on a fun-filled holiday. Tourism Concern together with VSO have shown the role NGOs can play in the prior education of visitors especially with regard to the in-flight videos they are producing together. Their first video concentrates on The Gambia and has been shown on Air 2000–First Choice flights since January 2000. This video helps to prepare visitors by raising issues of suitable dress, poverty and the value of spending money locally. Videos with similar themes are planned for other Third World destinations. Also within The Gambia, local NGO Gambia Tourism Concern circulates a pamphlet *Tips for Tourists* which highlights sensitive issues from the point of view of the local population. These include, for example, advice on some standard issues such as dressing appropriately and asking permission to take photographs, but also cover other interesting issues which are obviously of concern to local people. The following tip is a case in point:

8. Refusing to Associate
It is no big deal wanting to keep to yourself. Everyone has the right. However, too much of it may work against your holiday. If you are known for it, you may stay

ignorant about a lot of things which associating with local people could make possible. Associating is very important because it will expose you to the goings-on in town, demystify certain misconceptions and facilitate a healthy exchange of ideas for mutual benefit (*Tips for Tourists*, Gambia Tourism Concern, cited by Bah 1999/2000: 8–9).

To conclude this section a case study is provided of an eco-cultural tourism site in South Africa, the Tswaing Crater Museum. This provides a good example of what can be achieved in the development of a tourist site when there is collaboration between an NGO, in this case the Tswaing Forum (which includes representatives of local communities), and government agencies, the private sector and educational bodies.

Case study – Tswaing Crater Museum, South Africa

The Tswaing Crater Museum is an eco-museum which has been developed in a peri-urban area 40 kilometres from Pretoria, the capital of South Africa. According to de Jong and van Coller (1995: 58), 'An eco-museum is an active museum which uses its available resources to influence environmental attitudes and thereby helps to improve the life of the local community.' Tswaing is centred on a unique natural feature, a well-preserved meteorite crater, which is over 200,000 years old. The word 'Tswaing' is seTswana for 'place of salt', a reference to the lake of salty water which fills part of the crater. There is also a wetland area at the 2,000-hectare site, over 320 bird species and 420 floral species and the remains of a factory that produced soda ash and salt.

There are over 1 million people living in the vicinity of the eco-museum and many of them are impoverished. Prior to the museum's conception, Tswaing was an agricultural research station plagued by numerous cases of vandalism and poaching, with much damage caused by local residents. Clearly a successful eco-cultural tourism venture could not proceed without community support. The Tswaing Crater Museum's motto, 'For the People, By the People', explicitly draws attention to the degree of community participation being fostered in this enterprise (Figure 12.2). Community empowerment, along with provision for education, research and recreation at the site, are the main emphases of the project. The project intends to address elements of the South African government's Reconstruction and Development Plan by creating jobs, providing skills training, employing local people in construction and generating income for the local communities through tourism (de Jong and van Coller 1995).

An NGO, the Tswaing Forum, was created in order to pool resources and to plan for the eco-museum's development. The only criterion for membership of the Forum was an interest in developing Tswaing, thus members include amateur ornithologists, scientists, government officials and members of the largely impoverished surrounding communities. A number of steps were taken to encourage active participation of community members. For example, while English is the official language of the Forum, people can speak in any language and other members will interpret for them. Meanwhile the architects contracted to develop the

Figure 12.2   Tswaing Crater Museum's motto.

site had to present all plans and ideas to Forum meetings where they had to be approved, thus learning to express technical ideas in an easily comprehensible manner.

Within the Forum, community members play important roles in two sub-committees: the environment and tourism committee, and the planning committee. The planning committee worked with community representatives to devise a development plan for the project. First, however, capacity-building work was carried out to increase community participants' understanding of the planning process and to ensure they felt confident to participate. Practical skills such as how to run meetings and work as a team were also included. Community representatives thus learned about how economic decisions were made (for example, they had to choose a business philosophy from four options) and about regional planning, understanding how the proposed development would be accommodated in light of present and future infrastructural development in the area and population growth. A group of representatives also travelled to the Pilanesburg Reserve to see what design ideas did and did not work there. Later, strategic planning workshops were held to encourage a wide range of members of local communities to actively participate in needs identification. The environment and tourism committee meanwhile analysed Tswaing's potential as a tourist site, planning for Tswaing to be a tourism hub in the local area while also identifying other local attractions, such as a nearby Ndebele village (see Figure 8.2). When selecting additional tourism attractions in the area, key criteria were that the local community must benefit, natural and cultural resources must be protected and it must be a financially viable option.

To ensure that members of surrounding communities benefit economically from the eco-museum, various schemes have been devised. These include wood-cutting, to thin out sickle bush in the area, and trail construction. Ten people from each of the ten surrounding communities were given this work, with community leaders asked to send a representative selection of people including the young, the old, the main language groups and women. Future small business opportunities for nearby communities will improve once the eco-museum is fully operational, as it will include facilities for arts and crafts sales, cultural performances and possibly also a natural remedies centre and fresh produce market.

Furthermore, the architects contracted to design major buildings for the site, such as a visitor centre, education areas, accommodation and conference facilities, were told that the architectural design had to be 'done in such a way as to accommodate the skills, craftsmanship and capabilities of the local community whilst also uplifting their technical skills and knowledge' (Van Reit and Louw Landscape Architects 1997: 36).

Once again the leaders of surrounding communities were asked to nominate a representative selection of their residents, including both men and women, to engage in nine-week training courses in specific aspects of construction, such as masonry or electrical wiring. When construction begins, they will be employed under the guidance of fully qualified tradespersons. In order that the trainees may go on to apply their skills in the future, an agreement has been reached with a private business consultancy firm to run a free course for them on 'How to run your own business'. Development of entrepreneurial skills represents a real step forward for people from this area, especially women who feel their domestic skills, working as a 'house girl', are all they have to offer the workforce.

The 'For the People, By the People' motto is being taken seriously in the hope that some members of surrounding communities will benefit directly from economic opportunities arising from the eco-museum's development, and that many others will come to understand that preservation of such a site can benefit themselves as well as future generations.

Source: Kobus Basson, Tswaing Crater Museum Project Manager: Author's fieldwork, June 1998.

Strategies of tourism NGOs and local action groups concerned with the negative impacts of tourism

So far the discussion has examined the actions of NGOs which are assisting communities to engage with tourism in a positive manner. This section now moves on to consider a number of strategies utilised by both local action groups and NGOs which are primarily concerned with minimising the harm the world's largest industry, tourism, can impose on Third World peoples. There are of course some NGOs involved in both kinds of work. A number of strategies devised to

Table 12.2   Strategies of NGOs concerned with the negative impacts of tourism

Strategy	Activities	Examples
Monitoring tourism development and disseminating information	• Research on impacts of tourism and dissemination of relevant information • Watchdog roles • Building capacity of local people to do their own monitoring of tourism • Certification schemes • Organising conferences to bring together researchers, activists and industry representatives	• Equations (India) – monitors government policy and major new resort developments; provides training and information so communities can do their own monitoring • Tourism Concern (UK) – resource centre, publications, press releases, teaching resources • Consumers' Association of Penang – highlights concerns through publications such as *See the Third World While it Lasts*
Lobbying	• Lobbying to change government policy or ensure it is enforced • Involving local communities in international policy work • Lobbying to get international support for human rights causes, e.g. prosecuting in their home countries people who have sex with children while on holiday	• Rethinking Tourism Project (USA) – training project for indigenous peoples to develop critical thinking about global tourism, leading to participation in the UN's Commission for Sustainable Development and the Convention on Biological Diversity • Asian Women's Association (Tokyo) and End Child Prostitution in Asian Tourism (ECPAT) (Thailand) – anti-prostitution organisations that lobby both governments and the tourism industry
Protest	• Protest action or campaigns against, for example, multinational domination of the tourism industry, displacement of people from protected areas, or sex tourism.	• Public protests in Barbados force the government to halt further golf course development after concerns about the pressure of golf courses on the limited water supply • Vigilant Goan's Army (India) – operation to oppose luxury hotels' wastage of resources while local residents lack access to essential services such as water and electricity

Sources: Based on information from Hong (1985); Husbands and Harrison (1996); Singh and Singh (1999); http://www.equitabletourism.org; http://www.tourismconcern.org.uk; http://www.txinfinet.com/mader/ecotravel/resources/rtp/rtp.html.

lessen the negative impacts of tourism on local peoples and environments are summarised in Table 12.2, namely monitoring and disseminating information, lobbying and protest action. While the work of one NGO may be highlighted as an example of protest work, this is unlikely to be the only strategy they use. Most local action groups and NGOs engage in a range of activities.

Monitoring tourism development and disseminating information

The independence of the NGO sector places it in an important position to monitor the impacts of tourism, both positive and negative, and to disseminate relevant information. NGOs can also coordinate monitoring efforts and pass on appropriate monitoring skills to local people. It can be very empowering for communities to learn to collect and record information on a regular basis so that they build up a database which they can draw upon if they wish to lobby government about concerns they have about tourism development, for example.

Two Western-based NGOs engaged in monitoring and dissemination work are the Rethinking Tourism Project (RTP) and Tourism Concern. RTP's mission is '. . . to 1) develop community education about tourism, and 2) develop a global network of Indigenous and non-Indigenous support groups to share information and resources about tourism' (http://www.txinfinet.com/mader/ecotravel/resources/rtp/rtp.html). Through their e-mail discussion group and newsletters they share information on the impacts of tourism development around the globe, and what different groups are doing to boycott unsustainable and irresponsible tourism development. Similarly, Tourism Concern (UK) tries to keep people informed of the harmful effects of tourism by publishing a magazine on tourism, and providing a resource centre which acts as a clearing house for information on tourism. Tourism Concern also influences public perceptions of tourism through press releases and provision of teaching resources.

Well-organised and effective tourism monitoring and watchdog groups have emerged in a number of Third World locations as well. The Consumers' Association of Penang, for example, has been very concerned about the impacts of large-scale tourism development in Malaysia which often upsets local social and cultural norms. To publicise their concerns, they published *See the Third World While it Lasts: The social and environmental impact of tourism with special reference to Malaysia* (Hong 1985). This book criticises, among other things, tourists who take photos without asking and who 'invade' long houses, and businesses which put pictures of partially dressed indigenous people on the front of postcards. Meanwhile the Ecumenical Coalition on Third World Tourism (ECTWT) sponsored publication of *Alternative Tourism* (Holden 1984). ECTWT aims to raise awareness about tourism issues and to stimulate debate about how tourism can become more equitable, thus initiating a number of conferences and reports.

An example of effective monitoring of government policy and of large-scale tourism development, as well as passing monitoring skills on to local communities, is provided by Equations, an Indian NGO. They commissioned a report on the tourism policy of India, noting how environmental concerns and human rights considerations were swept aside in the drive for liberalisation of the economy, which involved encouraging foreign companies to invest in tourism in India. Equations also conducts an annual audit of the tourism industry's operations. However, empowerment of local communities so that they can decide what action to take regarding tourism development in their local area is

---

BOX 12.4

Equations' mandate to empower communities

Equations, an Indian-based NGO, takes a critical perspective on tourism; however, this organisation also believes tourism can work in the interests of local development if planned and implemented in an appropriate manner:

> We are working toward tourism which brings economic benefits directly to all segments of the host community, particularly including women and indigenous peoples; is subject to local, democratic control, so that communities are making their own decisions about how tourism should be permitted and regulated; is integrated into other community activities, so that it is culturally appropriate and sensitive to the inequities between hosts and guests; enriches both hosts (economically, developmentally and in terms of control) and guests (culturally, re-creationally)

Source: http://www.equitabletourism.org

---

also a key role of Equations (Box 12.4). For example, to make their information accessible to local communities, Equations produces basic fact sheets in English and in some local languages. They also produce lists of criteria for assessing tourism development initiatives. They provide training so that communities living in areas popular with tourists can, for example, learn how to lobby effectively and understand how to use the legal system to bring developers to task. Hands-on workshops show people how to communicate effectively using media such as newsletters and how to conduct participatory research (http://www.equitabletourism.org).

A potential new niche in which NGOs could apply their monitoring skills is in the assessment of good practice in the tourism industry. For example, there is talk of establishing criteria for fair trade in tourism, as discussed above, or for sustainable tourism practices, as discussed in Chapter 11. In such cases NGOs could be ideal agencies to provide independent monitoring and verification of tourism ventures. In addition, the credibility of commercial operations such as Green Globe would be enhanced if NGOs or local action groups were commissioned to carry out the monitoring work.

Lobbying

As noted in the previous section, information garnered from the monitoring of the impacts of tourism and the direction of government policy can be used as an effective tool when lobbying for change at official levels. Much lobbying of the tourism industry and governments has been carried out by NGOs specifically concerned with sex tourism, such as the Asian Women's Association of Tokyo, End Child Prostitution in Asian Tourism (ECPAT) in

Thailand, and the Coalition on Child Prostitution and Tourism. Such organisations do not always work explicitly to empower local people to lobby for change on their own terms, however, which is something that RTP tries to achieve. RTP works to ensure that the voices of indigenous communities are heard at official levels. For example, they trained community representatives to develop critical thinking skills with regard to global tourism so they could effectively participate in international forums such as the UN's Commission for Sustainable Development and the Convention on Biological Diversity (http://www.txinfinet.com/mader/ecotravel/resources/rtp/rtp.html).

Protest

In situations where lobbying of governments or tourism industry players does not seem to be the most effective strategy for airing grievances and concerns about tourism development, local action groups and NGOs are supporting communities in voicing their protests. McLaren (1998: 125) cites a number of forms of resistance by people in destination communities, from painting murals which demonstrate their concerns about tourism in prominent tourism spots, to organisations providing education programmes so that local people understand how they can limit numbers of tourists and exert control over tourism developers. A recent example of advocacy is work by protest groups in Thailand who made good use of the media and the internet in drawing attention to negative environmental and social consequences of filming of the Hollywood blockbuster *The Beach*, a film on backpacker culture, on one of their islands in 1999. The Thai government meanwhile was hoping this movie would make Thailand an even bigger drawcard for tourists.

Tourism protest groups in parts of the Third World have achieved some significant victories against big industry opponents in recent years. In Sri Lanka, the development of a large resort was stopped in 1994 after protests at the destruction of coconut plantations which would subsequently occur. Similarly, opposition in Barbados led the government to put a halt to further golf course development, because existing golf courses were already placing an enormous strain on the restricted, rainfed water supply of this island nation. Some protest initiatives have also had regional impacts. For example, a meeting of three service workers' organisations was held in Penang in 1995 and resulted in a resolution urging unions and their workers throughout Asia to reject tourism-related prostitution, especially that involving children (Husbands and Harrison 1996: 6).

Below, a case study documents the work of tourism protest and lobby groups in one region where they have been particularly active, that is, Goa.

Case study: Protests against tourism in Goa, India

Goa started developing as a popular tourist destination in the 1960s when Western hippies flooded into this beach-side haven. By the 1990s, however, it was not only backpackers crowding the beaches as package tourists both from within India and from countries such as Germany and England were also lured by the attractions of Goa (Wilson 1997). There was enormous growth in self-contained resort accommodation, in particular, to service the international package tourists. Meanwhile developers were keen to devise particular attractions, including bungee jumping, casinos, water parks and golf courses, to bring in even more tourists. The tourism minister, Churchill Alemao, claimed that casinos and golf courses would attract 'quality tourists' to Goa (Prabhudesai 1999), by which he meant tourists willing to spend large amounts of money.

It is important to identify specifically what the protest groups which have sprung up in Goa are concerned about. According to Singh and Singh (1999), Goans are not opposed to tourism per se, as the livelihoods of many families are at least partly dependent on tourist dollars. Rather, it is the nature of tourism development which bothers them. Goan people wish to see tourism which preserves biological diversity and '. . . increases people's control over resources and strengthens community identity' (Singh and Singh 1999: 72). As will be evident from the examples below, much protest is related to the growth in charter tourists, who typically buy package tours which include most of their food, accommodation and transport requirements, and thus bring few benefits to local small business people. While there have been complaints about the socially inappropriate dress and behaviour of backpackers, they are not the main target of protestors (Wilson 1997).

The most well-known tourism protest group in Goa is Jagrut Goenkaranchi Fauz (JGF), or Vigilant Goan's Army, '. . . whose struggle emerges from its socio-economic and sociocultural analysis of the phenomenon of modern tourism' (Singh and Singh 1999: 72). Three recent campaigns launched by the JGF are representative of their concerns. 'Operation Ecotage' is critical of the impacts on coastal ecology of the large luxury hotels and the pressure they place on water sources. The campaign named 'Our homes – their holidays' focuses on the need for strong local input into tourism planning to ensure that tourism does not undermine access of local residents to essential services and infrastructure, including water and electricity. A third campaign targets labour practices of the luxury hotels, attempting to ensure that workers gain the security of permanent jobs and wages rather than being exploited by being employed as 'trainees' whereby their only income is the tips they gain (Herald News Desk 1999).

At one stage JGF directly targeted incoming tourists, informing them of the impacts of tourism on Goan people and environments and requesting that the tourists go home. The opening paragraph from a letter the JGF handed out at the airport to German tourists travelling with the company Condor in November 1989, is provided below:

> So, you come yet once again, CONDOR, the large hungry Vulture, that you are, a vicious bird of prey! . . . Do NOT come to Goa. Our limited resources cannot be sacrificed to meet your lustful luxury demands. Our people, for example, thirst for drinking water while the same is provided by the hotels, for

Table 12.3   Reasons for protests over tourism in Goa

Source of protest	Examples
Behaviour of 'hippies'	Drug taking; immodest dress, including nudity on the beach; loud parties
Undermining of local livelihoods	Toddy tappers denied access to coconut trees on lands leased for hotels; luxury hotels attempt to restrict access of fisherpeople to the foreshore, even though officially the coast of India is public property
Lack of amenities for locals	Tourist hotels use water for swimming pools while nearby villagers suffer from a shortage of drinking water; power shortages in local villages
Bowing to demands of large Indian businesses and multinational corporations rather than local concerns and interests	Plans to develop casinos and golf courses in the State to attract high-spending tourists, regardless of potential social and environmental consequences. Locals unduly pressured to sell coastal land
Undermining the dignity of the people	Locals gain work in hotels as cleaners, guards and waiters – they are at the beck and call of others as opposed to the past when they were self-employed
Damage to the physical environment	Coastal environment has been degraded. There have been many violations of the law that no construction is allowed within 500 metres of the beach – sometimes 'in the interest of tourism and profits' certain development is allowed up to 200 metres from the shoreline

Sources: Based on information from Singh and Singh (1999); Magic Lantern Foundation (1999).

you to SWIM in (English translation of part of a letter in German, handed out by JGF at Dabolim Airport of Goa, 3 November 1989; cited in Lea 1993: 709).

Other groups in Goa which oppose mass tourism include: the Goa Foundation, which focuses on empirical research and publishing on the sustainable development of tourism; Citizens Concerned About Tourism, which is particularly concerned about backpackers undermining Goan cultural values; and Bailancho Saad, a women's collective striving for a just society (Singh and Singh 1999). These groups have protested over a number of aspects of tourism development in Goa, including negative social, economic and environmental issues (see Table 12.3). What is interesting is that all but the first source of protest listed in Table 12.3 applies to charter and luxury tourists, not backpackers.

Tourism lobby groups in Goa have had some success. This includes taking legal action against the construction of hotels and resorts within 500 metres of Goan beaches, stopping development on community land and ensuring that hotels do not erect fences which cut off the access of locals to the beach (Magic Lantern Foundation 1999). They have also networked with tourism lobby groups in other parts of the world and drawn international attention to their cause (Lea 1993; Singh and Singh 1999). It has been suggested, however, that Goan protest groups are dominated by educated people, and thus '. . . are not particularly representative of the community at large' (Lea 1993: 711).

Clearly community groups which act as watchdogs on tourism development can be very powerful advocates for appropriate local development, working to keep their local and national governments honest and to ensure that the interests of investors do not override the concerns of local residents.

Conclusion

A diverse range of subjects and interests are represented in the strategies of NGOs working in the tourism sector, as discussed above. The introduction to this chapter outlined Korten's framework of first-generation (welfare), second-generation (self-reliance through capacity-building) and third-generation (sustainable systems development) NGO strategies. As shown in the NGO activities outlined in Tables 12.1 and 12.2, it is clear that NGOs and local action groups concerned with tourism are mainly working at the second and third levels. They are developing the skills of community members so that they can effectively monitor tourism development and lobby or protest for change when tourism is affecting their lives adversely, and they are also providing training so that communities will have the ability to establish and manage their own tourism enterprises. The best NGOs and local action groups combine confidence-raising with capacity-building. While some NGOs focus on what we might call 'welfare' concerns, such as child prostitution, they do not follow first-generation strategies, rather, they are involved in advocacy work and attempts to influence national and international policy decisions. This is inspiring, as it appears that most NGOs working in the tourism sector are either trying to ensure that tourism development occurs in a way which maximises benefits to the local population or they are challenging existing inequities in society.

However, there is still need for caution when assessing the value of NGOs working on tourism issues. They may not be profit-making institutions, but this does not mean that their agendas automatically prioritise the interests of local people (Mowforth and Munt 1998).

It is also important to be aware of power imbalances between Third World and Western NGOs and between these NGOs, local action groups and local communities. According to Jon Tinker, President of the Panos Institute, Third World NGOs get 'seduced' into accepting and supporting the causes lavishly presented to them by Western NGOs with whom they have formed partnership agreements. NGOs with a commitment to conservation issues, in particular, seem apt to push their agendas on to Third World 'partners' even when they clash with the interests of local people. Tinker suggests that more support should be provided to Third World NGOs to '... prepare and disseminate their own analysis of development issues' (cited in Mowforth and Munt 1998: 186). Similarly, local action groups are often dominated by elites, albeit elites concerned about social and environmental interests. A challenge for these groups in the future is to ensure they are inclusive of a wide range of local people and thus, interests.

In addition, there are some areas which deserve more careful attention from NGOs, but which have been ignored at least partly because of their challenging nature. While NGOs have provided excellent support for alternative tourism enterprises both in terms of their establishment and promotion, there have as yet been few attempts to transform the mainstream, mass tourism industry, which accounts for the majority of travellers and at whose feet the bulk of responsibility for environmental damage and social decay through tourism, and inequity in benefits for local communities, must rest. Tour companies will need more encouragement to implement socially and environmentally responsible initiatives. Some NGOs, such as Voluntary Service Overseas and Tourism Concern, are taking steps to influence the practices of companies involved in the world's fastest growing industry, but a more coordinated and concerted response is needed if any real change is to come about. Both NGOs based in the Third World and in the tourist-generating countries and local action groups have roles to play and it will be particularly important to influence the 'big players' such as airlines, international tour operators and hotel chains.

Questions

1. Why are local action groups and NGOs well positioned to act as watchdogs regarding tourism policy and practice?

2. What kinds of resources and support can NGOs provide to communities which are interested in pursuing community-based tourism ventures?

3. Based on Korten's (1987) framework, provide two examples of tourism NGOs adopting second-generation strategies, and two examples of NGOs adopting third-generation strategies.

Suggestions for further reading

Barkin, D. and Pailles, C. 1999 'NGO-community collaboration for ecotourism: a strategy for sustainable regional development', *Tourism Recreation Research*, **24**(2): 69–74.

Mann, M. (for Tourism Concern) 2000 *The Community Tourism Guide*, Earthscan, London.

Turner, R., Miller, G. and Gilbert, D. 2001 'The role of UK charities and the tourism industry', *Tourism Management*, **22**(5): 463–72.

Useful websites

Rethinking Tourism Project:
www.rethinkingtourism.org

Equations (Indian tourism NGO). Their website includes 'hotspots', a section which highlights contentious issues regarding tourism development in selected areas:
www.equitabletourism.org/

An interesting article on NGO–community collaboration in a tourism project in Mexico:
www.planeta.com/planeta/99/0499huatulco.html

Note

1. Some tour operators do provide excellent pre-travel information on the culture(s) and environments of their destination and appropriate behaviour, as discussed in Chapter 11, but they are in the minority.

CHAPTER 13

Conclusion

The main aim of this book was to consider ways in which tourism can facilitate rather than impede development, particularly from the perspective of Third World communities. From an academic perspective it was seen as timely to take debates on Third World tourism beyond the level of critique in order to contribute to the search for appropriate livelihood strategies. Neopopulist theories on participation, empowerment and sustainable development have been particularly pertinent in this respect, helping to provide ammunition to support the contention of Mann (2000: x), author of *The Community Tourism Guide*, that: 'in the right circumstances, tourism *can* support local people, cultures, environments and economies, while still being exciting and enjoyable for us [tourists]'. Thus while concerns about tourism, both in its mass and alternative guises, have been raised throughout, this book has maintained a positive focus and shown how in a range of different contexts tourism can work effectively as a strategy for development.

This concluding chapter begins by presenting some of the key findings of this book, notably the need for Third World countries to pursue inward-oriented development strategies. This is followed by a discussion on ways forward, drawing from the case studies and examples highlighted herein which show how tourism can work for development, but also why appropriate support is needed for communities involved in tourism. In particular, attention is drawn to the vital place of empowerment in all strategies for development, including tourism, which seek to be both sustainable and equitable.

Key findings

Tourism should be inward-oriented

A clear message this book has delivered is that for tourism to work for development, it must not be focused around outward-oriented objectives. Tourism under neoliberalism responds to the whims of overseas tourists, the interests of foreign investors and the demands of supranational organisations. Continued dominance of the international tourism industry by Western interests is of major concern because '. . . decisions affecting destinations are made from afar. They are more likely to be concerned with profits than with the impacts on host environments and populations' (Cater 1995: 202). The alternative is for states to focus upon how tourism can meet national and local level needs and interests. As Parnwell (1998) asserts, it is possible for governments to challenge globalising forces, including tourism, and mould them to suit their own agendas.

However, this book does not advocate any perfect model or blueprint to be followed by those who wish to pursue tourism as a means to achieving development. Rather, the factors which determine what is an appropriate strategy for development will depend upon the context in which tourism is taking place, including cultural and social factors specific to certain communities, as well as the place of particular countries in the world today, economically and politically (Akama 1999). These contextual factors have a major bearing on a country's opportunity to engage successfully with the tourism process in ways that meet its needs at national and local levels. Indeed, such factors should be central to government planning regarding tourism, rather than allowing tourism growth and the nature of tourism development to be dictated by exogenous forces.

Inward-oriented or endogenous development requires that states should plan for tourism in an integrated fashion, placing it in the context of other development priorities such as small business development, environmental protection, devolution of political control to the community level, and providing economic opportunities for indigenous people (Brohman 1996a). Thus Chapter 9 argued that individual countries may find that they could gain more benefits from pursuing growth in domestic tourism than international tourism, as there is less seasonality among domestic tourists and a willingness to consume locally produced goods and services. Similarly, states wishing to encourage local entrepreneurship may find it useful to encourage backpackers who are keen to use homestay accommodation and frequent basic roadside restaurants.

The most successful examples of tourism being pursued by governments in ways which maximise local benefits are those few places that actively support community involvement in tourism (Namibia), or which have a clear mandate to pursue nature tourism or culturally oriented tourism (such as Bhutan, Samoa and the Maldives). In these cases it is the controls set by the state which have attracted tourists and in some cases led to premium prices being paid. Of concern is that in the future global trade bodies, citing agreements such as the GATS (Chapter 2), may try to clamp down on countries which have placed tight controls over the nature of tourism development or provided support for domestic investors and the informal sector.

In pursuing inward-oriented development, both alternative and conventional forms of tourism may offer appropriate paths.

Support for alternative *and* conventional forms of tourism

Chapter 1 demonstrated that it is neither correct nor constructive to set up mass tourism and alternative tourism as polar opposites, with the former imbuing all that is bad and the latter evoking all that is good about tourism from the perspective of local communities. Both offer potential for development through tourism and both should be accountable in terms of their social, economic and environmental effects. While there are greater problems associated with mass tourism at present (Shah and Gupta 2000), it also continues to be the dominant form of tourism around the globe accounting for the major share of tourist dollars, thus it is no surprise that both national governments and local communities remain keen to tap into this market. Well-designed and controlled forms of mass tourism are able to accommodate the demands of large numbers of tourists in ways which maximise revenue while minimising local disturbance. As argued by Brohman (1996a: 66):

> Even mass tourism need not be foreign controlled, enclavic, unplanned, short-term, culturally destructive, and environmentally unsustainable. With more selective and deliberate planning, community participation, and local control over development, tourism in general can be made to conform more to the objectives of an alternative strategy.

Chapter 11 revealed some innovative strategies in this respect, including the 'Adopt a Farmer' scheme in St Lucia whereby hotels purchased their fruit and vegetables locally and assisted farmers in producing more commercially lucrative varieties. Also inspiring was the fact that two very large tour operators in Britain were, along with a number of specialist small operators, judged very highly in terms of the pre-departure information which they provided to tourists about issues such as environmental and cultural sensitivity in the destination country and ways of supporting the local economy. The willingness of some charter companies to show in-flight videos to raise tourist awareness was similarly noted.

The case studies and examples in Part II of this book also suggested that small-scale forms of tourism which are based upon local skills and resources can be very beneficial for local communities. In particular, chances for active participation and empowerment of communities through tourism were enhanced in small-scale ventures, and these ventures also provided greater opportunities for involvement by marginalized people, such as women. Typically the objectives of these ventures go beyond economic gains with, for example, relationship-building being a critical component of both the Ladakh Farm Project and Global Exchange's Chiapas tour. At the political level, such forms of tourism can help to weaken core–periphery linkages and thus build the self-reliance of Third World communities (Khan 1997).

While new types of tourism, such as ecotourism, backpacker tourism and revolutionary tourism, hold much promise in terms of their potential to contribute to community development, what is most critical is the *process* by which tourism is approached. Without sufficient attention to issues such as class, gender and ethnicity, for example, new forms of tourism have the potential to be even more destructive than conventional forms, particularly as the newer forms of tourism encourage direct interaction between tourists and people in destination areas. Thus we should be wary of labels, particularly those which suggest a product is ethically or morally superior. An 'ecotourism lodge', for example, can be heavily reliant on Western investment and products, while a 'village visit' may involve a chief coercing his people to perform dances for tourists in order that he receives a small payment from the tour operator. Clearly it is the process, not the product necessarily, which makes both mass and alternative forms of tourism appropriate, or not, in terms of promoting local development.

However, alternative, small-scale and community-based forms of tourism development will not always provide an appropriate development strategy. Such forms of tourism do not generally earn a lot of revenue in the short term, and they require a community to have a wide range of business and marketing skills just to manage day-to-day operations. Thus it is not surprising that some ventures, even Sunungukai camp in Zimbabwe which has received an international accolade in the form of a British Airways Tourism for Tomorrow Award (Chapter 6), have not yet proven to be economically sustainable (Murphree and Nyika 1997; O'Hare and Barrett 1999). Dominance of the travel industry by Western-based companies with high degrees of horizontal and vertical integration makes it difficult for Third World tourism operators to compete.

In their struggle to find effective strategies for sustainable development in line with their particular interests and utilising the resources they have at hand, it is likely that Third World countries will need to be open to a diverse range of development strategies, which may include both mass and alternative forms of tourism. Whatever model of tourism development they choose to pursue, there are likely to be significant trade-offs to be made (Ashley *et al.* 2000: 9). For example, Chapter 10 showed how the Maldives sought to control the negative social impacts of mass tourism by only allowing resort development on islands not inhabited by locals, whereas in Samoa, interaction between locals and tourists was encouraged through a smaller-scale formula for tourism development which relies upon involvement of village communities. Undoubtedly the Maldives has achieved greater economic rewards from their strategy overall, but Samoa's unique model also has specific benefits in allowing the income from tourism to be more widely dispersed. Advantages of the latter approach could also include local retention of profits and a subsequent reduction in inequalities, improvement of rural living standards, development of business and management skills at the local level and a reduction in rural–urban migration (Brown 1998a).

Ethical practice within the tourism industry

The discussion thus far has demonstrated that governments need to play a key role in pursuing tourism as an inward-oriented strategy. However, in an increasingly globalised world where national governments have little control over exogenous factors such as the flow of capital internationally, if tourism is to work *for* development there must be more emphasis on ethical practice within the industry as well. Increasingly airlines, hotels and tour operators are supporting self-regulation through codes of conduct and certification schemes (Chapter 11). However, attention to issues of social sustainability, including justice and human rights considerations, needs to grow alongside the strong green consciousness which is developing. In addition, ethical practice should include support for the local economy in the destination area through maximising use of local goods and services.

Weaver and Oppermann (2000) suggest that 'new tourists' (Poon 1993), that is, those who search for meaningful experiences and are environmentally and socially responsible, could become the key tourist market in the future. We can only hope that this will eventuate, as further reform within the industry is likely to be largely dictated by consumer preferences and pressure. In the meantime it is vital that tourism NGOs and tourism businesses, such as guidebook companies, continue to raise consumer awareness about appropriate tourism development.

Local actors can influence tourism development

In addition to influencing tourism development through their preferences as consumers, civil society actors have exerted their agency by responding to inappropriate tourism development or attempting to influence the nature of tourism development in their area. Some have protested publicly and been successful in changing the direction tourism is taking in their area, forcing state and business interests to recognise their needs and concerns (Chapter 12). For example, action groups in Goa lobbied to ensure public access to the beach and to protect the rights of workers, while people in Barbados made the government aware of the extreme environmental problems being caused by too much golf course development. Such local protests clearly show how 'local forces contest global forces by harnessing tourism according to their own terms' (Teo and Chang 1998: 124). Others have chosen to initiate their own tourism enterprises and lobbied for support from the state. The women managing the Honda Bay Boatmen's Association in the Philippines, for example, worked through the city council to challenge a cartel of families who monopolised the local tour boat trade. They also filed complaints about illegal commercial fishing which was depleting the protected marine resource upon which tourism was based. It is much more likely that communities will be able to influence tourism development in such ways when they have strong internal organisations which encourage participation by a diverse range of interests, such as youths, women, traditional leaders and any minority groups.

In essence, this section on key findings has shown how actors from the government sector, private sector and civil society are all playing essential roles in determining how tourism can work as a successful strategy for development. The final section now concentrates on principles for working with communities in tourism destination areas in order to maximise the benefits and minimise the costs to them of tourism development.

Working with communities

As established above, there is no blueprint for ensuring that tourism will work for development. However, it is possible to identify a number of general principles for enhancing community benefits from tourism:

- promote empowerment as a precursor to community involvement in tourism;
- encourage active participation;
- identify both tangible and intangible benefits of tourism;
- share the benefits and costs of tourism;
- support diverse livelihood options;
- develop positive relationships between communities and other tourism stakeholders.

Promote empowerment as a precursor to community involvement in tourism

Empowerment is a means to determining and achieving socio-economic objectives. Empowerment can also help to break down the power gradient that usually sees external stakeholders having control over tourism initiatives. It should not, therefore, just be seen as a potential outcome of community involvement in tourism development. Women and men often need to be empowered, in terms of having access to a wide range of information about their options and the confidence to take part in discussions and negotiations, *before* they can effectively decide whether, or how, to pursue involvement in tourism. Communities have the right to say 'no' to tourism, even if it looks like it could reap major economic benefits. In this regard, it is essential that clear information dissemination occurs at the start to ensure that the community is aware of both the risks and constraints to the venture, and has realistic expectations of possible gains to be made. They also need to consider how potential costs and benefits will be shared among different interest groups (Akama 1996).

Empowerment of community members (through training courses, information sharing and participation on decision-making bodies) is necessary prior to and during tourism development, and must spread beyond a small number of their 'representatives'. When 'community participation' is largely limited to roles on decision-making bodies for the leaders and a few jobs for the masses, it is likely that influential community members will secure better access to the available resources at the expense of others: 'We have trouble eating this "community" pill as it is always presented by those people who get the cars and the salaries, speaking on behalf of "the community"' (Paulo Wandschneider, Delegation of the European Commission to Zambia: Author's fieldwork, July 1998).

Psychological empowerment, which ideally should mean that a community is confident in its ability to participate equitably and effectively in a given tourism development, has rarely been given credence in literature on community involvement in tourism. Yet in the Tswaing Crater Museum development in South Africa, it was only by holding capacity-building workshops and allowing community participants to speak in any language they were comfortable with that members of surrounding communities had the confidence to become active members of the planning committee for the museum (Chapter 12). Feelings of self-worth are essential if individuals are to feel that tourism is a viable process for them to engage in and if they are to move beyond being seen as just passive beneficiaries.

Encourage active participation

The rationale behind an agency's attempts to promote community involvement may speak volumes about whether that participation will be active or passive. 'Participation of local communities', as promoted by the private sector, conservation authorities and other agencies promoting involvement of local communities in tourism, can simply be a public relations exercise, useful for advertising purposes, or a means of placating the community to ensure they do not jeopardise the venture. Conservation agencies, such as the Natal Parks Board, are now rejecting exclusionary approaches to community involvement in the protected areas but may still need to put more effort into moving beyond passive participation of communities (Chapter 6). One way to do this is to ensure that communities participate in monitoring or any research which takes place. The Makuleke community, who have reclaimed part of the Kruger National Park, are ensuring this happens by asking that researchers involve young people from their community as research assistants. Another strategy for active involvement is to have community representatives sitting on local agencies which plan for tourism development, as occurs in the Annapurna Conservation Area Project (Chapter 6). Successful ways of exerting control over the form and function of tourism affecting their people include minimising invasiveness by siting tourist accommodation away from the village or by not allowing overnight stays, or limiting the size of tour parties and the times which they may visit the community.

It is important to realise that by including local communities as more active participants in tourism ventures, there will be increasing conflicts between them and higher-level agencies, including national interests (Wells 1996: 3). Finding effective ways of resolving such conflicts will be critical to the long-term success of such ventures.

Identify both tangible and intangible benefits of tourism

Communities which invest their energy and resources in tourism initiatives naturally want to see tangible benefits, including an early and continuous flow of income. This is something which agencies supporting community involvement in tourism need to be very aware of – it is simply unrealistic and unjust to expect impoverished communities to wait several years before realising any return for their hard work. As it is likely to be a long time before a planned tourism venture can be established, marketed and turn a profit, support agencies should look for alternative means of benefiting the community. They could, for example, ensure that local labour and materials are employed in any construction work, and encourage associated activities such as the manufacture of craft products which could be sold at other tourism sites until the community venture is established.

Decision-making bodies must also consider intangible benefits of community involvement in tourism:

> Intangible benefits, such as empowerment, skill development, perceptions of (in)security, community cohesion or conflict . . . are difficult to quantify and sometimes difficult for outsiders to perceive, but are likely to be significant to residents (Ashley and LaFranchi, 1997: 71).

This is a particularly important point for donors. Too often they are prepared to continue funding tourism initiatives based on tangible 'outputs' such as the construction of a guest house, but they rarely ask harder questions such as whether or not most of the local community actually supports the initiative and feels they will benefit from it. Similarly, government business development officers may be impressed with the nice shop and display area that the women involved in the Siyabonga cooperative have for their crafts (Chapter 8), but have they noticed the psychological empowerment which has occurred with a number of illiterate members now proudly enrolling themselves in school and setting higher goals? Chapter 7 meanwhile showed how liberating it could be for people to tell heritage tourists their own stories of past oppression, while Chapter 8 showed how the success of women entrepreneurs servicing the Himalayan trekking industry had led to men in their households assisting with domestic roles for the first time in their lives. In the case of CAMPFIRE (Chapter 5), it is intangible results, notably empowerment, self-determination and social capital, that are seen by some as the programme's greatest achievements

– not the revenue gained or the habitats conserved (Murphree and Nykia 1997).

Share the benefits and costs of tourism

While ideally community involvement in tourism should mean that benefits flow to most members of a community, this does not occur automatically. Thus when tourism is a strategy for community development, mechanisms need to be in place to ensure that the benefits are widely dispersed. If the divided and divisive nature of communities is accepted, it should be recognised that there are always disadvantaged groups within a community and their needs, in particular, should be targeted. Women often constitute a disadvantaged group because social norms inhibit their freedom to become involved in public forums and sit next to men in decision-making positions, but if efforts are made to allow their voices to be heard then their interests can be addressed. This was apparent in the case of women in the CAMPFIRE programme in Zimbabwe who argued successfully that household dividends should be paid to women-headed households, including to each of the wives in the case of a polygamous union and to divorced women, as well as to conventional male-headed house-holds (Fortmann and Bruce 1993).

In many cases only one person or household in a community has established a tourism business which is generating an income. This can lead to conflict within a community but, as was shown with the case study of Noah's tours in the Eastern Highlands of Zimbabwe, there are appropriate and mutually beneficial ways of spreading the benefits of tourism (Chapter 9). One option is for the individual or family to put a percentage of their profits into a fund for community development, leading to goodwill towards tourism and thus a friendly attitude towards tourists visiting the area. A second option is to involve more people in the venture by, for example, taking tourists to visit local artisans at work and giving them the opportunity to purchase crafts at these places. It is excessively romantic to suggest that all members of a community will benefit equally from any tourism venture; however, the opportunity for any venture to support equitable development and thus to be seen in a positive light by most residents will be increased significantly by encouraging active participation by wide segments of a community from the outset.

Equally important as sharing benefits is the need to minimise costs of tourism and to ensure that no group within a community has to bear a disproportionate share of the costs. While this should seem obvious, even cases of otherwise exemplary alternative tourism initiatives have failed to adequately address such concerns. Costs of tourism development which are likely to aggravate in particular those who have gained no benefits from tourism include the inappropriate behaviour of tourists, the inflationary effect of tourism on the prices of goods and services in their area, and being prohibited from harvesting resources from a newly designated protected area.

Support diverse livelihood options

The fact that tourism has costs as well as benefits should remind us of the danger of a community investing the majority of its energy, resources and skills into tourism projects. Where tourism is being pursued as a strategy for development it should ideally take its place alongside a range of livelihood options for the community, rather than superseding these other activities. Enthusiasm from donors and NGOs in supporting community involvement in tourism initiatives can sometimes be misleading for rural communities which have little experience in business and yet start to expect that tourism will bring immediate, and substantial, returns. Any business reliant primarily on overseas markets is vulnerable to fluctuations which may be due to factors such as political turmoil in the capital city or the nervousness of Western tourists in the wake of the 11 September 2001 terrorist attacks in the USA. Earlier chapters revealed that in places such as Fiji, during military coups, and South-east Asia, during the Asian economic crisis of the late 1990s, whole communities which were dependent on an income from tourism faced potential ruin.

It is thus very important that when tourism is promoted as an option for sustainable livelihoods in the Third World, it is not glorified or put forward as the only option for their development. Tourism should instead take its place alongside other livelihood strategies for the community. It is particularly important that pursuit of tourism should not unduly interfere with primary production such as agriculture and fishing which may provide a community with their only source of nourishment and income in times of economic downturn. Where activities such as agricultural production have been at the centre of a community's culture involving, for example, religious rituals and harvest festivals, it is also socially destructive if they are replaced by the new economic activity of tourism.

Develop positive relationships between communities and other tourism stakeholders

The discussion in Part III of this book, in particular, has drawn attention to the importance of communities working together with other stakeholders in order to maximise their benefits from tourism: 'partnerships between local people, the private sector and government open up a range of opportunities not restricted to any one group' (Wearing and Neil 1999: 133). Efforts by communities to enhance their own well-being through tourism ventures will rarely be successful without coordinated efforts involving other stakeholders. These stakeholders can help to ensure that the following requirements for community involvement in tourism are met:

- Capacity-building of high quality and an ongoing nature is provided.
- Capital is available on flexible terms.

- Communities have secure tenure over their land and other natural resources.
- Communities are educated about the tourism process and what tourists may expect through, for example, study tours.
- There is adequate support from qualified professionals such as lawyers, marketing specialists and small business experts.

A major contribution of this book has been to support the view espoused under neopopulism that civil society should play an important role in determining and working towards meeting sustainable development objectives for communities. There is very little written explicitly about the roles of NGOs in the tourism literature, despite the fact that Chapter 12 showed how vital NGOs can be in supporting the active involvement of communities in tourism initiatives. Thus for example, the Annapurna Conservation Area Project in Nepal used money from trekkers to provide capacity-building workshops for local people, while Gambia Tourism Concern published *Tips for Tourists* as well as lobbying their government to find ways of supporting community involvement in tourism rather than the all-inclusives market.

Communities can also benefit through partnership arrangements with operators which can provide expertise and assist with marketing endeavours (Chapter 11). For example, business partners can help to promote tourism to remote, hard to access areas, or simply to ventures which do not have the resources to produce glossy brochures and advertise in mainstream travel avenues. Both Damaraland campsite in Namibia and Rainforest Expeditions in Peru provide excellent examples of partnerships whereby there is profit-sharing with communities from the start and after a certain time, ownership of the venture passes to the community. However, it may be necessary to scrutinise the actions of private sector partners, to see whether they regard tourism as a means of promoting community development or whether they see involvement of communities as merely a means to developing tourism. In the first instance, the external stakeholder might provide capacity-building work for members of a community and take them on study tours of other tourism sites so they can determine what form of tourism may be appropriate for their community and plan for this appropriately. In the second instance, the stakeholder may seek the approval of the community leader to bring tourists to view distinctive natural or cultural attractions in the area, at the discretion of the tour operator rather than the convenience of the community, and with the only economic benefit coming from random craft sales to tourists. The latter option allows for minimal community control while the former centres on community control and benefits.

Working with a range of stakeholders also makes sense because for tourism to work for development it is necessary to have integration of local, national and international level strategies. Neopopulist strategies tend to focus at the local level, but local level initiatives are likely to fail unless strategies are concurrently enacted at national and international levels. Ideally governments should provide an appropriate policy environment, regulatory framework, infrastructure and support for small business development. They can also give priority to investors working to assist local communities, and grant communities secure tenure over their land and other resources as the Namibian government did when it devolved use rights over wildlife to people on communal lands (Chapter 10). Meanwhile at the international level tourism organisations can establish criteria to support socially and environmentally responsible tourism, as seen in Chapter 11, and consumers can put pressure on tourism operators to support tourism ventures which result in direct local benefits.

Final point

In conclusion, while tourism brings with it a myriad of potential pitfalls, it also offers considerable potential for bringing appropriate development to local communities. Ultimately it is vital to find ways in which tourism can work *for* development because it is the world's largest industry and it is continuing to grow, notably in Third World destinations. In addition, so many people within Third World communities are keen to be involved in tourism. Tourism is not *the* answer to development problems facing diverse communities throughout the Third World, but it may provide assistance in meeting the goals of a number of these communities. This idea has been supported both by agencies calling for a focus on pro-poor tourism as well as those campaigning for fair trade in tourism. As well as promoting economic development, tourism can help to meet social and political goals such as building capacity, strengthening community-level institutions, reinforcing cultural integrity and, ideally, self-determination. This book has shown that agencies supporting local development and other tourism stakeholders, including the private sector, can facilitate local involvement and try to ensure that tourism development occurs in an equitable and sustainable manner. Meanwhile local action groups and NGOs can monitor tourism development and put pressure on governments and the industry for change when the rights and well-being of local communities are under threat.

The critical issue for whether future tourism in Third World countries will contribute to or undermine local development rests on the nature of that tourism development. Local participation, involving both control over tourism and a fair share in the benefits of tourism, is the key, but this must be backed up by reform of the industry and its powerful players, as well as more responsible behaviour on the behalf of tourists themselves.

Questions

1. Is it possible that both mass tourism and alternative tourism could provide pathways to tourism *for* development in Third World countries? If so, under what conditions could this happen?

2. List three principles for appropriate tourism development in the Third World.

3. Explain the difference between empowerment as a precursor to community involvement in tourism and an outcome of community involvement in tourism.

Suggestions for further reading

France, L. (ed.) 1997 *The Earthscan Reader in Sustainable Tourism*, Earthscan, London.
Krippendorf, J. 1987 *The Holiday Makers*, Heinemann, London (Chapter 13: About the concept of a balanced tourist development).

Useful website

Fair Trade in Tourism – Forum Reports for 1999 and 2000:
http://www.tourismconcern.org.uk/fair%20trade/frame.htm

Bibliography

A'Bear, D.R., Henderson, C.H., Little, A.M., Louw, C.L. and Mander, J. 1993 *Management of Natural and Human Resources through Community Development in North Easter Natal, South Africa*, Occasional Paper 121, Institute of Natural Resources, Pietermaritzburg.

Abram, D. 1999/2000 'Guide books turn travellers into package tourists. Against: Dave Abram', *In Focus*, **34**: 5.

Acott, T.G., La Trobe, H.L. and Howard, S.H. 1998 'An evaluation of deep ecotourism and shallow ecotourism', *Journal of Sustainable Tourism*, **6**(3): 238–53.

Adams, J.S. and McShane, T.O. 1992 *The Myth of Wild Africa: Conservation Without Illusion*, Norton and Co., New York.

Adams, W. and Megaw, C. 1997 'Researchers and the rural poor: asking questions in the Third World', *Journal of Geography in Higher Education*, **21**(2): 215–29.

Adams, W.M. and Hulme, D. n.d. 'Conservation and communities: changing narratives, policies and practices in African conservation', unpublished paper.

Allen, J. and Hamnett, C. (eds) 1996 *A Shrinking World? Global Unevenness and Inequality*, Oxford University Press, Oxford, in association with the Open University, Milton Keynes.

Allen, J. and Massey, D. 1995 *Geographical Worlds*, Open University, Milton Keynes.

Akama, J. 1996 'Western environmental values and nature-based tourism in Kenya', *Tourism Management*, **17**(8): 567–74.

Akama, J. 1999 'The evolution of tourism in Kenya', *Journal of Sustainable Tourism*, **7**(1): 6–25.

Albuquerque, K. and McElroy, J. 1995 'Alternative tourism and sustainability', pp. 23–32 in M. Conlin and T. Baum (eds), *Island Tourism: Management, Principles and Practice*, Wiley, New York.

Altman, J. and Finlayson, J. 1993 'Aborigines, tourism and sustainable development', *Journal of Tourism Studies*, **4**(1): 38–50.

Anderson, D. and Grove, R. 1987 'Introduction: the scramble for Eden: past, present and future in African conservation', pp. 1–12 in D. Anderson and R. Grove (eds), *Conservation in Africa: People, Policies and Practice*, University Press, Cambridge.

Anderson, S. 1999/2000 'What's in a guide book?' *In Focus*, **34**: 6–7.

Arcadis Euroconsult 1998 *Combined Review of Strategic Support Through ZIMTRUST to the Communal Areas Management Programme for Indigenous Resources (CAMPFIRE) and Institutional Support to CAMPFIRE*, Royal Netherlands Embassy, Harare.

Ashley, C. 2000 *The Impacts of Tourism on Rural Livelihoods: Namibia's Experience*, Working Paper 128, Overseas Development Institute, London.

Ashley, C., Boyd, C. and Goodwin, H. 2000 'Pro-poor tourism: putting poverty at the heart of the tourism agenda', *Natural Resource Perspectives*, Overseas Development Institute, London, 51: 1–12.

Ashley, C. and Garland, E. 1994 *Promoting Community-Based Tourism Development*, Research Discussion Paper No. 4, Ministry of Environment and Tourism, Windhoek.

Ashley, C. and LaFranchi, C. 1997 *Livelihood Strategies of Rural Households in Caprivi: Implications for Conservancies and Natural Resource Management*, DEA Research Discussion Paper 20, Ministry of Environment and Tourism, Namibia.

Ashley, C. and Roe, D. 1997 *Community Involvement in Wildlife Tourism: Strengths, Weaknesses and Challenges*, Evaluating Eden Project, International Institute for Environment and Development, London.

Ashley, C. and Roe, D. 1998 *Enhancing Community Involvement in Wildlife Tourism: Issues and Challenges*, International Institute for the Environment and Development, London.

Australian Department of Foreign Affairs and Trade 2000 'Republic of the Fiji Islands: Country Brief, October 2000'. http://www.dfat.gov.au/geo/fiji/fiji_brief.html (downloaded 17 April 2001).

Aziz, H. 1999 'Whose culture is it anyway?' *In Focus*, Spring: 14–15.

Aziz, H. 1999/2000 'Guide books turn travellers into package tourists. For: Dr Heba Aziz', *In Focus*, 34: 4.

Badger, A., Barnett, P., Corbyn, L. and Keefe, J. 1996 *Trading Places: Tourism as Trade*, Tourism Concern, London.

Bah, A. 1999/2000 'Gambia's alternative guide', *In Focus*, 34: 8–9.

Baker, J. 1997 'Trophy hunting as a sustainable use of wildlife resources in Southern and Eastern Africa', *Journal of Sustainable Tourism*, 5(4): 306–21.

Barkin, D. and Pailles, C. 1999 'NGO–community collaboration for ecotourism: a strategy for sustainable regional development', *Tourism Recreation Research*, 24(2): 69–74.

Barrett, C. and Arcese, P. 1995 'Are integrated conservation-development projects (ICDPs) sustainable? On the conservation of large mammals in sub-Saharan Africa', *World Development*, 23(3): 1073–84.

Barron, P. and Prideaux, B. 1998 'Hospitality education in Tanzania: is there a need to develop environmental awareness?' *Journal of Sustainable Tourism*, 6(3): 224–37.

Bartis, H. H. 1998 'A national black heritage trail in the Eastern Cape Province, South Africa: is it an option?' pp. 17–28 in D. Hall and L. O'Hanlon (eds), *Rural Tourism Management: Sustainable Options*, Conference Proceedings, 9–12 September, Scottish Agricultural College, Auchincruive.

Baskin, J. 1995 'Local economic development: tourism – good or bad?' pp. 103–16 in *Tourism Workshop Proceedings: Small, Medium, Micro Enterprises*, 9–10 March, Land and Agriculture Policy Centre, Johannesburg.

Beaumont, N. 1998 'The meaning of ecotourism according to . . . is there now consensus for defining this "natural" phenomenon? An Australian perspective', *Pacific Tourism Review*, 2: 239–50.

Bell, R.H. 1987 'Conservation with a human face: conflict and reconciliation in African land use planning', pp. 79–101 in D. Anderson and R. Grove (eds), *Conservation in Africa: People, Policies and Practice*, University Press, Cambridge.

Belsky, J. 1999 'Misrepresenting communities: the politics of community based rural ecotourism in Gales Point Manatee, Belize', *Rural Sociology*, 64(4): 641–66.

Berno, T. 1999 'When a guest is a guest: Cook Islanders view tourism', *Annals of Tourism Research*, **26**(3): 656–75.

Bhattacharyya, D. 1997 'Mediating India: an analysis of a guidebook', *Annals of Tourism Research*, **24**(2): 371–91.

Blaikie, P. 2000 'Development, post-, anti-, and populist: a critical review', *Environment and Planning A*, **32**: 1033–50.

Blamey, R. 1997 'Ecotourism: the search for an operational definition', *Journal of Sustainable Tourism*, **5**(2): 109–30.

Boniface, B. and Cooper, C. 1994 *The Geography of Travel and Tourism*, Butterworth Heinemann, Oxford.

Boniface, P. 1998 'Tourism culture', *Annals of Tourism Research*, **25**(3): 746–9.

Bonner, R. 1993 *At the Hand of Man: Peril and Hope for Africa's Wildlife*, Alfred A. Knopf, New York.

Boo, E. 1990 *Ecotourism: The Potentials and Pitfalls*, World Wildlife Fund, Washington, DC.

Boyd, S. 1997 'Egos and elephants', *New Internationalist*, March: 16–17.

Boyd, S. 1999 'Tourism: searching for ethics under the sun', *Latinamerica Press*, **31**(33): 1–2, 10.

Bradt, H. 1995 'Better to travel cheaply?' *The Independent on Sunday*, 12 February: 49–50.

Bras, K. and Dahles, H. 1998 'Women entrepreneurs and beach tourism in Sanur, Bali: gender, employment opportunities and government policy', *Pacific Tourism Review*, **1**: 243–56.

Bras, K. and Dahles, H. 1999 'Massage, miss? Women entrepreneurs and beach tourism in Bali', pp. 35–51 in H. Dahles and K. Bras (eds), *Tourism and Small Entrepreneurs – Development, National Policy, and Entrepreneurial Culture: Indonesian Cases*, Cognizant Communications, New York.

Breen, C., Mander, M., A'Bear, D., Little, T. and Pollett, T. 1992 *Social Conceptions of the Roles and Benefits of National Parks*, Occasional Paper 119, Institute of Natural Resources, Pietermaritzburg.

Brennan, F. and Allen, G. 2001 'Community-based ectourism, social exclusion and the changing political economy of KwaZulu-Natal, South Africa', pp. 203–21 in D. Harrison (ed.), *Tourism and the Less Developed World: Issues and Case Studies*, CABI Publising, Wallingford.

Brinkcate, T.A. 1997 'People and parks: implications for sustainable development in the Thukela Biosphere Reserve, KwaZulu/Natal', Master of Science dissertation, University of the Witwatersrand, Johannesburg.

Britton, S. 1982 'The political economy of tourism in the third world', *Annals of Tourism Research*, **9**(3): 331–58.

Britton, S. 1987a 'Tourism in Pacific-Island states: constraints and opportunities', pp. 113–35 in S. Britton and W. Clarke (eds), *Ambiguous Alternative: Tourism in Small Developing Countries*, University of the South Pacific, Suva.

Britton, S. 1987b 'Tourism in small developing countries: development issues and research needs', pp. 167–89 in S. Britton and W. Clarke (eds), *Ambiguous Alternative: Tourism in Small Developing Countries*, University of the South Pacific, Suva.

Britton, S. 1991 'Tourism, capital, and place: towards a critical geography', *Environment and Planning D: Society and Place*, **9**: 451–78.

Britton, S. and Clarke, W. 1987 *Ambiguous Alternative: Tourism in Small Developing Countries*, University of the South Pacific, Fiji.

Brohman, J. 1995 'Universalism, Eurocentrism, and ideological bias in development studies: from modernisation to neoliberalism', *Third World Quarterly*, **16**(1): 121–40.

Brohman, J. 1996a 'New directions in tourism for the Third World', *Annals of Tourism Research*, **23**(1): 48–70.

Brohman, J. 1996b *Popular Development: Rethinking the Theory and Practice of Development*, Blackwell, Oxford.

Brown, D. 1998a 'In search of an appropriate form of tourism for Africa: lessons from the past and suggestions for the future', *Tourism Management*, **19**(3): 237–45.

Brown, D. 1998b 'Debt-funded environmental swaps on Africa: vehicles for tourism development?' *Journal of Sustainable Tourism*, **6**(1): 69–79.

Brown, N. 1992 'Beach boys as culture brokers in Bakau town, Gambia', *Community Development Journal*, **27**: 361–70.

Brundtland, H. 1987 *Our Common Future*, Oxford University Press, Oxford, for the World Commission on Environment and Development.

Brunt, P. and Courtney, P. 1999 'Host perceptions of sociocultural impacts', *Annals of Tourism Research*, **26**(3): 493–575.

Buckley, R. 1994 'A framework for ecotourism', *Annals of Tourism Research*, **21**(3): 661–9.

Burns, P. 1999a 'Dealing with dilemmas', *In Focus*, **33**: 4–5.

Burns, P. 1999b 'Paradoxes in planning: tourism elitism or brutalism?' *Annals of Tourism Research*, **26**(2): 329–48.

Butler, R. 1990 'Alternative tourism: pious hope or trojan horse?' *Journal of Travel Research*, **28**(3): 40–5.

Campbell, L. 1999 'Ecotourism in rural developing communities', *Annals of Tourism Research*, **26**(3): 534–53.

CAMPFIRE Association *c.*1998a 'Hunting: Funding rural development and wildlife conservation in CAMPFIRE', Fact sheet, CAMPFIRE Association and Africa Resources Trust, Harare.

CAMPFIRE Association *c.*1998b 'Women in CAMPFIRE: Shaping their own development', Fact sheet, CAMPFIRE Association and Africa Resources Trust, Harare.

Carlisle, L. 1997 'Conservation Corporation: an integrated approach to ecotourism', pp. 6–7 in G. Creemers (ed.), *Proceedings of a Workshop on Community Involvement in Tourism*, Natal Parks Board and KwaZulu-Natal Tourism Authority, Pietermaritzburg.

Carruthers, J. 1997 'Nationhood and national parks: comparative examples from the post-imperial experience', pp. 125–38 in T. Griffiths and L. Robin (eds), *Ecology and Empire: Environmental History of Settler Societies*, Melbourne University Press, Melbourne.

Carter, S. 1998 'Tourists' and travellers' social construction of Africa and Asia as risky locations', *Tourism Management*, **19**(4): 349–58.

Cartier, C. 1998 'Megadevelopment in Malaysia: from heritage landscapes to "leisurescapes" in Melaka's tourism sector', *Singapore Journal of Tropical Geography*, **19**(2): 151–76.

Cater, E. 1993 'Ecotourism in the Third World: problems for sustainable tourism development', *Tourism Management*, **14**(2): 85–90.

Cater, E. 1995 'Consuming spaces: global tourism', pp. 183–231 in J. Allen and C. Hamnett (eds), *A Shrinking World? Global Unevenness and Inequality*, Oxford University Press, Oxford, in association with the Open University, Milton Keynes.

Cater, E. 1996 *Community Involvement in Third World Ecotourism*, Discussion Paper No. 46, Department of Geography, University of Reading, England.

Cater, E. and Lowman, G. (eds) 1994 *Ecotourism: A Sustainable Option?* Wiley, Chichester.

Ceballos-Lascuráin, H. 1996 *Tourism, Ecotourism and Protected Areas*, International Union for the Conservation of Nature, Gland, Switzerland.

Chalker, Baroness 1994 'Ecotourism: on the trail of destruction or sustainability? A minister's view, pp. 87–99 in E. Cater and G. Lowman (eds), *Ecotourism: A sustainable Option?* Wiley, Chichester.

Chambers, R. 1997 *Whose Reality Counts? Putting the First Last*, Intermediate Technology Publications, London.

Chambers, R. and Conway, G.R. 1992 *Sustainable Rural Livelihoods: Practical concepts for the 21st Century*, IDS Discussion Paper No. 296, Institute for Development Studies, University of Sussex, Brighton.

Chant, S. 1992 'Tourism in Latin America: perspectives from Mexico and Costa Rica', pp. 85–101 in D. Harrison (ed.), *Tourism and the Less Developed Countries*, Belhaven, London.

Chant, S. 1997 'Gender and tourism employment in Mexico and the Philippines', pp. 120–79 in T. Sinclair (ed.), *Gender, Work and Tourism*, Routledge, London.

Chant, S. and McIlwaine, C. 1995 *Women of a Lesser Cost: Female labour, foreign Exchange and Philippine Development*, Pluto Press, London.

Cheong, S. and Miller, M. 2000 'Power and tourism: a Foucauldian observation', *Annals of Tourism Research*, 27(2): 371–90.

Cherry, M. 1993 'Phinda: making ecotourism profitable for the people', *Sunday Times*, Johannesburg, 30 May: 35.

Child, B., Ward, S. and Tavengwa, T. 1999 *Natural Resource Management by the People: Zimbabwe's CAMPFIRE Programme*, Environmental Issues Series No. 2, IUCN Regional Office for Southern Africa, Harare.

Clancy, M. 1999 'Tourism and development: evidence from Mexico', *Annals of Tourism Research*, 26(1): 1–20.

Cloke, P. 2000 'Tourism, geography of', pp. 840–3 in R. Johnston, D. Gregory, G. Pratt and M. Watts (eds), *The Dictionary of Human Geography*, Blackwell, Oxford.

Cohen, E. 1973 'Nomads from affluence: notes on the phenomenon of drifter-tourism', *International Journal of Comparative Sociology*, 14(1–2): 89–103.

Cohen, E. 1987 ' "Alternative tourism" – a critique', *Tourism Recreation Research*, XII(2): 13–18.

Cohen, E. 1988 'Authenticity and commoditization in tourism', *Annals of Tourism Research*, 15(3): 371–86.

Cohen, E. 1993 'Open-ended prostitution as a skilful game of luck: opportunity, risk and security among tourist-oriented prostitutes in a Bangkok *soi*', pp. 155–78 in M. Hitchcock, V. King and M. Parnwell (eds), *Tourism in South-East Asia*, Routledge, London.

Commonwealth Secretariat 1996 *Women and Natural Resource Management: A Manual for the Caribbean Region*, Commonwealth Secretariat, London.

Cone, C.A. 1995 'Crafting selves: the lives of two Mayan women', *Annals of Tourism Research*, 22(2): 314–27.

Conservation Corporation Africa (CCA) 1997 *Conservation Corporation Africa*, Johannesburg.

Cukier, J. 1996 'Tourism employment in Bali: trends and implications', pp. 49–75 in R. Butler and T. Hinch (eds), *Tourism and Indigenous Peoples*, International Thomson Press, London.

Cukier, J., Norris, J. and Wall, G. 1996 'The involvement of women in the tourism industry of Bali, Indonesia', *The Journal of Development Studies*, 33(2): 248–70.

Dahles, H. 1999 'Tourism and small entrepreneurs in developing countries: a theoretical perspective', pp. 1–19 in H. Dahles and K. Bras (eds), *Tourism and Small Entrepreneurs – Development, National Policy, and Entrepreneurial Culture: Indonesian Cases*, Cognizant Communication Corporation, New York.

Dahles, H. and Bras, K. (eds) 1999a *Tourism and Small Entrepreneurs: Development, National Policy and Entrepreneurial Culture – Indonesian Cases*, Cognizant Communications, New York.

Dahles, H. and Bras, K. 1999b 'Entrepreneurs in romance: tourism in Indonesia', *Annals of Tourism Research*, 26(2): 267–93.

Dann, G. 1996 'Images of destination people in travelogues', pp. 349–75 in R. Butler and T. Hinch (eds), *Tourism and Indigenous Peoples*, International Thomson Business Press, London.

Dasmann, R. 1988 'National parks, nature conservation and "future primitive"', pp. 301–10 in J.H. Bodley (ed.), *Tribal Peoples and Development Issues*, Mayfield, Calif.

Davies, K.J. 1997 'A review of the Natal Parks Board's neighbour relations policy and its implementation at Spioenkop Game Reserve', Master's thesis, School of Oriental and African Studies, London.

Deaville, B. 1997 'Preliminary report: the development of eco-tourism within the Communal Areas Management Programme for Indigenous Resources (CAMPFIRE), Zimbabwe', unpublished report, University of Derby.

De Beer, G. and Elliffe, S. 1997 *Tourism Development and the Empowerment of Local Communities*, Development Policy Research Unit, University of Cape Town, South Africa.

De Jong, R. and van Coller, H. 1995 'For the people – By the people', *Lantern*, Winter: 56–8.

De Kadt, E. (ed.) 1979 *Tourism: Passport to development?* Oxford University Press, Oxford.

De Kadt, E. 1990 *Making the Alternative Sustainable: Lessons from development for tourism*, DP 272, Institute of Development Studies, University of Sussex, Brighton.

Department of Environmental Affairs and Tourism 1997 'White paper on the conservation and sustainable use of South Africa's biological diversity', *Government Gazette*, 385(18163), Pretoria.

Dernoi, L. 1981 'Alternative tourism: towards a new style in North–South relations', *International Journal of Tourism Management*, 2: 253–64.

Dhliwayo, M. 1998 'The CAMPFIRE Project in Chipinge's Mahenye Ward', *CAMPFIRE News*, 17, March, 3.

Douglas, N. 1994 'They came for savages: a comparative history of tourism development in Papua New Guinea, the Solomon Islands and Vanuatu', Ph.D. thesis, University of Queensland, Brisbane.

Douglas, N. 1998 'Tourism planning in Vanuatu: an historical study', *Pacific Tourism Review*, 1: 201–9.

Drake, S.P. 1991 'Local participation in ecotourism projects', pp. 132–63 in T. Whelan (ed.), *Nature Tourism: Managing for the Environment*, Island Press, Washington.

Duffus, D.A. and Dearden, P. 1990 'Non-consumptive wildlife-oriented recreation: a conceptual framework', *Biological Conservation*, **53**: 213–31.

Eadington, W. and Smith, V. 1992 'Introduction: the emergence of alternative forms of tourism', pp. 1–12 in V. Smith and W. Eadington (eds), *Tourism Alternatives: Potentials and Problems in the Development of Tourism*, University of Pennsylvania Press, Philadelphia.

Ecotourism Society 1998 'Ecotourism Statistical Fact Sheet', http://www.ecotourism.org/textfiles/stats.txt.

Edwards, M. and Hulme, D. (eds) 1995 *Non-Governmental Organisations: Performance and Accountability*, Earthscan, London.

Else, D., Murray, J. and Swaney, D. 1997 *Africa – the South*, Lonely Planet, Hawthorn, Australia.

Elsrud, T. 2001 'Risk creation in travelling: backpacker adventure narration', *Annals of Tourism Research*, **28**(3): 597–617.

Enloe, C. 1990 *Bananas, Beaches and Bases: Making Feminist Sense of International Politics*, University of California Press, Berkeley.

Erb, M. 2000 'Understanding tourists: interpretations from Indonesia', *Annals of Tourism Research*, **27**(3): 709–36.

Evans, G. and Cleverdon, R. 2000 'Fair trade in tourism – community development or marketing tool?' pp. 137–53 in G. Richards and D. Hall (eds), *Tourism and Sustainable Community Development*, Routledge, London.

Fairburn-Dunlop, P. 1994 'Gender, culture and tourism development in Western Samoa', pp. 121–41 in V. Kinnaird and D. Hall (eds), *Tourism: A Gender Analysis*, Wiley, Chichester.

Fairclough, G. 1994 'No bed of roses: government tries to uproot prostitution from economy', *Far Eastern Economic Review*, September 15: 30.

Fennell, D. 1999 *Ecotourism: An introduction*, Routledge, New York.

Fennell, D. and Malloy, D. 1999 'Measuring the ethical nature of tourism operations', *Annals of Tourism Research*, **26**(4): 928–43.

Ferrar, T., Wynne, A. and Johnstone, M. 1997 *Community Based Tourism in the Northern Province*, Working Paper 62, Land and Agriculture Policy Centre, Johannesburg.

Font, X. and Buckley, R. 2001 *Tourism Ecolabeling: Certification and Promotion of Sustainable Management*, CABI Publishers, New York.

Food 2000 1987 *Global Policies for Sustainable Agriculture*, Report of the Advisory Panel of Food Security to the World Commission on Environment and Development, Zed Books, London.

Forsyth, T. 1995 'Business attitudes to sustainable tourism: self-regulation in the UK outgoing tourism industry', *Journal of Sustainable Tourism*, **3**(4): 210–31.

Fortmann, L. and Bruce, J. 1993. *You've Got to Know who Controls the Land and Trees People Use: Gender, Tenure and the Environment*, Occasional Paper NRM 1/1993, Centre for Applied Social Science, University of Zimbabwe, Harare.

France, L. (ed.) 1997a *The Earthscan Reader in Sustainable Tourism*, Earthscan, London.

France, L. 1997b 'Introduction', pp. 1–22 in L. France (ed.), *The Earthscan Reader in Sustainable Tourism*, Earthscan, London.

France, L. 1997c 'The role of governments', pp. 213–14 in L. France (ed.), *The Earthscan Reader in Sustainable Tourism*, Earthscan, London.

Frank, A.G. 1975 *On Capitalist Underdevelopment*, Oxford University Press, New York.

Friedmann, J. 1992 *Empowerment: The Politics of Alternative Development*, Blackwell, Cambridge.

Friesen, R. 1997 'Management audit of Sunungukai eco-tourism camp', unpublished report.

Gamat, Prakash 1999 'Goa government drafting 25-year tourism plan', *Economic Times*, 14 April.

Garrod, B. and Fyall, A. 1998 'Beyond the rhetoric of sustainable tourism?' *Tourism Management*, **19**(3): 199–212.

Gauthier, D.A. 1993 'Sustainable development, tourism and wildlife', pp. 97–109 in J.G. Nelson, R. Butler and G. Wall (eds), *Tourism and Sustainable Development: Monitoring, Planning, Managing*, Department of Geography, University of Waterloo.

Ghimire, K. (ed.) 2001 *The Native Tourist: Mass Tourism Within Developing Countries*, Earthscan, London.

Gibbons, S. and Selvarajah, C. 1994 'A study of the international backpacker visitor to New Zealand: building a profile to assess value and impact', unpublished report, Department of Management Systems, Massey University, Albany.

Gibson, C. and Marks, S. 1995 'Transforming rural hunters into conservationists: an assessment of community-based wildlife management programs in Africa', *World Development*, **23**(6): 941–57.

Goldsmith, E. 1991 'The seductive language of development', *Adult Education and Development*, September.

Goodwin, H., Kent, I., Parker, K. and Walpole, M. 1997 *Tourism, Conservation and Sustainable Development*: Volume 1 – *Comparative Report*, Final Report to the Department for International Development, London.

Goodwin, H., Kent, I., Parker, K. and Walpole, M. 1998 *Tourism, Conservation and Sustainable Development: Case Studies from Asia and Africa*, Wildlife and Development Series No. 12, International Institute for Environment and Development, London.

Goudie, S.C., Khan, F. and Kilian, D. 1999 'Transforming tourism: black empowerment, heritage and identity beyond apartheid', *South African Geographical Journal*, **81**(1): 22–31.

Greenpeace Australia Pacific and Oliver, P. 2001 *Caught between Two Worlds: A Social Impact Study of Large and Small Scale Development in Marovo Lagoon, Solomon Islands*, Greenpeace Australia Pacific, Suva.

Guevara, J. 1996 'Learning through participatory action research for community eco-tourism planning', *Convergence*, **24**(3): 24–40.

Gurung, D. 1995 *Tourism and Gender: Impact and implications of tourism on Nepalese Women – A Case Study from the Annapurna Conservation Area Project*, Mountain Enterprises and Infrastructure Discussion Paper, 95/03, International Centre for Integrated Mountain Development, Kathmandu.

Hadjor, K. 1993 *Dictionary of Third World Terms*, Penguin, London.

Haigh, R. 1995 *Backpackers in Australia*, Occasional Paper No. 20, Bureau of Tourism Research, Canberra.

Hall, C. 1992 'Sex tourism in South-east Asia', pp. 64–74 in D. Harrison (ed.), *Tourism and the Less Developed Countries*, Belhaven, London.

Hall, C. 1998a 'Historical antecedents of sustainable development and ecotourism: new labels on old bottles', pp. 13–24 in C.M. Hall and A.A. Lew (eds), *Sustainable Tourism: A Geographical Perspective*, Longman, Harlow.

Hall, C. 1998b 'Making the Pacific: globalization, modernity and myth', pp. 140–53 in G. Ringer (ed.), *Destinations: Cultural Landscapes of Tourism*, Routledge, London.

Hall, C. and Butler, R. 1995 'In search of common ground: reflection on sustainability, complexity and process in the tourism system', *Journal of Sustainable Tourism*, 3(2): 99–105.

Hall, C. and Page, S. 1999 *The Geography of Tourism and Recreation: Environment, Place and Space*, Routledge, London.

Hampton, M. 1998 'Backpacker tourism and economic development', *Annals of Tourism Research*, 25(3): 639–60.

Hardie-Boys, N. 1999 'Nature conservation and aid in Samoa', pp. 185–98 in J.D. Overton and R. Scheyvens (eds), *Strategies for Sustainable Development: Experiences from the Pacific*, Zed, London.

Harrison, D. (ed.) 1992 *Tourism and the Less Developed Countries*, Wiley, Chichester.

Harrison, D. (ed.) 2001 'Tourism and less developed countries: key issues' pp. 23–46 in D. Harrison (ed.), *Tourism and the Less Developed World: Issues and Case Studies*, CABI Publishing, Wallingford.

Hasler, R. 1996 *Ecotourism: A Comparative Analysis of findings from Kenya, Zimbabwe and South Africa*, University of Zimbabwe, Centre for Applied Social Sciences, Harare.

Hawkins, D. and Khan, M. 1998 'Ecotourism opportunities for developing countries', pp. 191–201 in W. Theobold (ed.), *Global Tourism*, Butterworth Heinemann, Oxford.

Helu Thaman, K. 1994 'Environment-friendly or the new sell? One woman's view of ecotourism in Pacific Island countries', pp. 183–91 in A. Emberson-Bain (ed.), *Sustainable Development or Malignant Growth? Perspectives of Pacific Island Women*, Marama Publications, Suva, Fiji.

Hemmati, M. (ed.) 1999 *Gender and Tourism: Women's Employment and Participation in Tourism*, Report for the United Nations Commission on Sustainable Development, 7th Session, April 1999, New York, United Nations Environment and Development Committee of the United Kingdom, London.

Herald News Desk 1999 'JGF will oppose upmarket tourism', *The Herald*, 27 September.

Herliczek, J. 1996 'Where is ecotourism going?' *The Amicus Journal*, 18(1): 31–5.

Hitchcock, M., King, V. and Parnwell, M. 1993 'Introduction', pp. 1–31 in M. Hitchcock, V. King and M. Parnwell (eds), *Tourism in South-East Asia*, Routledge, London.

Hitchcock, R. and Brandenburgh, R. 1990 'Tourism, conservation, and culture in the Kalahari Desert, Botswana', *Cultural Survival Quarterly*, 14(2): 20–4.

Holden, Peter (ed.) 1984 *Alternative Tourism*, Report of the Workshop on Alternative Tourism with a Focus on Asia, Chiang Mai, Thailand, 26 April–8 May, Ecumenical Council on Third World Tourism.

Holder, J. 1996 'Maintaining competitiveness in a New World Order: regional solutions to Caribbean tourism sustainability problems', pp. 145–73 in *Practising Responsible Tourism: International Case Studies in Tourism Planning, Policy, and Development*, Wiley, New York.

Honey, M. 1999 *Ecotourism and Sustainable Development: Who owns Paradise?* Island Press, Washington DC.

Hong, Eveleyne 1985 *See the Third World While it Lasts: The Social and Environmental Impact of Tourism with Special Reference to Malaysia*, Consumers' Association of Penang.

Hoogvelt, A. 1997 *Globalisation and the Postcolonial World: The New Political Economy of Development*, Macmillan, Basingstoke.

Hughes, G. 1998 'Tourism and the semiological realization of space', pp. 17–32 in G. Ringer (ed.), *Destinations: Cultural Landscapes of Tourism*, Routledge, London.

Humane Society of the United States 1997 *CAMPFIRE: A close look at the costs and Consequences*, Humane Society of the United States/Humane Society International, Washington, DC.

Hunter, C. 1995 'Key concepts for tourism and the environment', pp. 52–92 in C. Hunter and H. Green (eds), *Tourism and the Environment: A Sustainable Relationship?* Routledge, London.

Hunter, C. 1997 'Sustainable tourism as an adaptive paradigm', *Annals of Tourism Research*, 24(4): 850–67.

Husbands, W. and Harrison, L.C. 1996 Practicing [*sic*] responsible tourism: understanding tourism today to prepare for tomorrow', in L.C. Harrison and W. Husbands (eds), *Practising [sic] Responsible Tourism: International Case Studies in Tourism Planning, Policy, and Development*, Wiley, New York.

Hutnyk, J. 1996 *The Rumour of Calcutta: Tourism, Charity and the Poverty of Representation*, Zed, London.

Hvenegaard, G. 1994 'Ecotourism: a status report and conceptual framework', *Journal of Tourism Studies*, 5(2): 24–35.

Hvenegaard, G. and Dearden, P. 1998 'Linking ecotourism and biodiversity conservation: a case study of Doi Inthanon National Park, Thailand', *Singapore Journal of Tropical Geography*, 19(2): 193–211.

IIED 1994 *Evaluating Eden: An Overview of Community Approaches to Wildlife Management*, a report by the International Institute for Environment and Development, London.

Inskeep, E. 1997 'Tourism planning in Bhutan', pp. 227–31 in L. France (ed.), *The Earthscan Reader in Sustainable Tourism*, Earthscan, London.

Jafari, J. 1989 'An English language literature review', pp. 17–60 in J. Bystrzanowski (ed.), *Tourism as a Factor of Change: A Sociocultural Study*, Centre for Research and Documentation in Social Sciences, Vienna.

Jamieson, T. 1996 ' "Been there – done that": identity and the overseas experience of young Pakeha New Zealanders', Master of Arts in Social Anthropology, Massey University, Palmerston North.

Jangid, R.C. 1997 'Breaking "the dream" ', *In Focus*, 24: 4–5.

Jeffrey, P. 1999 'Rebuilding brigades', *Latinamerica Press*, 31(33): 4.

Joekes, S., Green, C. and Leach, M. 1996 *Integrating Gender into Environmental Research and Policy*, Institute for Development Studies, University of Sussex, Brighton.

Johnson, S. 1998 'Bookmark', *Resource Africa*, 1(5): 11.

Johnston, R. 2000 'Community', pp. 101–2 in R. Johnston, D. Gregory, G. Pratt and M. Watts (eds), *The Dictionary of Human Geography*, Blackwell, Oxford.

Joppe, M. 1996 'Sustainable community tourism development revisited', *Tourism Management*, 17(7): 475–9.

Kalén, C. and Trägårdh, N. 1998 *Sustainable Use of Wildlife: A Case Study from the Campfire Programme in Zimbabwe*, Swedish University of Agricultural Sciences, Uppsala.

Kalisch, A. 2000 'The GATS and fair trade in tourism', Briefing paper for Tourism Concern, London. http://www.tourismconcern.org.uk/fair%20trade/gats_tourism.htm

Kavita, E. 2000 'The economic fall-out of apartheid', *In Focus*, 36: 8–10.

Khan, M. 1997 'Tourism development and dependency theory: mass tourism vs. eco-tourism', *Annals of Tourism Research*, **24**(4): 988–91.

Kindon, S. 1999 'Contesting development', pp. 173–202 in R. Le Heron, L. Murphy, P. Forer and M. Goldstone (eds), *Explorations in Human Geography: Encountering Place*, Oxford University Press, Auckland.

Kindon, S. 2001 'Destabilising "maturity": women as tourism producers in Southeast Asia', pp. 73–92 in Y. Apostopoulos, S. Sonmez and D.J. Timothy (eds), *Women as Producers and Consumers of Tourism in Developing Regions: Issues, experiences, Policies*, Praeger, Westport.

Kinnaird, V. and Hall, D. (eds) 1994 *Tourism: A Gender Analysis*, Wiley, New York.

Kinnaird, V. and Hall, D. 1996 'Understanding tourism processes: a gender-aware framework', *Tourism Management*, **17**(2): 95–102.

Kinnaird, V., Kothari, U. and Hall, D. 1994 'Tourism: gender perspectives', pp. 1–33 in V. Kinnaird and D. Hall (eds), *Tourism: A Gender Analysis*. Wiley, New York.

Koch, E. 1994 *Reality or Rhetoric: Ecotourism and Rural Reconstruction in South Africa*, Discussion Paper DP54, United Nations Research Institute for Social Development, Geneva.

Koch, E. 1997 'A vision of tourism for the new southern Africa: why tourism matters', paper prepared for the launch of Action for Southern Africa's People-First Tourism campaign, 5 July 1997.

Koro, E. 1999a 'Zimbabwe's CAMPFIRE programme promotes conservation and development', *Resource Africa*, **1**(8): 3.

Koro, E. 1999b 'Namibian rural residents reclaim wildlife heritage', *Resource Africa*, **1**(6): 4.

Korten, D. 1987 'Third generation NGO strategies: a key to people-centred develop-ment', *World Development*, **15** (Suppl.): 145–59.

Krippendorf, J. 1987 *The Holiday Makers: Understanding the impact of leisure and Travel*, Butterworth Heinemann, Oxford.

Lama, W.B. 1998 'CBMT: Women and CBMT in the Himalaya', submitted to the Community-Based Mountain Tourism Conference, as posted on the Mountain Forum Discussion Archives on 5.08.1999: http:www2.mtnforum.org/mtnforum/archives/document/discuss98/cbmt/cbmt4/050898d.htm. Downloaded 23.9.1998.

Lea, J. 1988 *Tourism and Development in the Third World*, Routledge, London.

Lea, J. 1993 'Tourism development ethics in the Third World', *Annals of Tourism Research*, **20**: 701–15.

Leheny, D. 1995 'A political economy of Asian sex tourism', *Annals of Tourism Research*, **22**(2): 367–84.

Lélé, S. 1991 'Sustainable development: a critical review', *World Development*, **19**(6): 607–21.

Levy, D. and Lerch, P. 1995 'Tourism as a factor in development: implications for gender and work in Barbados', *Gender and Society*, **5**(1): 67–85.

Lew, A. 1996 'Adventure travel and ecotourism in Asia', *Annals of Tourism Research*, **23**(3): 723–4.

Lew, A. 1998a 'Ecotourism trends', *Annals of Tourism Research*, **25**(3): 742–6.

Lew, A. 1998b 'The Asia-Pacific ecotourism industry: putting sustainable tourism into practice', pp. 92–106 in C.M. Hall and A.A. Lew (eds), *Sustainable Tourism: A Geographical Perspective*, Longman, Harlow.

Lew, A. 2001 'Tourism development in China: the dilemma of bureaucratic decentrali-sation and economic liberalisation' pp. 109–20 in D. Harrison (ed.) *Tourism and the Less Developed World: Issues and Case Studies*, CABI Publishing, Wallingford.

Ley, D. 2000 'Postmodernism', pp. 620–2 in R. Johnston, D. Gregory, G. Pratt and M. Watts (eds), *The Dictionary of Human Geography*, Blackwell, Oxford.

Lieper, N. 1998 'Cambodian tourism: potential, problems, and illusions', *Pacific Tourism Review*, 1: 285–97.

Lillywhite, M. and Lillywhite, L. 1991 'Low impact tourism: coupling natural/cultural resource conservation, economic development, and the tourism industry', pp. 89a–89r in J. Kusler (ed.), *Ecotourism and Resource Conservation: A Collection of Papers*, Vol 1. From the 1st International Symposium on Ecotourism, 17–19 April 1989, Merida, Mexico, and the 2nd International Symposium on Ecotourism and Resource Conservation, 27 November–2 December 1990, Miami, Florida.

Lindberg, K. and Enriquez, J. 1994 *An Analysis of Ecotourism's Economic Contribution to Conservation and Development in Belize*: Volume 2 – *Comprehensive Report*, World Wildlife Fund, United States, and Ministry of Tourism and the Environment, Belize.

Lindberg, K., Enriquez, J. and Sproule, K. 1996 'Ecotourism questioned: case studies from Belize', *Annals of Tourism Research*, 23(3): 543–62.

Little, A. 1991 *The Impact of Tourism on the Environment and the Culture of the Local Population*, Occasional Paper 69, Institute of Natural Resources, Pietermaritzburg.

Liu, J. 1994 *Pacific Islands Ecotourism: A Public Policy and Planning Guide*, Pacific Business Center Program, University of Hawaii.

Loker, L. 1993 *The Backpacker Phenomenon II: More Answers to Further Questions*, James Cook University, North Queensland.

Loker-Murphy, L. and Pearce, P. 1995 'Young budget travelers: backpackers in Australia', *Annals of Tourism Research*, 22(4): 819–43.

Long, V. and Kindon, S. 1997 'Gender and tourism in Balinese villages', pp. 91–119 in T. Sinclair (ed.), *Gender, Work and Tourism*, Routledge, London.

Lumsdon, L.M. and Swift, J.S. 1998 'Ecotourism at a crossroads: the case of Costa Rica', *Journal of Sustainable Tourism*, 6(2): 155–72.

Lyon, J. 1997 *Maldives*, Lonely Planet, Hawthorn, Australia.

MacCannell, D. 1973 'Staged authenticity: arrangements of social space in tourist settings', *American Journal of Sociology*, 79: 589–603.

MacKenzie, J.M. 1987 'Chivalry, social Darwinism and ritualised killing: the hunting ethos in Central Africa up to 1914', pp. 41–62 in D. Anderson and R. Grove (eds), *Conservation in Africa: People, Policies and Practice*, University Press, Cambridge.

MacKenzie, J.M. 1988 *The Empire of Nature: Hunting, Conservation and British Imperialism*, Manchester University Press, Manchester.

Macleod, D. 1998 'Alternative tourism: a comparative analysis of meaning and impact', pp. 150–67 in W. Theobold (ed.), *Global Tourism*, Butterworth Heinemann, Oxford.

McKercher, B. 1993 'Some fundamental truths about tourism: understanding tourism's social and environmental impacts', *Journal of Sustainable Tourism*, 1(1): 6–16.

McLaren, D. 1998 *Rethinking Tourism and Ecotravel: The Paving of Paradise and What You Can Do to Stop It*, Kumarian Press, West Hartford.

McManus, P. 2000 'Environmental audit', p. 212 in R.J. Johnston, D. Gregory, G. Pratt and M. Watts (eds), *The Dictionary of Human Geography*, Blackwell, Oxford.

McMinn, S. and Cater, E. 1998 'Tourist typology: observations from Belize', *Annals of Tourism Research*, 25(3): 675–99.

McNeely, J.A., Thorsell, J.W. and Ceballos-Lascuráin, H. 1992 *Guidelines: Development of National Parks and Protected Areas for Tourism*, World Tourism Organization, Madrid, and United Nations Environment Programme, Paris.

Magic Lantern Foundation 1999 *Goa under Siege* (Video distributed by Tourism Concern, UK), New Delhi.

Malloy, D. and Fennell, D. 1998 'Codes of ethics and tourism: an exploratory content analysis', *Tourism Management*, **19**(5): 453–61.

Mandalia, S. 1999 'Getting the hump', *In Focus*, **31**: 16–17.

Mander, M. and Steytler, N. 1997 *Evaluating Eden: Assessing the Impacts of Community Based Wildlife Management – the South African, Lesotho and Swaziland Component. Phase 1*, The World Conservation Union and International Institute for Environment and Development, London.

Mann, M. (for Tourism Concern) 2000 *The Community Tourism Guide*, Earthscan, London.

Mansperger, M. 1995 'Tourism and cultural change in small-scale societies', *Human Organization*, **54**(1): 87–94.

Marchand, M. and Parpart, J. 1995 *Feminism/Postmodernism/Development*, Routledge, London.

Marshment, M. 1997 'Gender takes a holiday: representation in holiday brochures', pp. 16–34 in T. Sinclair (ed.), *Gender, Work and Tourism*, Routledge, London.

Mas, I. 1999 'Sua Bali: a pilot project on sustainable village tourism on Bali', pp. 101–12 in M. Hemmati (ed.), *Gender and Tourism: Women's Employment and Participation in Tourism*, Report for the United Nations Commission on Sustainable Development, 7th Session, April 1999, New York. United Nations Environment and Development Committee of the United Kingdom, London.

Massey, D. 1995 'Imagining the world', pp. 5–51 in J. Allen and D. Massey (eds), *Geographical Worlds*, Open University, Milton Keynes.

Matowanyika, J. with Serafin, R. and Nelson, J. 1992 *Conservation and Development in Africa: A Management Guide to Protected Areas and Local Populations in the Afrotropical Realm*, Heritage Resources Centre, University of Waterloo, Ontario.

Mayo-Anda, G., Galit, J. and Reyes, A. 1999 'The women's hand in a boatmen's co-operative: organizing the Honda Bay tour boat operators in Palawan, Philippines', pp. 90–100 in M. Hemmati (ed.), *Gender and Tourism: Women's Employment and Participation in Tourism*, Report for the United Nations Commission on Sustainable Development, 7th Session, April 1999, New York. United Nations Environment and Development Committee of the United Kingdom, London.

Medeiros de Araujo, L. and Bramwell, B. 1999 'Stakeholder assessment and collaborative tourism planning: the case of Brazil's Costa Dourada Project', *Journal of Sustainable Tourism*, 7(3/4): 356–78.

Medlik, S. 1993 *Dictionary of Travel, Tourism and Hospitality*, Butterworth Heinemann, Oxford.

Middleton, T. and Hawkins, R. 1998 *Sustainable Tourism: A Marketing Perspective*, Reed, Oxford.

Milne, S. 1998 'Tourism and sustainable development: exploring the global–local nexus', pp. 35–48 in C. Hall and A. Lew (eds), *Sustainable Tourism: A Geographical Perspective*, Longman, New York.

Mitchell, L. and Murphy, P. 1991 'Geography and tourism', *Annals of Tourism Research*, **18**(1): 57–70.

Momsen, J. 1994 'Tourism, gender and development in the Caribbean', pp. 106–20 in V. Kinnaird and D. Hall (eds), *Tourism: A Gender Analysis*, Wiley, Chichester.

Moore, D. 1996 *A River Runs Through It: Environmental History and the Politics of Community in Zimbabwe's Eastern Highlands*, NRM Series, Occasional Paper, Centre for Applied Social Sciences, University of Zimbabwe, Harare.

Morgan, N. and Pritchard, A. 1998 *Tourism Promotion and Power: Creating Images, Creating Identities*, Wiley, Chichester.

Morrison, K. and Robinson, J. 1995 'Sunungukai camp recommendations', unpublished report, November 1995.

Moscardo, G. and Pearce, P. 1999 'Understanding ethnic tourists', *Annals of Tourism Research*, 26(2): 116–31.

Mowforth, M. and Munt, I. 1998 *Tourism and Sustainability: New Tourism in the Third World*, Routledge, London.

Munt, I. 1994 'Eco-tourism or ego-tourism?' *Race and Class*, 36(1): 49–60.

Murphree, M. and Nyika, E. 1997 *Investigation into the Performance of Non-Lease Tourism Projects in the Communal Lands of Zimbabwe*, Synthesis Report, October 1997, IRT/SPECISS Consulting Services, Harare.

Nabane, N. 1996 *Lacking Confidence? A Gender-Sensitive Analysis of CAMPFIRE in Masoka Village*, Wildlife and Development Series No. 3, International Institute for Environment and Development, London and Africa Resources Trust, Harare.

Natal Parks Board 1996 *Natal Parks Board Policy: Ecotourism and Protected Areas*, 30 November 1996, Pietermaritzburg.

Natal Parks Board 1997 *Annual Report 1996/1997*, Pietermaritzburg.

Ndlovu, R. and Mashumba, F. 1998 *Report on the 6th Peer Exchange Visit for Parliamentarians, Mahenye, Zimbabwe, 9–14 February 1998*. United States Agency for International Development and SADC Natural Resources Management Project, Harare.

Nelson, C. 2000 'A Kenyan sees his heritage', *Manawatu Evening Standard*, 8 January: 8.

Nelson, J.G. 1993 'An introduction to tourism and sustainable development with special reference to monitoring', pp. 3–24 in J.G. Nelson, R. Butler and G. Wall (eds), *Tourism and Sustainable Development: Monitoring, Planning, Management*, Heritage Resources Center, University of Waterloo, Canada.

New Internationalist 1999 'The adding up problem: why the environment suffers from debt', *New Internationalist*, May: 16.

Norberg-Hodge, H. 1991 *Ancient Futures: Learning from Ladakh*, Rider, London.

Noronha, F. 1999 'Culture shocks', *In Focus*, Spring: 4–5.

Obua, J. and Harding D. 1996 'Visitor characteristics and attitudes towards Kibala National Park, Uganda', *Tourism Management*, 17(7): 495–505.

O'Connor, J. 2000 'The big squeeze', *In Focus*, Summer: 4–5.

O'Grady, R. 1981 *Third World Stopover: The Tourism Debate*, World Council of Churches, Geneva.

O'Hare, G. and Barrett, H. 1999 'Regional inequalities in the Peruvian tourist industry', *The Geographical Journal*, 165: 47–61.

Oppermann, M. 1992 'International tourism and regional development in Malaysia', *Tijdschrift voor Economische en Sociale Geografie*, 83: 226–33.

Oppermann, M. 1999 'Sex tourism', *Annals of Tourism Research*, 26(2): 251–66.

Oppermann, M. and Chon, K-S. 1997 *Tourism in Developing Countries*, International Thomson Business Press, London.

O'Rourke, D. *c.*1987 *Cannibal Tours* [video recording] O'Rourke and Associates, Lindfield, NSW, Australia.

Pagdin, C. 1995 'Assessing tourism impacts in the Third World: a Nepal case study', *Progress in Planning*, **44**: 185–266.

Panos 1995 'Ecotourism: paradise gained, or paradise lost?' Panos Media Briefing 14, Panos Institute, London.

Parnwell, M. 1998 'Tourism, globalisation and critical security in Myanmar and Thailand', *Singapore Journal of Tropical Geography*, **19**(2): 212–31.

Paskal, C. 2000 'Island management: setting limits', *In Focus*, **37**: 11.

Pattullo, P. 1996 *Last Resorts: The Cost of Tourism in the Caribbean*, Cassell, London.

Pearce, D. 1992 'Alternative tourism: concepts, classifications, and questions', pp. 15–30 in V. Smith and W. Eadington (eds), *Tourism Alternatives: Potentials and problems in the Development of Tourism*, University of Pennsylvania Press, Philadelphia.

Pearce, D. and Wilson, P. 1995 'Wildlife-viewing tourists in New Zealand', *Journal of Travel Research*, **34**(2): 19–26.

Pearce, P. 1995 'From culture shock and culture arrogance to culture exchange: ideas towards sustainable socio-cultural tourism', *Journal of Sustainable Tourism*, 3(3): 143–54.

Phillimore, J. 1998 'Gender, tourism employment and the rural idyll', pp. 409–31 in *Rural Tourism Management Sustainable Options*, International Conference, 9–12 September, SAC Auchincruive, Scotland.

Picard, M. 1993 'Cultural tourism in Bali: national integration and regional differentiation', pp. 71–98 in M. Hitchcock, V. King and M. Parnwell (eds), *Tourism in South-East Asia*, Routledge, London.

Pleumarom, A. 1994 'The political economy of tourism', *The Ecologist*, **24**(4): 142–8.

Pobocik, M. and Butalla, C. 1998 'Development in Nepal: the Annapurna Conservation Area Project, pp. 159–72 in C.M. Hall and A.A. Lew (eds), *Sustainable Tourism: A Geographical Perspective*, Longman, Harlow.

Polit, J. 1991 'Ecotourism: proposals and reflections for a community development and conservation project', pp. 357–61 in J. Kusler (ed.), *Ecotourism and Resource Conservation: A Collection of Papers*, Volume 1. From the 1st International Symposium on Ecotourism, 17–19 April 1989, Merida, Mexico, and the 2nd International Symposium on Ecotourism and Resource Conservation, 27 November–2 December 1990 Miami, Florida.

Poon, A. 1993 *Tourism, Technology and Competitive Strategies*, CAB International, Wallingford.

Potter, R., Binns, T., Elliott, J. and Smith, D. 1999 *Geographies of Development*, Longman, Harlow.

Prabhudesai, Sandesh 1999 'Churchill plans to save Goa with casinos and golf courses', *Goa News*, 25 September.

Pretty, J. 1995 'The many interpretations of participation', *In Focus*, **16**: 4–5.

Pritchard, A. and Morgan, N. 2000 'Constructing tourism landscapes: gender, sexuality and space', *Tourism Geographies*, 2(2): 115–39.

Pruitt, D. and Lafont, S. 1995 'For love or money: romance tourism in Jamaica', *Annals of Tourism Research*, **22**(1): 422–40.

Purdie, N. 1996 'Reasserting the local in the global: local livelihoods and sustainable development in the proposed East-Rennell World Heritage Site, Solomon Islands', unpublished M.Phil. thesis, Massey University, Palmerston North.

Raguraman, K. 1998 'Troubled passage to India', *Tourism Management*, **19**(6): 533–43.

Ranck, S. 1987 'An attempt at autonomous development: the case of the Tufi guest houses, Papua New Guinea', pp. 154–65 in S. Britton and W. Clarke (eds), *Ambiguous Alternative: Tourism in Small Developing Countries*, University of the South Pacific, Suva.

Rangan, H. 1996 'From Chipko to Uttaranchal', pp. 205–26 in R. Peet and M. Watts (eds), *Liberation Ecologies: Environmental, Development, Social Movements*, Routledge, New York.

Rees, W. 1990 'The ecology of sustainable development', *The Ecologist*, 20(1): 18–23.

Republic of South Africa 1997 *Statistics in Brief*, Central Statistics Service, Pretoria.

Richards, G. and Hall, D. (eds) 2000 *Tourism and Sustainable Community Development*, Routledge, London.

Richter, L. 1989 *The Politics of Tourism in Asia*, University of Hawaii Press, Honolulu.

Richter, L. 1995 'Gender and race: neglected variables in tourism research', pp. 71–91 in R. Butler and D. Pearce (eds), *Change in Tourism: People, Places, Processes*, Routledge, London.

Richter, L. 1998 'Exploring the political role of gender in tourism research', pp. 391–404 in W. Theobold (ed.), *Global Tourism*, Butterworth Heinemann, Oxford.

Riley, P. 1988 'Road culture of international long-term budget travelers', *Annals of Tourism Research*, 15: 313–28.

Ringer, G. 1998 'Introduction', pp. 1–16 in G. Ringer (ed.), *Destinations: Cultural Landscapes of Tourism*, Routledge, London.

Rose, J. 1998a 'Hiti Tau', OneWorld News Service (http://www.oneworld.org/news/reports98/tahiti.html).

Rose, J. 1998b 'Fanau tourism', OneWorld News Service (http://www.oneworld.org/news/reports98/tahiti2.html).

Ross, J. 1999 'The "revolutionary tourist" ', *Latinamerica Press*, 31(33): 5.

Ross, S. and Wall, G. 1999 'Evaluating ecotourism: the case of North Sulawesi, Indonesia', *Tourism Management*, 20: 673–82.

Rossel, P. (ed.) *Tourism: Manufacturing the Exotic*, International Working Group for Indigenous Affairs, Copenhagen.

Rostow, W. 1960 *Stages of Economic Growth*, Cambridge University Press, Cambridge.

Rudkin, B. and Hall, C. 1996 'Unable to see the forest for the trees: ecotourism development in the Solomon Islands', pp. 203–26 in R. Butler and T. Hinch (eds), *Tourism and Indigenous Peoples*, International Thomson Business Press, London.

Ryan, C., Jeffcoat, M. and Jeffcoat, S. 1998 'Visitor and host perceptions of tourism on Niue', *Pacific Tourism Review*, 1: 189–99.

Said, E. 1977 *Orientalism*, Phaidon, New York.

Sanchez-Gonzalez, C. 1999/2000 'For once . . . ignore the instructions!' *In Focus*, 34: 16–17.

Sandwith, T., in conjunction with Toucher, L. and the Community Conservation Reference Group and Task Team 1998 *Community Conservation Programmes: Towards the Development of a New Policy and Strategic Plan* (Draft 7, March 1998), KwaZulu-Natal Nature Conservation Service, Pietermaritzburg.

Scheyvens, R. 1999a 'Ecotourism and the empowerment of local communities', *Tourism Management*, 20(2): 245–9.

Scheyvens, R. 1999b 'Siyabonga craft cooperative, South Africa', pp. 149–57 in M. Hemmati (ed.), *Gender and Tourism: Women's employment and participation in Tourism*, Report for the United Nations Commission on Sustainable Development, 7th Session, April 1999, New York. United Nations Environment and Development Committee of the United Kingdom, London.

Scheyvens, R. 2000 'Promoting women's empowerment through involvement in ecotourism: experiences from the Third World', *Journal of Sustainable Tourism*, 8(3): 232–49.

Scheyvens, R. (forthcoming, a) *The Potential for Ecotourism to Facilitate the Empowerment of Local Communities in Southern Africa: A Summary Report using Selected Case Studies*, Institute of Natural Resources, Pietermaritzburg.

Scheyvens, R. 2002 'Backpacker tourism and Third World development', *Annals of Tourism Research*, 29(1): 144–64.

Scheyvens, R. and Purdie, N. 2000 'Discarding the green lenses: support for a livelihoods approach to sustainable development', *Journal of Pacific Studies*, 24(2): 229–51.

Seifert-Granzin, J. and Jesupatham, S. 1999 *Tourism at the Crossroads: Challenges to Developing Countries by the New World Trade Order*, Equations, Bangalore and Tourism Watch, Leinfelden-Echterdingen, Germany.

Selwyn, T. 1993 'Peter Pan in South-East Asia: views from the brochures', pp. 117–37 in M. Hitchcock, V. King and M. Parnwell (eds), *Tourism in South-East Asia*, Routledge, London.

Shah, K. and Gupta, V. (and C. Boyd, ed.) 2000 *Tourism, the Poor and Other Stakeholders: Experience in Asia*, Overseas Development Institute and Tourism Concern, London.

Simon, D. 1997 'Development reconsidered: new directions in development thinking', *Geografiska Annaler*, 79B(4): 183–201.

Sinclair, M. (ed.) 1997 *Gender, Work and Tourism*, Routledge, London.

Sinclair, M., Alizadeh, P. and Onunga, E. 1992 'The structure of international tourism and tourism development in Kenya', pp. 47–63 in D. Harrison (ed.), *Tourism and the Less Developed Countries*, Wiley, Chichester.

Sindiga, I. 1995 'Wildlife-based tourism in Kenya: land use conflicts and government compensation policies over protected areas', *Journal of Tourism Studies*, 6(2): 45–55.

Sindiga, I. 1996 'Domestic tourism in Kenya', *Annals of Tourism Research*, 23(1): 19–31.

Sindiga, I. 1999 'Alternative tourism and sustainable development in Kenya', *Journal of Sustainable Tourism*, 7(2): 108–27.

Singh, T.V. and Singh, S. 1999 'Coastal tourism, conservation, and the community: case of Goa', pp. 65–76 in T.V. Singh and S. Singh (eds), *Tourism Development in Critical Environments*, Cognizant Communication, New York.

Smith, V. (ed.) 1978 *Hosts and Guests: The Anthropology of Tourism*, Blackwell, Oxford.

Sobania, I. 1999 'Turning green? A case study of tourism discourses in Germany in relation to New Zealand', Master's Thesis, Waikato University, Hamilton (NZ).

Sofield, T. 1993 'Indigenous tourism development', *Annals of Tourism Research*, 20: 729–50.

Spano, Susan 2000 'Project benefits turtles and travellers', *Sunday Star-Times*, 16 January: C11.

Spreitzhofer, G. 1998 'Backpacking tourism in South-East Asia', *Annals of Tourism Research*, 25(4): 979–83.

Stevenson, A. 1997 'A spiritual journey', *The Royal Geographical Society Magazine*, June: 9–16.

Stonich, S. 1998 'Political ecology of tourism', *Annals of Tourism Research*, 25(1): 25–54.

Stonich, S., Sorensen, J. and Hundt, A. 1995 'Ethnicity, class and gender in tourism development: the case of the Bay Islands, Honduras', *Journal of Sustainable Tourism*, 3(1): 1–28.

Stonza, A. 1999 'Learning both ways: lessons from a corporate and community ecotourism collaboration', *Cultural Survival Quarterly*, **23**(2): 36–9.

Sturma, M. 1999 'Packaging Polynesia's image', *Annals of Tourism Research*, **26**(3): 712–15.

Sutcliffe, W. 1999 *Are You Experienced?* Penguin, Harmondsworth.

Swain, M. 1993 'Women producers of ethnic arts', *Annals of Tourism Research*, **20**: 32–51.

Swain, M. 1995 'Gender in tourism', *Annals of Tourism Research*, **22**(2): 247–66.

Tapela, B. and Omara-Ojungu, P. 1999 'Towards bridging the gulf between wildlife conservation and rural development in post-apartheid South Africa: the case of the Makuleke community and the Kruger National Park', *South African Geographical Journal*, **81**(3): 148–55.

Taylor, G. 1995 'The community approach: does it really work?' *Tourism Management*, **16**(7): 487–9.

Teo, P. and Chang, T. 1998 'Critical issues in a critical era: tourism in Southeast Asia', *Singapore Journal of Tropical Geography*, **19**(2): 119–29.

Theopile, K. 1995 'The forest as a business: is ecotourism the answer?' *Journal of Forestry*, **93**(3): 25–7.

Thomlinson, E. and Getz, D. 1996 'The question of scale in ecotourism: case study of two small ecotour operators in the Mundo Maya region of Central America', *Journal of Sustainable Tourism*, **4**(4): 183–200.

Tibet Information Network 2000 'Tibetan tour guides under new political pressure', *Rethinking Tourism Project – Electronic Newsletter* (RTProject@aol.com) 1 June 2000.

Timothy, D. 1999 'Participatory planning: a view of tourism in Indonesia', *Annals of Tourism Research*, **26**(2): 374.

Timothy, D. and Wall, G. 1997 'Selling to tourists: Indonesian street vendors', *Annals of Tourism Research*, **24**(2): 322–40.

Tourism Concern 1999a 'Adopting farmers', *In Focus*, **32**: 12, 19.

Tourism Concern 1999b 'Gambia bans all-inclusives', *In Focus*, **33**: 12.

Tourism Concern 2000 *What's the Difference between Backpacking and Mainstream Tourism?* Brochure produced by Tourism Concern, London.

Trask, H.K. and Trask, M. 1992 'The aloha industry', *Cultural Survival Quarterly*, Winter: 50–1.

Trousdale, W. 1998 'Tourism development control: a case study of Boracay Island, Philippines', *Pacific Tourism Review*, **2**: 91–6.

Trousdale, W. 1999 'Governance in context: Boracay Island, Philippines', *Annals of Tourism Research*, **26**(4): 840–67.

Truong, T-D. 1990 *Sex, Money and Morality: Prostitution and Tourism in Southeast Asia*, Zed, London.

Turner, R., Miller, G. and Gilbert, D. 2001 'The role of UK charities and the tourism industry', *Tourism Management*, **22**(5): 463–72.

Uriely, N. 1997 'Theories of modern and postmodern tourism', *Annals of Tourism Research*, **24**(4): 982–5.

Urry, J. 1990 *The Tourist Gaze: Leisure and Travel in Contemporary Societies*, Sage, London.

Valentine, G. 2001 'Whatever happened to the social? Reflections on the "cultural turn" in human geography', Keynote address, *2001: Geography, A Spatial Odyssey*. New Zealand Geographical Society and the Institute of Australian Geographers Joint Conference, University of Otago, Dunedin, 29 January–2 February 2001.

Vallely, B. 1990 *1001 Ways to Save the Planet*, Penguin, Harmondsworth.

Van der Cammen, S. 1997 'Involving Maasai women', pp. 162–3 in L. France (ed.), *The Earthscan Reader in Sustainable Tourism*, Earthscan, London.

Van Reit and Louw Landscape Architects 1997 *Tswaing Crater Museum: Development Plan*, Natural Cultural History Museum and Department of Public Works, Pretoria.

Voluntary Service Overseas 1999 *Travelling in the Dark: VSO's WorldWise Campaign Survey of Travel Advice*, VSO, London.

Wainwright, C. and Wehrmeyer, W. 1998 'Success in integrating conservation and development? A study from Zambia', *World Development*, **26**(6): 933–44.

Wall, G. 1996a 'Gender and tourism development', *Annals of Tourism Research*, **23**(3): 721–2.

Wall, G. 1996b 'One name, two destinations', pp. 41–57 in L. Harrison and W. Husbands (eds), *Practicing Responsible Tourism: International Case Studies in Tourism Planning, Policy, and Development*, Wiley, Chichester.

Wall, G. 1998 'Landscape resources, tourism and landscape change in Bali, Indonesia', pp. 51–62 in G. Ringer (ed.), *Destinations: Cultural landscapes of tourism*, Routledge, London.

Wall, G. and Long, V. 1996 'Balinese homestays: an indigenous response to tourism opportunities', pp. 27–48 in R. Butler and T. Hinch (eds), *Tourism and Indigenous Peoples*, International Thomson Business Press, London.

Wallerstein, I 1974 *The Modern World System: Capitalist Agriculture and the Origins of the European World Economy in the Sixteenth Century*, Academic Press, New York.

Warren, J. and Taylor, N. 1994 *Developing Eco-tourism in New Zealand*, New Zealand Institute for Social Research and Development, Wellington.

Watts, M. 2000a 'Development', pp. 166–71 in R. Johnston, D. Gregory, G. Pratt and M. Watts (eds), *The Dictionary of Human Geography*, Blackwell, Oxford.

Watts, M. 2000b 'Neo-liberalism', pp. 547–8 in R. Johnston, D. Gregory, G. Pratt and M. Watts (eds), *The Dictionary of Human Geography*, Blackwell, Oxford.

Wearing, S. 2001 *Volunteer Tourism: Seeking Experiences that Make a Difference*, CABI Publishing, Wallingford.

Wearing, S. and Larsen, L. 1996 'Assessing and managing the sociocultural impacts of ecotourism: revisiting the Santa Elena Rainforest Project', *The Environmentalist*, **16**: 117–33.

Wearing, S. and Neil, J. 1999 *Ecotourism: Impacts, Potentials and Possibilities*, Butterworth Heinemann, Oxford.

Weaver, D. 1998a 'Peripheries of the periphery: tourism in Tobago and Barbuda', *Annals of Tourism Research*, **25**(2): 292–313.

Weaver, D. 1998b *Ecotourism in the Less Developed World*, CAB International, Oxford.

Weaver, D. 1998c 'Strategies for the development of deliberate ecotourism in the South Pacific', *Pacific Tourism Review*, **2**: 53–66.

Weaver, D. 1999 'Magnitude of ecotourism in Costa Rica and Kenya', *Annals of Tourism Research*, **26**(4): 792–816.

Weaver, D. 2001 'Mass tourism and alternative tourism in the Caribbean' pp. 161–74 in D. Harrison (ed.), *Tourism and the Less Developed World: Issues and Case Studies*, CABI Publishing, Wallingford.

Weaver, D. and Oppermann, M. 2000 *Tourism Management*, Wiley, Brisbane.

Wells, B. and Brandon, K. 1992 *People and Parks: Linking Protected Area Management with Local Communities*, World Bank, WWF and USAID, Washington, DC.

Wells, M. 1994/5 'Biodiversity conservation and local people's development aspirations: new priorities for the 1990s', *Rural Development Forestry Network*, Paper 18a.

Wells, M. 1996 *The Economic and Social Role of Protected Areas in the New South Africa*, Policy Paper 26, Overseas Development Institute, London and Land and Agriculture Policy Centre, Johannesburg.

Wen, Z. 1997 'China's domestic tourism: impetus, development and trends', *Tourism Management*, 18(8): 565–71.

Wenham, R. and Wenham, J. 1984 'Just travel: an experiment in alternative tourism', pp. ATCM09/1–ACTM09/4 in P. Holden (ed.), *Alternative Tourism*, Report of the Workshop on Alternative Tourism with a Focus on Asia, Chiang Mai, Thailand, 26 April–8 May. Ecumenical Council on Third World Tourism.

Wheat, S. 1999/2000 'Editorial', *In Focus*, Winter: 3.

Wheat, S. 1999a *Travelling to a Fairer World: Can Tourism Help Combat Global Poverty?* Voluntary Service Overseas, London.

Wheat, S. 1999b 'Editorial', *In Focus*, 34: 3.

Wheat, S. 1999c 'To go or not to go to Indonesia?' *In Focus*, 33: 5.

Wheat, S. 1999d 'Tourism Concern interview', *In Focus*, 33: 16–17.

Wheeller, B. 1997 'Tourism's troubled times: responsible tourism not the answer', pp. 61–7 in L. France (ed.), *The Earthscan Reader in Sustainable Tourism*, Earthscan, London.

Whelan, T. 1991 'Ecotourism and its role in sustainable development', pp. 3–22 in T. Whelan (ed.), *Nature Tourism: Managing for the Environment*, Island Press, Washington, DC.

Wilkinson, P. and Pratiwi, W. 1995 'Gender and tourism in an Indonesian village', *Annals of Tourism Research*, 22(2): 283–99.

Wilson, D. 1997 'Paradoxes of tourism in Goa', *Annals of Tourism Research*, 24(1): 52–75.

Wood, E. 1996 'An economic assessment of local community craft markets near protected areas in KwaZulu-Natal, South Africa', Master's dissertation, Environmental and Resource Economics, UCL.

Wood, K. and House, S. 1991 *The Good Tourist*, Mandarin, London.

Wood, R. 1993 'Tourism, culture and the sociology of development', pp. 48–70 in M. Hitchcock, V. King and M. Parnwell (eds), *Tourism in South-East Asia*, Routledge, London.

Wood, R. 1998 'Bali: cultural tourism and touristic culture', *Annals of Tourism Research*, 25(3): 770–1.

Woodley, A. 1993 'Tourism and sustainable development: the community perspective', pp. 135–47 in J. Nelson, R. Butler and G. Wall (eds), *Tourism and Sustainable Development: Monitoring, Planning, Managing*, Heritage Resources Center, University of Waterloo, Canada.

Woodwood, S. 1997 'Report – "Cashing in on the Kruger": the potential of ecotourism to stimulate real economic growth in South Africa', *Journal of Sustainable Tourism*, 5(2): 166–8.

World Tourism Organization 1995 *Global Tourism Forecasts to the Year 2000 and Beyond*, Madrid.

World Tourism Organization 1998 *Tourism: 2020 Vision – Executive Summary Updated*, Geneva.

WWF 2000 'Tourism certification struggling for credibility', Press release, 29 August 2000. http://www.wwf-uk.org/news/news148.htm

Xu, G. 1998 'Domestic tourism and its economic effect in Beidaihe, the largest seaside resort of China', *Pacific Tourism Review*, **2**: 43–52.

Yeung, Y. 1998 'The promise and peril of globalization', *Progress in Human Geography*, **22**(4): 475–7.

Zambia National Tourism Board 1998 'The village comes to tourism', *News Flash*, Lusaka, Zambia, July: 3.

Ziffer, Karen 1989 *Ecotourism: The Uneasy Alliance*, Conservation International, Washington, DC.

Index

Note: Index references for tables and figures occur in *bold italics*.